MIRANDA SAWYER

OUT OF TIME

MIDLIFE, IF YOU STILL THINK YOU'RE YOUNG

4th ESTATE · London

4th Estate
An imprint of HarperCollinsPublishers
1 London Bridge Street
London SE1 9GF
www.4thEstate.co.uk

First published in Great Britain by 4th Estate in 2016
This 4th Estate paperback edition 2017

1

A catalogue record for this book is available from the British Library

ISBN 978-0-00-752108-1

Typeset in Stone Serif and Stone Sans

Printed and bound in Great Britain by Clays Ltd, St Ives plc

MIX
Paper from
responsible sources
FSC™ C007454

FSC™ is a non-profit international organisation established to promote
the responsible management of the world's forests. Products carrying the
FSC label are independently certified to assure consumers that they come
from forests that are managed to meet the social, economic and
ecological needs of present and future generations,
and other controlled sources.

Find out more about HarperCollins and the environment at
www.harpercollins.co.uk/green

MIRANDA SAWYER is a journalist and broadcaster. Besides her features and radio criticism for the *Observer*, her writing has appeared in *GQ, Vogue* and the *Guardian*. She makes documentaries for TV and radio.

Praise for *Out of Time*:

'Sawyer is at her best articulating with honesty the angst many of this generation feel about getting older . . . the Morrissey of her journalistic generation'   *Sunday Times*

'Easily the most modern, clever and true thesis I've read on middle age . . . While unsparingly honest, Sawyer's book is entertaining and ultimately cheering'   *The Times*

'Miranda Sawyer is a genius'   *Spectator*

'I spent a lot of time nodding along in agreement to this book as if it was my favourite record*'   Jeremy Deller

* 'Hallelujah' by Happy Mondays (Weatherall & Oakenfold remix)

Also by Miranda Sawyer

Park and Ride

Contents

Contents

For S, P and F

'Death is the dark backing that a mirror needs
if we are to see anything'
                    Humboldt's Gift, Saul Bellow

'You're going to have to fucking swallow this
whole fucking life and let it grow inside you
like a parasite'
                    Malcolm Tucker, *The Thick of It*

1. Is This It?

The start is always quiet. Even when the event is catastrophic, when it's sudden and violent and crashes in, a meteor blazing from the sky to change everything you know – even then, what people say is: 'It happened out of the blue. Everything was normal. Nothing seemed any different. It was a complete shock.'

When what is happening is gradual, when it seeps under the door, like water or smoke, then the start is even quieter. It's silent. You don't notice it at all.

Middle age is a time of settled status, when your achievements, your experience and your knowledge knit together to create sustenance and prestige, and you are taken seriously, valued as a high-contributing member of society.

'You're a smelly bum-bum,' says F, my daughter. Her face is full of sneer and delight. 'And when you die, I can have all of the sweeties that are in the tin up there. And I can go to Africa to see the funny cows that Miss told us about. And I can have your shoes that are sparkly.'

We were talking about us not having a garden, about moving flat maybe, probably not. I was feeling frustrated.

'But, you know, feelings aren't facts,' said my husband, S. He had been saying this a lot to me: 'Feelings aren't facts.'

What you feel is not what is actually happening here.

S is an emotional man, and he uses his mantras to reassure himself as much as me. He was right. The facts remained; they were unchanging. How I felt about them – how I feel about them – makes no difference. The sun rises, the day begins, the school opens, the children go out and then they come back, I work, ideas are sent off, plans are made, the plans succeed or they don't, meals are eaten, and off to bed, and again, and again. Time passes, more quickly than you dare to think about.

These are the facts. I am in my forties. I have a job. I am married. We have children and a flat with no garden, and a mortgage and a fridge-freezer and a navy blue estate car. None of this is a surprise. Is it?

Except . . . a mood can gradually take over, change the way you feel about the facts. Warp them into something different. You know how it is to fall out of love with someone? How the simple reality of them walking into a room, or the way their teeth clink on a mug as they drink their tea can make you hate everything about them, even though they are the very same person you once found so bewitching? I did not feel this about my husband. I was wondering if I felt it about myself. About my life, and who I had become.

There were other feelings. A sort of mourning. A weighing up, while feeling weighed down. A desire to escape – run away, quick! – that came on strong in the middle of the night.

But the main feeling I had came in the form of a moving picture, a repeat action. I am standing in a river, the water flowing, cold and silver, bubbling and churning around my feet. It's lovely, really lovely, and I'm plunging my hands in, over and over, trying to catch something. Have I dropped it? Is it a ring? Or was it a fish I wanted?

No. It's the water itself. It's so beautiful. I want to hold it in my palms, bring it up close, clutch it to my heart. I want to stop it rushing past me so fast.

A crisis sounds so thrilling. A breakdown. A revolution. A sudden change, institutional collapse. Something dramatic.

One that happens in your forties? Hmm. Less so. We all know what that is. We see the outward gesture – the new car, the extreme haircut, the unusually positioned piercing – and we smile. We patronize. Look how silly he is, in his baseball cap, on his motorbike, with his new lover on his arm. Not dashing, not carefree, not youthful. Sad. And see her, with her tragic attempts to slow time, the clothes that are too young for her, the organic diet, the new lips. Ridiculous. Laughable.

Under the showiness of the exterior, there is a change within. All the stuff we see, no matter how clichéd: that's just telling the world.

No show, here, however. I wasn't running off with a Pilates expert. I didn't blow thousands on a trip to find myself. I didn't even get a shit tattoo. There was nothing to witness. From the outside, all remained the same. Work, kids, marriage, mortgage, blah. The facts didn't change.

If the crisis seeps in, if the start is silent, you need a jolt to realize it. Having F was my jolt.

Our second child, she arrived late (five years after P, our son), a quarter-year before I turned 44. S and I knew we were very lucky. No matter what age you are when you have children, if they are healthy, you are lucky; and no matter what age you are when you have children, their arrival makes you feel young and old at the same time. The difference is, if you have them in your forties, the old part is more of a head-nag.

The jolt. I can pinpoint it. It happened one day when I was in the kitchen, working on my laptop. F was only a few months old. She was a good baby, cheerful and self-contained. She liked her bouncy chair and I would put it on the kitchen floor so we could smile at each other as I wrote. I typed, the washing machine spun, she bounced and grappled with a toy monkey called Monkey. All was serene. We were happy in our tiny life.

I looked at her as I wrote and I thought, You are amazing.

And then I thought, By the time you're 18, I will be over 60.

I stopped writing.

I thought, When you're 18, I will just about have the strength to push you out of the front door and into your adult life before I have to check into an old people's home.

I thought, What about university fees? What if you don't leave home completely, and want to move in again? We'll need to sell the flat to get the money for the old people's home.

Then I thought: If I'm tired now, that is nothing compared to how knackered I'm going to be dealing with two teenagers in my mid to late fifties. Plus, I still have all these things I need to do! Like . . . well, I don't know. But things that are important for me and my development. Also, we really need to get the front gate mended.

I looked at F and she looked at me, smiling, kicking her legs. She said, 'De du da de du,' and twisted her hands in front of her as though she were changing channels on a 1980s TV. I thought: That's an old-school motion right there. Then I thought: You're showing your age.

What F made me realize was that I was over halfway through. At 40, I could still convince myself that, with a decent diet and some luck when crossing the road, I could well have more than forty years to go. It's a lot harder to do that at 44.

I looked at F and I suddenly knew – really knew – that I had less time to go than I had already lived. That the time I had was a limited resource, that life was an astonishing gift and both were diminishing every day.

Lots of people get weird around this age, I did realize that. If you don't get Fear of Forty, then Fear of Fifty will do it. The Fear: of everything that you have become, and everything you have not.

Eugene O'Neill, in *A Long Day's Journey Into Night*, wrote: 'None of us can help the things life has done to us. They're done before you realize it. And once they're done, they make you do other things until at last everything comes between you and what you'd like to be and you've lost your true self for ever.'

(What has life done to me? What have I done? What would I like to be?)

Victor Hugo wrote this: 'Forty is the old age of youth; 50, the youth of old age.'

I thought about this a lot. So what happens in those ten years in between? And who wants to be a young old person? Even though that is all we ever are?

I'd had my jolt. I'd clocked my unmarked midpoint; I knew that time was running out . . . But what to do about it? Life is busy in your forties, whether or not you have children. It's hard to keep everything tied down. Most days, I felt like Dorothy in *The Wizard of Oz* when the twister hits and the house goes up, gazing out of the window as essential parts of her life whirl past. Her family, her friends, adversity (witchy Miss Gulch on the bike), livelihood (the cow – all out of control, spiralling towards the future, out of Dorothy's reach and remit. She can't help them, though she knows she must.

That is how my life is in middle age. So many people to take care of, so many jobs to do. A lot to catch and tether, and who can grab hold of anything when all the important bits are constantly in motion? Round and round, faster and faster. Are we moving forward or just spinning on the spot?

What I really wanted was for everything to stop, for the house to land, with me still inside. I wanted to arrive in a sun-lit place, to be celebrated as a new magical queen, and to have the time to enjoy it. A place made of sweets, where the small people who surrounded me – let's call them my children – all sang in tune and did what I told them to. Also, that when I landed, I'd crush the life out of my enemy, whoever my enemy is. That would be brilliant. Splat, gone, byeee. Gimme your shoes. And when you die, I can have your shoes that are sparkly.

Now that F is no longer a baby, she talks about death all the time. She kicks it around in her head, riffs on it to delay me putting her to bed. She doesn't want to go to bed. Too much to do, and she's scared of the dark (of death). She talks about death as though it's a cool result. To her death has glamour, because it's frightening and exotic and it won't happen.

The idea of death. In your teenage years, your twenties, it becomes an existential concept. Actually, it can be a comfort: nothing matters, because we're all going to die anyway. We're all going to die, so what's the point in learning quadratic equations, or cleaning under the bed?

When we're young, we like to be scared by death, because it seems so remote. But in your middle years, it starts moving closer, nearer to you. Coming into focus. Becoming real.

When F was still a baby, after that moment in the kitchen, death started doing weird things in my head. It kept merging with maths. I was adding and subtracting, calculating how long I had left, how little time I had to do what I thought I had to do. Earn money. Fulfil my potential. Do whatever it was I should be doing, rather than worrying about my age and my life and what that meant.

Death maths. I was doing my death maths and I didn't like the way the sums were adding up.

I started noticing the middle-aged men who said, 'I'm going to live to a hundred.' There were quite a few. The head of Condé Nast said this. A French actor. Eddie Izzard said it to me, in an interview, in a fabulously positive way.

'I'm going to live to a hundred. Why not?' he said, a man who ran 43 marathons in 51 days, at the age of 47, for a laugh. And then ran 27 marathons in 27 days, at the age of 54, for another giggle. Why not indeed? When Eddie said it, I was almost convinced. Maybe I, too, still had a long way to go.

But one day, when I was meant to be doing something else, I bothered to look up the stats. I saw the true death maths, and the death maths was clear. If you were born in the UK between the late 60s and late 70s, and you're a man, then all the research says that your life expectancy is 80. If you're a woman, it's 83.

You can probably add on a few years if you're middle class and don't smoke. I thought that, too. After I'd read the research, I looked around online and found a more accurate life expectancy questionnaire. I filled it in. Carefully, I totted up my nicotine years, how much I drink, how much I exercise; I converted stones into pounds and pounds into kilograms. There were no boxes that referenced illegal drugs, or rubbish food, or terrible housing or love-life decisions. The questionnaire gave my life expectancy as . . . 88.

So. It doesn't matter if you have just run the furthest you ever have in your life, or you neck kale smoothies every day, or you know some brilliant DJs. It doesn't even matter if you yourself are a brilliant DJ, or if you are Eddie Izzard. At some point between the ages of 40 and 50, you and I will have lived more than half our lives. We have less time left than we have already lived. The seesaw has tipped. There are the facts. And these are the feelings.

It was the death maths that did for me, the pinpointing of the years left, that new (old) knowledge. It started a revving in my head, a pain behind my eyes, a loss of nerve so strong I could barely move. I'm not sure that anyone knew, though. I had dark circles round my eyes, I was tired, but so is every parent of a child under one. And, yes, I was tired because of F, but also because the panic – that dark, revving provocateur – came at night.

I would wake at the wrong time, filled with pointless energy, and start ripping up my life from the inside. Planning crazy schemes. I'd be giving F her milk at 4 a.m. and simultaneously mapping out my escape, mentally choosing the bag I'd take when I left, packing it (socks, laptop, towels of all types), imagining how long I'd last on my savings (not long, because I'd had children, so I didn't have any savings). I'd be leaving the kids behind. Rediscovering the old me, the real one that was somewhere buried beneath the piles of muslin wipes and my failing forty-something body. I'd be living life gloriously. Remember how I was in my twenties? The travelling I did? That, again, but with wisdom . . .

Then I'd remember that I couldn't leave the kids behind, because I loved them so much, and I'd start planning a different escape.

Even while I was doing it, I knew it was vital not to get involved in such thinking, that I really needed to stay put, to look forward. Certainly not hark back. If you keep staring at your past, believing your best times are done, you'll be facing the wrong way for the next few decades. You'll reverse into death, arse-first.

And, anyway, hadn't I'd done those best times wrong? I would consider my younger self and shake my head. I'd decide on the turning points of my life and then spend hours bemoaning the way I'd dealt with them. What had I been thinking, refusing that job? Why did I waste so much time on that deadbeat dickhead? Why didn't I prioritize what I really enjoyed, rather than trying to please other people? Why didn't I push myself? What a waste! What a waster!

Sometimes, during the day, as I performed all the tiny, repetitive actions required of an adult when children are young – the wiping, the kissing, the picking up, the starting again – my mind would wander. Worse: it would *assess*. (No new parent wants assessment: they just want to get through.) I would assess my efforts – my life – so far, and all would come up juvenile and insubstantial. Grown-up epithets burnt in my mind, as though they were absolute truths. It would have been better to have your kids young. Buying a house with a garden is adulthood's be-all-and-end-all. A good steady job, a good steady love life and a good steady pension are all vital for you to function in today's world, and you should have established all of those by the time you were 30. At the latest.

In contrast, when I held up my own long-standing beliefs to the light, they seemed broken. The belief that convention was just that, conventional. That, if you and your family weren't starving, money couldn't make you much happier. That you were always better to go out than stay in. That a life packed full of experiences was more valuable than one packed full of possessions. I'd rushed around in my twenties and thirties because I'd wanted to enjoy myself out there, to live in the big world, rather than a small one based around acquisition. Where was the pleasure in contemplating the polished wondrousness of a wooden table, or a neatly maintained lawn?

In the middle of the night, when I wasn't planning to run away, I found myself contemplating those pleasures with envy. We didn't have a big table, or any outside space. We lived in a stuffed, scruffy flat.

I'd stuck with so many old prejudices – a hatred of wheelie suitcases, of drawer tidies for cutlery drawers – that I'd started to believe my prejudices were my personality. But my new-found late-night hobby of demented self-deconstruction made me see that they were not. They were merely affect-ations, kickbacks against my childhood and upbringing, the reactions of an overgrown teenager. An overgrown teenager with a family, a mortgage, a fridge-freezer, all that.

And part of my panic was caused by what a friend calls 'the baby-cage stage' – how small your world becomes when your child is small, and how manic and locked into it you are – and part of it was the fear of being over halfway through, and part of it was realizing that all the plans I had would remain un-fulfilled.

Because I was middle-aged.

Still, could I be, really? There is something about middle age that is terrifically embarrassing. So embarrassing, in fact, that it cannot apply to me. Or you, either. We are of the mind to be young or old. There is cachet in both, even dignity. But not in between. Not in the middle.

Because we know middle age. It belongs to Jeremy Clark-son. It's blouson leather jackets. Terrible jeans. Nasty out-of-date attitudes manifesting themselves in nasty out-of-date jokes. Long-winded explanations of work techniques that everyone else bypassed years ago. Micro-management of events that mean nothing – e.g. a cake sale. Useless com-petitiveness about useless stuff that actually boils down to an argument about status, such as Whose Child Is The Most Naturally Gifted? or How Amazing Was Your Holiday In That Villa Of Your Really Rich Mate? or Have You Seen Our New Kitchen? Christ. Who'd want any of that?

Nobody. Or at least nobody I know. I'm surrounded by people my own age who are convinced they're not middle-aged. They know they're not young – they sort of know they're not young – but they're definitely not middle-aged. And they're boosted in this belief by mad midlife journalism. There are a lot of articles out there about how middle age doesn't start until your fifties. Or your sixties. Or never. Everyone over 49 is shagging rampantly while shovelling in the drugs, apparently, just as they were in their twenties, thirties, forties . . .

Fine by me. Because that means it's possible that they – that I – will switch easily from their youthful selves into well-maintained, sexy, eccentric, yet wise older citizens. No worries about middle age for us. Suddenly – preferably overnight, if that can be arranged – we will all transform into Helen Mirren and Terence Stamp (looking good!), with the added bonus of Bill Murray's wit and insouciance. We will merely walk out of one room (marked Young) and into another (Old). No corridors in between, no panicked running from room to room, opening the wrong doors, searching for the exit.

Around this time, the death-maths time, I went for lunch with an old friend. In the 90s, he was a scabrous, hilarious journalist, a man who'd be sent to a far-right politics convention or a drugs den because he'd come back with something funny. Now, he was the same but different (like me, like us all). He was travelled, rather than travelling. And he, too, was struggling with midlife.

I told him of how hard I found it to combine work with little kids. He told me he would like to have children, 'because then you know what to live for, what the whole point of everything is'.

We had a great lunch and he recommended a book to me. It was about survival. It told the tales of people who have successfully come through extreme events (successfully, meaning they didn't die). The book was designed to inspire others to reassess their approach to life, meant to excite us boring people into living without fear.

The book was jam-packed with action. A woman was shot by her husband in front of her children. A man was attacked – part-eaten! – by a bear. Another woman had a daughter, a healthy, beautiful, 4-year-old daughter, who caught a virus and died.

God, I hated that book. But there was an image in it that stayed. I can't remember now why it was mentioned, how it came up, but it was about a chess game. I'll tell it as I saw it – as I see it – in my head. It's like a recurring dream.

I am in a bar. It's a great bar, filled with stimulating people I know a little, but not so well that they've heard all my best anecdotes. Someone convivial invites me to play a chess game. 'Hell, yes!' I shout, and sit down, slopping my caipirinha as I do so. It doesn't matter. I am funny, good-looking and clever. Everyone in the room loves me. I am sure to win, but also, as I don't really care about chess, I'm going to win simply by playing as I wish. No strategy, no sell-out, but many thrilling, unexpected moves that simply pop into my head. Because I'm great!

After about an hour when, in truth, I haven't really been concentrating on what's been going on, I go out of the room for a moment. When I come back, the atmosphere is different. The bar seems colder. All the exciting people have disappeared. The lights have dimmed; the person I'm playing chess with is hard to make out clearly.

I look down at the chessboard and see that my hot-headed, non-strategic play has meant that I have lost some vital pieces: a bishop, both rooks, a knight, several pawns. Where did they go? How could I have discarded them so unthinkingly? My armoury is diminished. Moves have taken place that I didn't even notice, and now my position is weak.

I can see that it's going to be tough to get anything at all out of this particular match. I've played it too casually. I've played it all wrong.

I say, with a smile: 'Perhaps I could start again?'

And someone – my opponent, my conscience, God – answers me, in a voice that's quiet and calm, but that fills the room, makes my ears ring, my stomach shudder: 'No. This is the game.'

This is the game.

So I did the only thing I could think of that didn't involve running away: I wrote about how I was. The fact of being over halfway through my life, and the feelings that fact created. The *Observer* ran the article I wrote, accompanied by a photograph of me, in a lot of make-up, looking younger than I usually do. This was very kind, though not so useful for the piece.

The article's title was 'Is This It?' And it was, I suppose. Except I couldn't seem to shake off the uncomfortable feeling, the anxiety itch.

I was still in the grips of my teeny tiny *crise d'un certain age* (French = more exciting), and it still didn't show. No alarms and no surprises. I yearned for my desperation to become more flamboyant; I was like the child with stomach-ache who wants a bruise, a plaster, an ambulance rush to A&E. Nothing occurred.

It was pathetic. Who was I kidding? I didn't pack my bag anywhere except in my head. I couldn't leave, and a quiet crisis seems, to everyone outside it, like no crisis at all. Why couldn't I turn my panic into flight – abandon my home, even for a few months – to have a true middle-aged catastrophe? Why didn't I shag a builder, or a bendy yoga dullard? Why wasn't I taking a long, solo hike across an unfamiliar landscape, pausing only to meet authentic people who would tell me the meaning of life?

I talked to S about this. I said: 'Would you mind if I staged a midlife drama, if I left you and wandered around a bit for a couple of months?'

He said: 'Not a bother. As long as you take the kids.'

On the radio, I heard a writer talking. There was a five-part series of his musings, inspired by the lengthy hikes he takes across cities. An imposing man, he mostly walks at night. I quite fancied this, but it's a different prospect, going for solo rambles in the early hours when you're a shortish woman. I thought about cycling, or going for 3 a.m. drives, but both seemed pointless – plus slowing down to talk to a pedestrian when you're in a car at night could easily give the wrong impression. Also, I still had the days to get through, sorting the kids and earning a living; and S was going away for work, so – babysitting bills.

Still. As a result of the 'Is This It?' article, I got a deal from a publisher to write a book about midlife. A book. *This* book. And I tried to write it. God, I tried. I would bundle P to school and F to the child-minder, and then I would go to the kitchen and sit in front of my laptop, and put my coffee next to it to the right and my phone (switched to silent) to the left; and I would try to write. But the words didn't come easy, and I had to earn a living, so I would put the book aside and go back to journalism. The quick turnaround kept me busy.

It might have been the head-mush you get when your children are small. Or denial, I suppose. But for some reason, I didn't seem to be able to approach middle age face on. I couldn't see it clearly. The panic was there, the Fear, the feelings. I knew how to write about them. But the fundamental crisis seemed to be happening off-camera, just out of sight, weaving itself in and around my everyday life without ever becoming distinct.

*

For a while, instead of writing, I talked to people. I tried to separate the personal from the more universal. Some of what I was churned up about seemed only to do with me, and some of it was timeless, a classic midlife shock and recalibration, and some of it was hooked into the time I was in, where we all were right now.

There is an element of middle age that is the same for anyone who thinks about it. Not just the death maths, but how the death maths affects your idea of yourself. Your potency and potential. Your thrusting, optimistic, silly dreams, such as they are. As they were . . . They've been forced to disappear. Suddenly, you've reached the age where you know you won't ever play for your favourite football team. Or own a house with a glass box on the back. Or write a book that will change the world.

More prosaically, you can't progress in your job: your bosses are looking to people in their twenties and thirties because younger workers don't cost so much or – and this is the punch in the gut – they're better at the job than you are. Maybe you would like to give up work but you can't, because your family relies on your income, so you spend your precious, dwindling time, all the days and weeks and months of it, doing something you completely hate. Or you sink your savings into a long-nurtured idea and you watch it flounder and fail. Or your marriage turns strange. You don't understand each other any more.

In short, you wake one day and everything is wrong. You thought you would be somewhere else, someone else. You look at your life and it's as unfamiliar to you as the life of an eighteenth-century Ghanaian prince. It's as though you went out one warm evening – an evening fizzing with delicious potential, so ripe and sticky-sweet you can taste it on the air – you went out on that evening for just one drink . . . and woke up two days later in a skip. Except you're not in a skip, you're in an estate car, on the way to an out-of-town shopping mall to buy a balance bike, a roof rack and some stackable storage boxes.

'It's all a mistake!' you shout. 'I shouldn't be here! This life was meant for someone else! Someone who would like it! Someone who would know what to do!'

You see it all clearly now. You blink your eyes, look at your world, at your gut, your ugly feet in their awful shoes and think: I've done it all wrong.

I joined internet forums about midlife crisis where men – it was mostly men – lamented their mistakes.

'I could have done more, been more successful, been a better person,' said one. 'I used to be someone but now I'm just part of the crowd.'

'Maybe,' said another, 'I should just resign myself to the fact that I'm not what I used to be. But, see, this is my problem, I can't . . .'

Women talked too. A friend's Facebook status: '. . . the slow realization over the past year that I've messed it up. I've had a crap start in life and I went on to make a series of poor decisions, so now I've made my bed, I've got to lie in it. I could be so much more than a fat, grey, toothless, 44-year-old harpy living in a fucking council house with one child who despises me, another who will never live independently, and a marriage that will forever be in recovery . . . I know it's up to me to change things. What's not entirely clear is how to choose the right path. Because I don't know where I'm going . . .'

I spoke to a friend who said: 'I wonder if we messed it up for ourselves, having such a good time when we were young.'

We are each of our age. We share a culture, whether *The Clangers*, or *Withnail*, or 'Voodoo Ray'. Our heroes are communal, our references the same. Everyone has their own story, but it's shaped by the time in which it's told.

I've always enjoyed being part of something bigger. In the late 80s, I believed in rave and the power of the collective. Even now I like crowds, especially when music is playing; I love gigs, clubbing, festivals, marches, football matches, firework displays. I'm not mad about the hassle of getting to those places, but once I'm there, I'm fully in. As long as it isn't too mediated, so that you can feel in and of an experience or an audience, so you are there, singly, but also consumed within a whole other entity, the crowd. The crowd has its own emotions, its own rhythm.

It's good to lose yourself in that. I find it comforting to feel as others do, to share a moment; to know that I'm unique, but not that special. I like to know that what I'm going through, while personal to me, is also part of a pattern.

I thought about the 90s. I was very social. Always out, usually with other people. Most of my twenties took place then, in that time when youth was celebrated, where youth culture came in from the side, where the mainstream was altered by the upstart outsiders. And we – me, my friends, the crowd of us all – felt the rush of it, the need for speed. There was an up-and-out head-fuck that we searched for, constantly. Was that still within us, even now? That weird hyperactivity, the hunt for the high, a hatred of slowing up? A desire to escape the mundane, to be busy and crazed with endorphins. Even now?

In the 90s, drugs were involved in this, of course, and I thought about the people I know who have continued their hedonism into their forties. There were others who waited until middle age to start what used to be called dabbling. Others had given up everything – no booze, no drugs – but seemed driven to find other highs, through exercise: running, cycling, triathlons. Or they turned their drug obsessiveness into a new delight in food. Tracking down the most exclusive, carefully sourced ingredients from an expert, then taking such trouble over the preparation and timing that the moment of ingestion dominated their whole week . . . I noticed that all the new gadgets had names like ecstasy tablets. The Spiralizer. The Thermomix. The Mirage. The Nutribullet, made by a company called the Magic Bullet.

If you were young in the 90s, how does that affect your middle age?

I tried to think about this as I got up in the mornings, laid the table, helped small limbs in and out of uniforms, checked homework. S was away a lot, at this time, and I was alone with the kids. That was okay. Once you've had a child, and that child goes to nursery, or school, or a child-minder, you become plugged into a system. I had numbers to call, in case my arrangements fell through. And F was still little. Until she started crawling, I took her to meetings, showed her off like a new handbag. She was a good distractor.

My thoughts came and went. They mostly turned into questions.

Music was one, of course. I don't think I know anyone who doesn't believe in music, in what it can do. I'm of a generation that knows that music can save your life, give your life meaning, express the inexpressible, alter your course. People came into nightclubs while on a train track to normality and left believing they could be anything they liked. Their minds were opened up to a different way of living, a new way to work. They rejected the norm, the factory job, the lawyer training. Freelance creativity was their way out.

But what does music mean when you're older? How does freelance feel when you've reached your forties, when you're in a position where other people – your children – are relying on your work being stable, on the regular pay cheque that comes in every month? The internet had changed most of the creative jobs: journalism, media, photography, books, film-making, acting, fashion, comedy, music. There were fewer jobs and they paid less. All the work that seemed like an escape when we were young wasn't proving to be so now.

Music, creativity, community, getting out of it. These were more than the habits of a generation: they were – they are – our touchstones. They had been how we got through life, what we had used to help us negotiate its pitfalls and terrors. It could be that part of my midlife angst was concerned with whether the old ways – our old beliefs – were effective any more. And what I could do if they weren't having the same effect. If they don't work, if they make it worse, then what?

In Bristol I gave a talk at a Festival of Ideas. I wasn't sure I had any ideas worth festivalizing, but as what I'd been thinking about was midlife, I talked about that. I brought up death maths, and expensive bikes, drinking too much, and mourning the rush, and middle-aged sex lives. I made jokes about spiralizers.

Afterwards, there were questions from the audience. One man in his early 40s put his hand up and said, 'I still feel 22.' ('Feelings aren't facts!' I didn't say.) He had recently bought a skateboard. He didn't know whether to learn skateboarding or hammer the skateboard to the wall, as a decoration.

How can we make our minds, which insist that we're still 22, match up with our bodies, which are twice that age? How do we get rid of the sense of having missed out? How can we stop worrying about looking silly, because of our age? What should we do with our old MA1 jackets, or 12-inch remixes, or twisted Levi's jeans? Does it matter if we don't like new pop music? Is it okay to go to all-nighters if we go with our kids? What if we haven't had kids?

I did my best with the questions. But I hadn't studied mindfulness or sociology. I'm not a self-help guru. I can never tell if a new moisturizer makes any difference at all to my wrinkles. I was uncertain about many things, including time and consciousness and whether my mood (which was upbeat) was due to the warmth of the hall or the peri-menopause.

I wondered, what is an adult? We stretch our youth so far, so tight. We pull it up over our ageing bodies, like a pair of Lycra tights. We all do it to a certain extent, and yet we're cruel to those who seem to hold on too hard for too long. We laugh about MAMILS (middle-aged men in Lycra) and cougars (middle-aged women sleeping with younger men). We mock women who have Botox and surgery, even as we urge them to stay as young-looking as they can. We giggle at dad-dancing, post up patronizing 'Go on, my son!' clips of grey-haired ravers on Facebook.

But it's double standards. Because didn't we, in our hearts, believe that youth is better than middle age? I think we did. I think we do. And our youthful ideals were clashing with our ideas of adulthood. There was a fight going on, inside and out. We take our children to festivals and get more trashed than they do.

'What do you do in nightclubs?' asked P. 'I know you dance, but how long for? Can you choose the music? Why does everyone drink alcohol if it makes them ill?'

P once had a severe dancing-and-sugar comedown after a wedding. He danced for hours, fuelled on Coca-Cola and sweets. In the morning, he woke, white as a sheet, was sick, and had to go back to bed. He actually said, 'I'm never doing that again, Mum. Never.' His hangover was textbook, even though he didn't drink.

I was great in nightclubs, but what did that qualify me for now? Could I continue with what I did – writing about popular culture, especially music – now that I was twice the age of those I talk to? A music writer. A critic. These jobs are as old-fashioned as being a miner, and as destined for redundancy. That's a proper hangover.

Anyway, weren't clubs partly about fancying people? I seemed to have a shifting sense of who I am. If you're settled in a relationship, what does that mean? How does middle age affect your idea of love, of sex, of faithfulness? What about money? Not only did I know many people who earned a lot more than me, money, in general, seemed to have changed its meaning.

And what of the shallower stuff? How I looked. What my body could do, how it worked. My blood still pumped, I still bled. Did my body bleed as it used to?

Gradually, gradually, in between the bubbling, same-old rigmarole of everyday life, I came up with a plan. I would look back for a short time. (What's the phrase? 'Looking back is fine but it's rude to stare.') I would look back quickly, just long enough to investigate my prejudices and assumptions about adulthood. I would recall my twenties, check in on my thirties. There would be no beating myself up about wrong decisions, I would merely tell the tale. And then, I would arrive at my forties and I would look at that. At this middle decade, between the old age of youth and the youth of old age.

I would think about what I looked like. What my body can do. What marriage means, what happens when it changes over time. Work, and how our 90s' assumptions might affect how we work now. Money. Money, which leads to jealousy. Anger, and patience, how they grow or die.

How children impact on your life in the everyday. Not the love – the love is assumed, we know the love – but what having children means for those who care for them, the routine of them, the stability. Parents. Family.

And death, I suppose. Time. The time left.

If I couldn't tie these subjects down, catch them, skewer them with a ready pin for labelling and exhibition, then at least I could watch them fly. I could marvel at their existence. I might even see them settle (from the corner of my eye), and then I might glimpse their colours.

2. Adult-ish

January is always a bastard. Not only because it's January, but because it's my birthday, on the 7th. Exactly one week after New Year's Eve, two weeks after Christmas Eve, when nobody wants to go out, or drink alcohol, or spend money, or see anyone they know well ever again, other than to tell them precisely what they think of them and their crappy idea of a gift or a joke or a long-term partner. S has used up all his present ideas for me over Christmas. And even if I do celebrate my birthday, the next day when I wake up, guess what? It's still January.

But, you know, the kids love a birthday. They love giggling outside our bedroom door and then sneaking up to the bed with all the noiseless subtlety of piglets in mining boots. They love nudging each other – 'You go, go on, one, two, three' – before shouting, 'HAPPY BIRTHDAY, MUM,' and singing the birthday song and its coda: 'How old are you now? How old are you now? How old are you NO-OW? How old are you now?' They know the answer. Those birthday bumps would break your back.

Downstairs, on the kitchen table, my array of presents is minimalist. A card from my mum. A printout of a photo of the four of us from S, with a promise to 'buy you something later'. Two packets of Haribo Tangfastics, my favourite sweets, from P, wrapped wonkily in Christmas paper. Not exactly bumper. But you know what? It's fine.

I take the kids to school and F tells everyone it's my birthday, and my age. This is also fine. I'm not going to start lying about it. How old am I no-ow? I am 44. I am 45. Or 46, 47, 48. Not much has changed in the past few years. I am an adult. Whatever that is.

I watch P as we walk to school. Though I often forget how old I am, and when I remember it pulls me up short, he is of an age when every birthday is vital, when how many years (months, days) you've lived add up to power. When two years' age difference is a chasm, an insurmountable status gap. Another small boy, a head taller than my son, just another kid to me, is as thrillingly attractive and powerful to P as a pop star. He keeps trying to play football with the older boys. He trots faster to catch up with them. I can see them tolerating his breathless jokes, bearing his presence, but only just.

P's birthday parties involve football, usually; sometimes the cinema or Laser Quest. What did I do when I was his age? How about older? 15? I can remember my 17th birthday (in a Scout hall) and my 21st party (above a pub) and my 30th, and my 40th, just a few years ago. My 40th birthday party was very like my 30th. The main difference was that when a stranger offered me ecstasy, I didn't take it.

I don't want a party like that now. I'm not sure why. Some time over the past few years I lost the desire to be the centre of attention and the stamina required for all the organizational palaver. I wouldn't mind a party in the summer, maybe, with champagne cocktails and up-and-at-'em music, around a heated open-air swimming pool. A barbecue. Nicely dressed young people topping up drinks. In Los Angeles.

But in January, in London, in an expensive, cramped, roped-off area of a pub that you have to vacate at 11 p.m. or share with whichever punters decide to wander in?

No, thanks. Maybe I'll think differently when I'm 49 and a half.

Our idea of adulthood is formed by our youth. Adults were a puzzle to me when I was young. I looked at them and thought: How did they ever get married? Who could love these enormous, slow-moving creatures, with their pitted skin and springy hair? Their trousers hung loose over their flattened behinds. Their chipped, crumby teeth were like the last biscuits in the tin. When they were close, unpleasant smells leaked from hidden places. They talked a lot, in booming voices, about nothing important. They sat down. Then they stayed sitting down.

('Come on, Mum!' says F, in frustration. 'Stop talking! Let's PLAY!')

Not all adults were the same. I settled on my dad's lap and put my hands on the outside of his hands. I tried to force them together, to make him clap. He'd resist, hold steady, until suddenly, he relaxed, and let my pushing win. Blapp! His big hands, cupped, made the most impressive noise I'd ever heard. A gunshot, a crack that split the air, indoors or out. I used to try to copy him. But the Dad Power Clap cannot be made by the young. Only dads, with their dad hands, can create such thunder.

I liked my dad's smell. He smelt of nothing much, Swarfega sometimes, toast sometimes, talc. He didn't wear aftershave. My mum didn't wear perfume. She had a bottle of Chanel No 5, which I played with, but the liquid was orange, the scent was off. Sometimes, she smoked in the car on the way from work and her clothes smelt, not like fire, but chemical, metallic. She hid her cigarettes from us in her handbag. 'Death sticks', some people called them. I took them one by one, from the golden box, examined them, slit them open to scrutinize the curling tobacco slivers. Death looked a lot like wood shavings.

She stood in front of me and my brother and said, 'Look, my thighs join all the way up, too.' This was to my brother. He was weird about his legs, because mine were a different shape, and he was younger and wanted to be like me. I knew it didn't matter – who cared what your legs looked like? It was whether you could run fast that was important – but it was another reason to lord over him. I liked to emphasize our differences, though we were very similar. Our bodies were small and strong. We hung them upside-down from anything.

My mum wore no make-up. Her cosmetics bag contained one brown mascara, old and dried up, one lipstick and some shiny blue eye shadow. She rarely used any of them. Not when she went to work, as a secondary-school teacher, not when she saw friends. Only on special birthdays, when we went out to a restaurant to sit quietly and worry over cutlery selection. She wore trousers, no heels. In heels, she towered over my dad.

Neither of my parents put much effort into their appearance – odd, when we lived in a suburb that judged you by what you wore when you put out the bins – but, still, I thought they looked good. Handsome, rather than cute. Slightly 1960s, even in the 70s and 80s. My mum changed her hairstyle a lot: in the space of five years, she had a long orangey bob; a cap of sleek, dark curls; a blonde Purdey-style crop. She wore blouses that looked like shirts, nothing girly, no florals.

And, even when my dad got burnt in the sun, when his stomach reddened in stripes where the skin had folded as he'd sat reading, I thought he was fantastic. (His feet burnt too, so after one day of holiday he wore socks and sandals, like the university lecturer he was.) He was great at sport: football, cricket, throwing and catching, crazy golf, anything to do with a ball. Also, card games, building dens, drawing. He worked out the Rubik's Cube in a matter of minutes. He could skim a stone so it bounced seven times. He had a side parting and his hair flopped over his right eye.

When I was P's age, my mum was 37, my dad 40. When I think of my parents, I think of them then, and a little older, as I grew into my teens. I see them in their middle age. Was that their prime? It seemed so, to me.

Now, their elderliness comes as a surprise. How careful they are as they get out of the car, the time it takes, the probing for the pavement with extended foot, how they grip the door frame to pull themselves up and out. Every time they come to stay, and I notice their slowed movements, I have to readjust my image of them, overlay it with the reality. They have changed shape. My dad, once slim as a reed, is rounder. My mum has grown thinner. Their hair, their teeth, all different. They have the accessories of the senior citizen. Age-related discount cards. Spectacles: off-the-shelf, from Boots. Mouth plates, with odd teeth on them, like sparse standing stones. Hearing aids. Sudoku.

Despite all this, they are not as old to me as they once were. When I was a child, when my parents were younger than I am now, they were ancient. But now the gulf is not as wide.

I knew that my parents – my adults – were not like other grown-ups. They were special because they were mine. They loved me, as I loved them. Though I couldn't truly fathom how they could love each other – not as a separate unit, not without us children to mediate, to inspire passion. I loved my parents in a devoted but patronizing way, convinced that nobody else could want such battered specimens. They were like old teddies. The only people who valued them were those who'd cared for them for a long time.

Other children's adults were bewildering. Their nostrils were enormous – you could see the hairs in there, sometimes the bogeys. They breathed at you and asked you questions to which there were no proper answers, such as: Haven't you grown? How's school? (I do this now.)

They told you off for different faults from the ones your parents chose. Leave your shoes out the back! Don't blow bubbles in your drink! Use a teaspoon for the sugar! The women wore make-up that made their faces all slidy, the men dressed exclusively in shades of mud-brown, from shoes to spectacle frames. Those slurpy noises they made when they drank their tea, the 'oof' when they sat down, said in a comedy voice, to get a giggle. How old were they? Who knew? 25? 42? 117?

At junior school, I loved a few teachers. Mr Buckley, who had a beard and liked a laugh. Miss Braben, who taught us stories. Matronly, shaped like a peg doll, with a shelf bosom and padded hips. Once, she stopped the class to tell us all to look through the window. There was a horse, somehow free to roam south Manchester, galloping past the school, sweaty and wild-eyed. Its enormous head flicked and twisted through the air, its legs glistened; an astonishing sight. We stared. Then we went back to *I Am David*.

But most teachers – most adults – were scary. Horror-story characters. The headmaster resembled a giant winged insect, striding around in his billowing black gown, leading us in succinct, reasonable prayer at assembly: 'Dear Lord, we ask you to grant us . . . a GOOD day . . . Amen.' When I went to senior school, there were science teachers with stains on their shirts; a maths teacher who smelt so rank that, when you asked a question, you held your breath as he talked you through what you should be doing. He crouched down to check we understood, kind, careful man that he was; we let out our breath dramatically when he moved on.

One teacher had an enormous pus-filled spot that moved daily from the side of his nose to the space between his eyebrows. One, who taught sports, a woman, made sexy jokes that we didn't quite understand. One, a Latin teacher, eccentric and funny, was so well-known as a pervert that whenever he told me, or any of my gang of five girlfriends, to stay behind for being naughty, another of us remained too. We didn't even talk about it, just made sure there were two of us. We backed around the desks as he advanced.

Though I liked many of them – the Latin teacher was one of my favourites – they were all, fundamentally, repellent. Coarse, bloated, unsmooth, hairy. But it wasn't just their looks. They were Other, a different species from me and my friends, and we were happy with that. I was an anti-adult bigot. I believed in child/grown-up apartheid. I didn't want to think of them as anything other than alien. I didn't want them to think of me at all.

Even as I grew into my early twenties, adults remained off-putting. They operated outside us, in their different world. We were in our own gated community, within theirs. This suited us. We looked inwards, we liked our prison. But sometimes our elders would crash across the invisible fences. It was always uninvited, always a surprise.

During the summer I was 21, I worked for a few weeks teaching English as a foreign language in a residential school in Kent. The school was like a stately home, and we taught children from all lands: Italy, Japan, Israel, what was then Yugoslavia. Any child whose rich parents chose to go off shopping in London rather than risk a week's holiday with their offspring.

At the end of the three weeks, there was a staff party. All of us teachers got drunk; I jumped, fully clothed, into the swimming pool. In the corridor by the kitchens, another teacher, our team leader, a man in his forties, said something

irrelevant and plonked his lips on mine. He had a moustache.
It was like having your mouth explored by an adventurous
damp nailbrush – as sexy as that.

That same summer, I used my TEFL money, plus cash
I'd earned as a cleaner, to get a train to Barcelona with three
girlfriends. We hung out on the Ramblas, at a square where
tourists mingled with black-clad heroin addicts. Another
middle-aged man with another moustache: this one grabbed
me on the way to some restaurant toilets.

Why did drunk older men think that snogging was an
inevitable consequence of having fun? The way they kissed
wasn't sexual, but controlling. It was as though they clamped
their mouths on yours to shut you up. But we hadn't even
noticed them before they talked to us.

Adults are outsiders in young people's real lives, until we
make ourselves known, by forcing our way in, by telling them
what to do. Until we blunder over, unwelcome gate-crashers
at the party.

On the front of a magazine, I see this: 'Adults Suck and Then
You Are One'. A slogan on a jumper. I would like to own
this jumper.

Because now I am an adult – one of those inappropriate,
frightening, physically bizarre people. I'm quite good at talking to kids, but isn't there something creepy about that?
There's no hiding my sagging skin, my English teeth. I don't
stick my tongue down anyone's throat unless I'm married to
them. But when I grab my son's friends as a joke, pretend
to chase them round the kitchen for a kiss, COME HERE,
LITTLE BOY, MWAH MWAH MWAH, a lumbering dinosaur
great-aunt, I wonder: Is this funny or am I properly freaking
them out?

What is it about adulthood that is still so unappealing? I don't want to go back to school, with its bewildering, kid-enforced social rules, so rigid they couldn't be broken, so fluid they changed every day. But I don't want to be like the grown-ups I grew up with. So . . . separate, in such an unappealing world. Dull. Rule-bound. Constricted by paying bills and by convention. Even in what you wore: no one had many clothes then, and what adults wore was practical, designed not to stand out, except on special occasions. Despite the outré flamboyance of some grown-ups' going-out wear, their working clothes were joyless: suits and sensible skirts, overalls, pinnies.

Adults, teenagers and children were all demarcated when I was young. But something happened between then and now. Children got older (they gained status within the family) and parents got younger – if not actually younger, then in the way they looked, their approach to life. Everyone's a teenager now, and for a lot longer. The teenager has become revered, absorbed into our normal. Parents and their older children go to the same places to eat, to dance, to hang out. They listen to the same music.

Those teenage tenets of non-conformity, of staying true to your beliefs, rather than compromising them for an easy life, of rebelling against rules that you know are worthless and mean nothing . . . These are now the attitudes that we all respect. Even in adults, even in *politicians*. Authenticity is all, and authenticity means an anti-establishment, punching-up strength of character. Tedious, conventional adulthood, that refuge of phoneys and scoundrels, of lecherous old men with moustaches, of the boring, the selfish, the power-hungry – that doesn't cut it any more. We have extended youth so far that its values have become universal and nobody interesting can ever fully grow up.

3. Never Mind the 90s

Back then, culture was relentless. New music, new ways of dressing and dancing and being would rise with sudden force, crash and break and sweep away all that had gone before. You would see a band in some horrible dive, or hear a track on a dance floor and that was it: everything changed. And somehow everyone knew about it, though there was no internet, no mobile phones. There were magazines, but they came out monthly, or once a week. There were pagers, but they were for drug dealers or on-call doctors, not for telling everyone about a brilliant club that had opened, a squat that was holding free parties, a place where it was all going off. There were radio shows that helped, record shops to hang around in, hand-drawn flyers, but really . . . We just all knew.

It felt like we were constantly on the cusp of something. A revolution. A change. We'd push at doors and they would open easily. We would be let into places that only weeks before had kept us outside, pulling faces through the windows. And the new kept on coming.

The beginning can be so enthralling, so thrilling, you forget that, for anything to start and thrive, another thing must weaken. The end of the old way is still a death. Something fades, gives up, sits down and never gets up again. Or it fights and dies anyway.

*

In 1988, I got my first proper job – not cleaning, not TEFL, not working in a shop – and it was the best job ever. I started working for *Smash Hits* magazine, as a writer. In my job interview, the editor asked me if he should put Elton John on the cover of the new issue (Elton was Number 1 at the time). I said, 'No way, you should put Brother Beyond on instead.' That was my lucky break: the editor had, in fact, just done that very thing. I got the job because I wasn't too far from being one of the pop fans who pored over *Smash Hits*. This was because I was a pop fan who pored over *Smash Hits*.

It was the era of Kylie and Bros, and the *Smash Hits* office was above the BOY shop in Carnaby Street. On my first day, I arrived at 9 a.m., and had to sit on the step outside for an hour until anyone else turned up. Once in, I was installed on a spare chair, in front of an electric typewriter, within a room that appeared to have been attacked by a litter bomb. Every single surface was piled high with paper and 12-inch singles and cassettes and overflowing ashtrays.

Almost all of the staff were from outside London – from Perth, Dublin, Belfast, Dundee, Liverpool – and none of them seemed so different from me. I kept looking around the room, peering between the teetering debris, wondering where the grown-up was – the suit, the scary person in charge. There wasn't one. Perhaps that was why everyone stayed so late. They were having fun: a new concept when it came to work, for me. I soon joined in, and I didn't really leave that room – not during weekday daylight hours – for the next two years.

The start of the 90s was marked by my flat burning down. It was a rented flat, three storeys above a pharmacy in south London. At the time, the road was a market street, full of fruit and veg stalls run by shouty locals. On weekends we would wait until the market was ending, then go out and blag cheap vegetables.

I shared the flat with four friends. Two of them plus another mate were in when the fire started. It was very quick. ('In the time it takes to build a spliff but not light it,' said D.) They had to climb out of a back window onto a roof. They were still in their pyjamas.

We never found out how the fire had started, though we had our suspicions. It had begun in N's room, and she favoured floaty curtains, also candles, also leaving the iron on. But we all smoked, so who knows? Her room was at the front, on the first floor, directly above the shop. The fire took hold there and raged upwards, the central staircase that spiralled up the building acting like a very efficient chimney. The blaze took out every single room. Except mine, right at the top at the back. I'd shut my door when I'd left. It was a bank holiday weekend and I'd gone to see my parents.

N phoned me at my mum's. She said: 'I've got nothing left. It's back to the brick in my room. We left your window open to let out the smell of smoke.'

That night someone climbed in through my window and robbed the flat of what was left: Levi's jeans, Technic decks, trainers. Also my tickets to see Prince. I told the police which seats they were for. I thought they would send someone to pick up the ticket-holders, arrest and question them about the robbery. Maybe an undercover officer in Nike Jordans and a Keith Haring T-shirt. They didn't do anything.

When I got back into the flat, I clambered up the floors, thinking I could salvage stuff. But everything was covered with soot so thick that it wouldn't come off when you tried to clean it. It just streaked and striped, ingrained itself deeper. The water was cold, the electricity cut. In the bathroom, the disposable razors on the side of the bath had twisted in the heat, curled up like small orange snakes.

I climbed the black stairs to my room and shut the door. Nothing much in there had changed. Some of the photos had fallen down, my trainers and tickets were gone. But otherwise it was exactly as I had left it. It felt like a dream. Around the top of the door, scorch marks stretched, pushing out from the frame and on to the wall. They looked like the black fingers of a monster, scrabbling to get in.

After the fire, everything was different. We were uprooted, homeless. It felt liberating, rather than sad. That group of people split, some coupled up, some left London. I slept on mates' floors. I left *Smash Hits*, for reasons I can't remember now, and I bought a black London taxi. Its top speed was 55 m.p.h. I drove to France in it with N. We played the Stone Roses' 'One Love' as we chugged, very slowly, into Paris.

But we fell out over a bloke. So I drove around France by myself for a month, met up with friends of friends, slept wherever they were, or bedded down in the back of the taxi on the floor. I spent a lot of time on my own in it, rumbling along long, straight roads through tall, straight trees, winding across plains, over mountains. In the evenings, I would drive into the middle of towns, park up and go out to the local bars. Play pool. Talk to people. One time, when I woke, mucky and hungover and too hot, having parked in a lovely quiet square, a whole market had been put up around the cab.

When I got back to London, I met someone who became my boyfriend. I stayed with him in a mate's room, with all my mate's stuff still in it. Our stuff made no impression; we didn't have many possessions to add. When my dad came to visit, he cried.

I sold my taxi to an *NME* photographer who drove it to the south of Spain and swapped it for a bag of Es. I had no job, nowhere proper to live. Everything was in flux.

All around was fun, though. Raves in film studios that you got to at midnight, locked out until everyone stormed the doors and you were carried in on the tide of people.

Gigs: small, drunk, violent events where the lead singer would throw himself off speaker stacks and roll around on the floor and the drummer turned his head to be sick offstage and wouldn't miss a beat. Afternoons in Soho parks and pubs that would carry on into the evening and some do over east: grubby and empty then, apart from the beigel shops. A squat party at Brockwell Park lido where people were climbing over the walls to get in, sliding down the drainpipes in the corners. I saw a bloke on a bike ride straight into the swimming pool. And then try to carry on cycling along the pool floor.

There were sudden blags – a mate passing an ID bracelet past the PR frontline over and over until we were all in backstage. Festivals where it didn't rain and you nicked a pass so you could park backstage, with pop stars arriving in helicopters right next to your tent. And you lost all your mates and then you found one, at 6 a.m., trying to put on a top hat by placing it upside down on the ground and falling onto it head first.

Everything kept getting swept aside. Acid house swept away rare groove. Madchester took over. Indie bands – shoegazing and baggy – were suddenly irrelevant when 'Smells Like Teen Spirit' came out. Somehow everything was allowed, except poodle rock and bad pop. Dance music was mushrooming and morphing, taking in rock and hip-hop and ambient and prog and perfect pop and film scores and songs from children's TV. It churned them all up and spat them out. The beats got faster, darker; the sounds became scary.

Some time in the middle of the decade, *Parklife* and *Definitely Maybe* and then *The Great Escape* and *(What's the Story?) Morning Glory* became a competition, and that side of stuff died, really. Britpop became Cool Britannia and was hijacked by the tabloids. Antics that seemed like a laugh when they happened in front of a small group of like-minded people were suddenly a national talking point. Jarvis jumping onstage during Michael Jackson's performance to make fart signs came from the same instinct as sometime Pulp member Antony Genn streaking during Elastica's gig at Glastonbury that same year. But it was different because more people were watching. People who didn't think the same way.

Still. At the beginning of the decade you would see the Roses and the Mondays on *Top of the Pops* and it would feel like victory. Or Jarvis would wipe the floor with everyone on *Juke Box Jury* and you would punch the air. Or the Chemical Brothers would get to Number 1, with a video where a girl became a saucer-eyed dancing devil . . . Something was changing. Someone as quixotic and wild and other as Tricky became a genuine pop star for a few moments.

You couldn't quite believe that the stuff that was brilliant – and it was patently brilliant – was pushing through into the centre, that the mainstream was taking notice, that bands you knew were amazing but off-beam and awkward were being adopted by everyone. But they were. And the feeling it brought was . . . correct. We knew we were right.

There was a slow creep upwards during the 80s and early 90s until, *whoosh*, everything tipped over the edge. And we were rollercoastering, zooming down, arms in the air, our bodies whipped to the side and flung up so quick that we lost our stomachs as we flipped over and over.

No one really had a proper job. Some people were not working much at all, doing the odd day helping out at a mate's promotions company, or taking shifts at a record store. I was freelancing, writing for *Smash Hits*, and then other magazines: *Q, Time Out, Select, The Face*.

Select, a magazine that wrote about alternative music in a pop way, was on the floor above *Smash Hits*. It was populated by young men, which was a change for me – *Smash Hits* was mostly women. The *Select* boys knew a lot about music in a trainspottery way. The only way to push past their knowledge, to be noticed at all, was to talk a lot and never sit down. So I did: I stood up for days and days, chatting, making jokes. I wrote at home, at night.

Select, like *Smash Hits* before it, was a laugh. But unlike *Smash Hits*, which had a big circulation and a never-ending array of pop stars willing to be photographed with pineapples on their heads, *Select* had a limited star squad. The same people on rotation, really. Our job was to come up with interesting feature ideas, because there weren't enough bands who'd talk to us. We did features on groupies and ecstasy, and how porn was taking over. I wrote pieces about bootleg T-shirts, about stars' other halves. Once, an entire issue run of 60,000 copies had to be pulped because an article on legal highs included Feminax. The publishers thought a reader might overdose and die (on Feminax! Even if you snorted it, as my friend Gavin did, you only got a little tickle).

I wrote for *The Face* about boy-racer teenagers and posh students. You could write about anything for *The Face*. They sent me – a writer with no fashion knowledge – to write about Fashion Week. After traipsing between several sniffy, dull events, I got to go to an Alexander McQueen show. It was in a warehouse and it was exactly like going to a rave: the scramble outside, the flat impossibility of entry. But I knew clubs. I knew what to do. I pushed to the front, talked my way in on the door. It was easy.

Nathan Barley had nothing on *The Face* back then. We gave out free wallpaper, designed by Björk: just the one magazine-sized piece. I think we thought readers would buy loads of copies so they could cover a wall. My flatmate started playing *Tomb Raider* and I watched him manoeuvre pixel-pixie Lara Croft, with her square-muscled bum and swingy ponytail, through *Raiders of the Lost Ark* caves to fight dragons. I thought: We should put her on the cover! We did: not a human version, the cartoon-game version of Lara. On the inside spread she wore Versace and Gucci.

We once did a fashion shoot that featured models wearing nothing at all. You were meant to infer the clothes from the marks they left on the models' skin – the crease marks around the wrist, the redness left by a belt. But the printing was so bad you couldn't see the detail. The shoot was naked models, accompanied by captions about what they weren't wearing. A 90s' version of the emperor's new clothes.

All those kind-of friends you met through going out, who made films or music or danced so hard they made a club change its atmosphere, or were just funny and great-looking, had a way with clothes or a knack of being everywhere first . . . All those people, they were making the stories. Pushing the horrible youth establishment (Dave Lee Travis!) off their pedestals, forcing their own agenda.

We were so good at having a good time. Everyone noticed. Everyone wanted to join in. We didn't mind too much. When you see your friends and friends of your friends take over music and art and magazines and modelling and comedy and films and books and clubs, you think, Great. This is what we want. We are going to win.

'You know who you remind me of?' says a mum in the playground. 'You know those girls who used to be on TV, the tomboy ones. Zoë Ball, Denise Van Outen . . . They had a name for them . . .'

I remember the name: ladettes. I know the story of the 90s. I've made documentaries about it for radio. I've been interviewed about it for TV. My memories are my own, but they fit with the history that's usually told, as long as they're edited.

But the turning points are different, for me. Nobody really cared about Blur v. Oasis, except in an oblique way: look how BIG everything's got! The people who made it in the 90s were from alternative culture. Not all of them – not Chris Evans, not the Spice Girls – but those who kept music close to their hearts. And that meant that when everything got big, when the full glare of the tabloids was trained on them, they didn't like it. They couldn't really cope. Even the ones who seemed to truly desire it – Oasis, Kate Moss, Damien Hirst, Damon Albarn – they had to move away from that light. It was too much. The establishment, the mainstream is scary and intolerant and more powerful than you might expect. It reduces everything to its basest motive: money-sex-power. Which is fun, for a time, but it's not everything you want. It's not what you're about. You're trying to make something new.

Blur fractured; Graham limped away. Oasis changed their entire line-up, apart from the Gallagher brothers. Pulp splintered. Suede stuttered. Elastica collapsed. Other bands had members kill themselves, or get very ill, or become overwhelmed with addiction, or withdraw.

The drugs changed. No more poppers and speed, no more weed and mushrooms and Feminax. Ecstasy, of course, cocaine, ketamine, and then, heroin. Weird stuff like PCP, which gave you flashbacks of little green men explaining the meaning of life. People started falling through the cracks, disappearing. Some were sectioned. Some died. Some went away and never came back. I wrote a piece about heroin and smoked it, though I hated downers, only liked the stuff that took you up and out. I got a cab home, was sick outside our gate and slept for fifteen hours. People got cross with me about the feature. Someone phoned me up and shouted at me about revealing he used heroin, even though I didn't mention him at all, even though I hadn't known he was on it.

I got shouted at quite a bit because of my articles. In one, I got methadone and methadrine mixed up, and a lead singer bawled me out backstage at a Rollercoaster event. In another,

I put in a quote from one singer wanting another singer to die of AIDS and it caused huge problems. You just didn't know what would blow up, really. I still thought I was only writing for people like me. People who were relaxed about drugs, who got the joke, who knew that the important bit was the music and the characters around it, and the highs and spin-outs and stupid stuff that came with it all.

The mainstream changed to accommodate us. It really did feel like we'd won. A Labour government got in, for the first time since the 70s. Bars started opening until 2 a.m., and some, all night. Working-class people were celebrated, allowed to be exceptional. Extraordinary ordinary people had become our heroes, and, after they moved aside, *Big Brother* started and reality TV became the way to make everyday amazingness into stars.

The other day, I came across a piece I'd written for *The Face* in 1996. It was called 'Where Were You When the 90s Happened?'. It made me laugh when I saw it. It's so hard to assess an era or a state of mind when you're in the middle of it. It redefines itself from a distance, over the years.

The important thing about the 90s was that I was in my twenties, I suppose. We were good at being young. Our belief in change was the same belief that all young people have, but we were lucky. Our generation had the circumstances, the impetus, the gold-plated opportunity to be able to push our beliefs out into the world. Many of our ideas are still around.

At the end of the 90s, I'd moved flat ten times, got through four cars, two serious love affairs and a few not-so-serious. I'd gone away a lot, for work (Las Vegas, LA, New York) and for me, because I'd needed to open up my head. I'd been to Cuba, to Mexico, to Iceland, to the Scottish islands, to Australia, to Nova Scotia, all around Europe. I'd done a bit of telly presenting (I never saw the shows because I was always out), I'd interviewed a lot of musicians, I'd written umpteen features on going out and staying up, on trainers and driving. I'd danced all night, then carried on to the next night, over and over. I'd written a book, about suburbia. In the summer of 1999, on a tour designed to take books into nightclubs, prove that the chemical generation liked to read, I'd met S, who I'm now married to.

So much change, so much energy. I know it was me, but it feels like it wasn't. And, God, it sounds exhausting.

4. Carry On

We left the 90s behind and continued in much the same way as before. (When are you meant to stop? Is there a signal? How do you know?) On New Year's Eve 1999, we met up at a friend's flat and then rushed to the South Bank to goggle at the fireworks, high on the crowd – excitable, international, cuddly – as well as the exploding sky.

Afterwards, in the early hours of the new millennium, a group of us bunched across a packed bridge, straggled through closed-to-traffic tunnels to get to a club. We were blitzed, so it took us quite a while; anyone watching might have been reminded of *Monty Python*'s 100-yard race for people with no sense of direction. One or two of us freaked out on the way – everyone held hands and ran until it was better, like 5-year-olds in the park. And then we were there.

I don't know how long we lasted, but long enough for the evening to splinter, to turn into individual adventures that you recounted later when you bumped into each other at the horse-trough washbasins, when you fell on your friends as though you'd been parted for years, rather than hours. Were we playing hide and seek at one point? Did we kick our legs out from behind pillars, like stupid pole-dancing ponies? As the sun rose, S and I went to an after-party in a bar off Leather Lane. It had a spiral staircase and a minor film star was there. We slumped on squishy sofas, teased the film star, made each other laugh.

We took photos of ourselves on our digital camera when we got home, thinking we were beautiful, but we looked sweaty and mad. Not that it mattered. We dragged the duvets to the sofa and watched nature films all day.

A few days later, I turned 33. And gradually, gradually, things began to change. Friends were finding partners, leaving house-shares, settling into new places with each other. Or they were leaving the country, resettling in a different way. We were still going out: just up the road, to Basement Jaxx's Rooty in the George IV, or miles away, to Glastonbury, or Ibiza. We got excited about bands. The Strokes: I remember seeing them at Heaven, gorgeous cartoons, rock-star Muppets. The Libertines, not so much. UK garage gradually warped into what would become grime, which I really liked, but I danced to it in my kitchen or at festivals, not at clubs.

The money I got from writing the book on suburbia meant that I could put a deposit on a flat, so I did, and moved in with two flatmates. We tiptoed around the new place, marvelling at how grown-up it seemed: the previous owners were a family, and everything was painted and maintained. The rented flat we were leaving was not so pretty. There, the walls were beige anaglypta, fingerprinted, smudged. The kitchen was orange with grease. In the bathroom, part of the ceiling had collapsed and was held up by the shower rail. When you went to the toilet in there, you had to wear a cycle helmet, in case the whole thing came down completely (health and safety). The new flat had Victorian fireplaces, sash windows, stripped wooden doors with china handles, and it seemed astonishing, solid and artily bohemian, an entry point to a proper life.

And so it proved. After a few months in our new palace, one friend moved out; then S moved in; then, a year or so later, the other friend left. Now there's no more moving: we still live in the same flat, S and I and our kids.

There were weddings, on and off over the decade. There were kids, too, to join the children a few people already had. A range of ages of parents and offspring, but a sudden rush of births after I was 36. We left everything to the final deadline, squeezed in adulthood as late as we could.

Time was doing what it does, ticking on, disappearing, bit by bit by bit. Opportunities were opening up as others were shutting down. There are people who are good at knowing when to move on, the best time to leave, the new thing to follow, where to go and when. They seem born with excellent timing. They'd somehow bought two-bedroom flats while they were in their early twenties. They were busy setting up companies, or were selling the ones they'd already established (when? how?). They were 'moving into digital'.

But there are those of us who make decisions too quickly, or too slowly, or who don't even realize there are decisions to be made. We continue with what we're doing because it's what we do, or because we like it, or we're loyal to something that perhaps is long gone. Or we sack it all on a whim, move from job to job, changing but not progressing, trying out new versions of the same thing.

I'd been working for the *Observer* since the mid-90s, as a regular writer, but I was still a freelancer. This suited me, though I wasn't always good at it. I said yes to jobs I was awful at, turned down opportunities that seem life-changing now. And when I got a new job, I couldn't work out, always, how I was meant to behave, what I was supposed to be doing. I needed an editor, a producer; a mentor, maybe. I wasn't concentrating. I landed another book deal, for a biography, but I couldn't deliver. I wrote dramas that didn't work out. I helped with online start-ups, I mentored teenagers who wanted to be journalists. I wrote columns and my columns were okay. But other columnists came along and they were sharper, funnier or more surreal: they were better.

S and I had met in 1999, and we gave each other an excuse to carry on going out, to continue with what we'd been doing separately (we'd been going to the same places, sometimes even the same parties, we'd discovered) but now with each other. We extended our work trips and went to Thailand, to China and New Zealand. We found the cheapest flights we could to Trieste, Amsterdam, Cornwall, the Pyrenees.

I'm not so good at remembering what happened when we went away, what we saw. S tells me tales of our trips and it's as though I never went. I remember the feelings, though.

'God, do you remember how much we used to argue?' I say to S. 'How could we be arsed?'

Our relationship wasn't smooth. It was difficult in the early years: we were both used to doing what we liked; our backgrounds were different; we found it hard to compromise into partnership. But we were cheap to run, we loved each other. Lucky us. Some of our friends had hooked up with the wrong person. Years of their time had been invested in a partner who suddenly didn't want to stay around, or who was already attached and never leaving their partner, or who was playing them against someone else. Often, it was women who suffered the fall-out. There were emergency rescues from outside bars, long phone calls at odd hours, evenings spent drinking, bitching, comforting.

Love lives, always hard to make sense of, were becoming even more difficult, weighted down with future pressure. Where were these affairs going, what was the point if they weren't going to make it? And it wasn't only love affairs. Friends (and us) were losing jobs; there were pregnancies and non-pregnancies, sudden illnesses, dying parents, sick kids, debt. Adult problems that we weren't qualified to deal with.

'I feel like we've been sitting at the back of the class, messing about,' said my friend L. 'And now we've looked up, and everyone else has been knuckling down for ages, without us noticing. They're going to pass the exams. We're the only ones left back here.'

There were so many changes, behind the scenes, in front of our faces. And yet it's easy to think that your thirties are not so different from your twenties. We thought this. You're just carrying on, refining, tweaking, but essentially remaining the same.

Maybe you look better than you did in your twenties because you're not slathered in make-up or wearing clown clothes. You've grown into your face; you know which haircut suits you. You can understand oblique conversational references ('She's grand,' meaning, 'I hate her'); you realize when jobs are being offered or are about to be taken away (be wary of any conversation that begins 'I don't know if you've heard our news?'). You don't burst into tears quite so much. You speak up when you feel something's wrong. You have less time for people you can't get on with and they have less time for you.

The side-tracking is still there, though. The diversions. The wandering around town in the afternoons, the not-answering your phone, the lunches that turn into evenings that turn into weekends. The belief that you're still an outsider, some sort of rebel *manqué*, sitting on the edges sniping at The Man. But The Man will only notice you if you're doing something worth noticing.

What's strange is that you do no more side-tracking than you did in your twenties, not really. You probably do less. You certainly spend less time drunk. But time is moving faster. It is, it is.

*

At that particular moment, the internet began to make a difference, to music and to books and to the media. The magazines I worked for started to close, one by one. *Select* shut down in 2000; *The Face* in 2004; *Smash Hits*, 2006. The *Mirror* launched a magazine in 2002, and I wrote a column for it; it was shuttered two years later. The *Observer* remained, and its sister paper, the *Guardian*. Both changed their size from broadsheet to Berliner in 2005. The new-sized printing presses cost £80 million, which was deemed a worthwhile investment, as though printing equipment was like London property.

Though most newspapers were still alive, there was pressure on fees, a blanket ban on contracts. One paper gathered together all its regular freelance writers and photographers to tell them it valued them highly but their rates would be cut in half from then on. A hundred per cent of the work; fifty per cent of the pay.

The internet had already messed up the music business, that no-longer-warbling dead canary in the goldmine. Music was all over the place. The money to be made in it was shifting from albums to gigs; record companies and promoters were haggling over what they thought was their share. At one point, mobile phone ringtones were deemed to be the way to wring profits from songs. In 2001, Apple launched iTunes and the iPod, and the iTunes store in 2003. Albums were unbundled, non-singles rendered worthless.

Still, to us, our ways of working remained the best. They had glamour, they were fun. We understood what to do, what the results meant. (Were our ways the old ways? Hadn't we only just invented them?) We laughed and bitched, as the earth was shifting beneath our feet.

In September 2008, I did an interview with Grace Jones. We met in a chi-chi bar-restaurant in Notting Hill that had lots of small rooms and sparkly fairy lights. It was a Monday night. Grace was hours late – her manager and I had a lovely meal while we waited – and, after she arrived, insisted on smoking, which made the waiters mad. At the end of the interview, which wasn't really an interview but an oblique chat in which Grace drank red wine, shouted, 'I am the ink in the squid,' and waggled her legs at me so I could feel how skinny her ankles were – anyway, at the end of that, we went to the bar.

Grace paid for the meal in cash (the only pop star I've ever interviewed who has done so) and ordered Sambuca for us both. She said, 'Father, Son and Holy Ghost,' and we biffed the drinks. Then she stuck her tongue down my throat: an unexpected move, which made me burst out laughing. Her lips were very soft. Grace stroked my face and grabbed my breast and said, 'It's a full moon, I feel horrrrrny' (to be fair, she had shouted this all evening). She wondered if I wanted to come to her hotel, and when I did not, she didn't seem that bothered.

She gave me her phone number. 'File it under Grrrr,' she said, so I did.

I helped her down the stairs – she was very drunk, did I mention? – and we went out into the wide Notting Hill street, the buildings like glistening celebration cakes, the street empty and quiet. Grace ran down the middle of the road, her arms stretched wide, her black outfit billowing around her, howling at the moon.

I thought: They don't make pop stars like that any more.

(They don't. We don't. Do we still want them?)

As Grace ran and howled, without apology, in London, over in New York Lehman Brothers was collapsing. Suddenly, the world of money imploded and shrank, and everything in its orbit got sucked into its black hole, never to escape.

All the bubbles were bursting. There was an election and the coalition got in. The day before the election, I'd interviewed Gordon Brown, prime minister incumbent, for the *Mirror*. I'd gone to the seaside, where he'd made a great speech. But he was impatient during our interview, which, for reasons I forget, took place in a static helicopter in the middle of a field. Afterwards, we had our photograph taken together. Then Brown took off in his helicopter, leaving me and the photographer alone. In a field. We had to find a taxi and file on the hoof. I transcribed the interview on a train, bashed it out in Starbucks. But I couldn't get the Starbucks internet to work on my laptop. My editor started shouting at me down the phone.

I asked a young techy guy if I could hop onto his wi-fi so I could file my copy.

'Sure,' he said. 'What's the article about?'

I told him.

'Who's Gordon Brown?' he asked.

I used to tell this story as an anecdote, a tale of the young and stupid, like a joke. I now think the butt of the joke wasn't the techy guy but me. Old-fashioned me, stranded in a field, rushing to a café, borrowing a dongle, writing about an already-forgotten Labour politician for a left-wing printed newspaper.

Money had changed. It no longer seemed to be real. Instead of it adding and subtracting in a way I understood, it had become a slippery, unsolid commodity. Work, too, was becoming less easy to comprehend, its relationships – between employer and worker, effort and resulting pay – becoming murky and unclear. Also, who owned what was done? Contracts were drawn up that gave employers rights over everything made, whether on the net, across the universe, across time, forever.

We were brought up in a world where jobs for life were rare. But they existed (teachers, council workers), and stability was accepted. Even when Thatcher destroyed the unions, dismantled the mining communities, she herself remained. She didn't budge. She stayed for years, to be followed by Major, who stayed almost as long. We thought New Labour would do the same, but it collapsed so quickly; disappeared, black-holed.

When I was young, my mum and dad worked hard, and were paid for what they did. The maths of their money worked: when they'd paid the bills and there was money left over, we went on holiday. When there wasn't, we didn't. We never went out for meals, but we didn't care about that. At university, if I went more than two hundred pounds overdrawn, the bank wouldn't give me any cash. I had to negotiate long and hard to get fifty pounds a week, which I got by turning up at a particular branch on a Monday and writing a cheque.

Those years seem so close. But they are a decade away, more.

Hitting 40 wasn't momentous. I remember feeling a small twinge of something – fear? Regret? Reflux? – but then I went to see Jarvis Cocker play a solo show and thought, He's older than me, and he's still great. It's not the birthday that matters: it's whatever is going on at the time of the birthday. And at that time, things were OK.

P was small, but there was only one of him and he wasn't at school, so we could warp and weave our lives around him pretty easily. He was difficult but, in hindsight, only in the way that babies are. He didn't do what I thought he would do (I think I thought he would act like a small child); scarily, he didn't do what the books said. He cried a lot. In the mornings, after breakfast, we would put him on a play mat and after a while he would cry. So we would try everything to make him stop: play him music, pick him up, jig him about, put him in his chair, dance about in front of him, give him a jangly toy, maybe some food. Nothing worked. And then someone said, 'Put him back to bed for a nap,' and that worked.

We were applying hectic solutions to a non-hectic situation, because that was how we'd lived up until then. We were still narcissistic enough to believe that a child was an extension of our personalities (he'll love staying up late, because we do; he'll love company for the same reason; he'll like this music because we played it a lot when I was pregnant; oh, look, he's a champion burper – it's a family trait). He lived to our timetable and that timetable remained flexible. Having a child stopped our late nights, mostly; but the major life rhythms, the when and where we were doing what we did, they were still as up and down as we were, as varied as the state of our finances. P seemed to fit in well.

I shared my fortieth birthday do. Two friends and I took over a pub, including the downstairs dance floor. It was a great party. Afterwards, I lay on the pavement outside and stared at the stars, searching out their sparkle between the high rises, looking past the restricted view, out to the enormous sky.

Between 2000 and 2010, I didn't move house once. I got married, I gave birth to two children. I acquired and held on to a flat, a microwave and a dishwasher, and a mortgage on that flat. How did that happen? Is this the person I am now? God, how dreary.

5. This is a Low

Here we are now. (Entertain us.)

The dramas of life change when you have children. They expand to the vastness of your terrified imagination. They reduce to the size of a raggedy toy cat.

'Where's Kitty?' wails F.

'What's she lost?' whispers S. 'That grey rat thing?'

'*Cat*, not rat,' I say. '*Kitty*.'

These dramas take up time, and mind-space. They don't leave much room for your own. This can be a good thing – gone are the hours spent worrying about what you said at a party, mostly because you don't go to parties – but also frustrating, when your own drama is about trying to work out where you're at. And how to go on from there.

I am fitting my drama into specified time slots. I have read that this is one of the best ways to approach unmanageable concerns, to contain the things in the day that keep you awake at night. In the mornings, you consider your anxieties, examine them properly for twenty minutes, then you store them and get on with your day. I contemplate my fears. I'm unsure how deep I should go, how dark and twisted, how specific (unemployment, divorce, the loss of The Point). Or should I be grateful for them, tell them I'm happy they've come into my life? Hold them in my virtual hand, before rolling them up like socks and putting them away tidily in their drawer – the virtual drama drawer (next to the wardrobe of worries)?

The next hour is spent frantically opening real-life drawers and boxes, untidying rooms, checking pockets, under sofas, trying to find a grey toy cat.

In the British Library, I am researching my drama.

In 1965, Canadian psychoanalyst and psychologist Elliot Jaques coined the now much-used epithet 'midlife crisis'. Jaques interviewed a group of successful people and realized that many were feeling the effects of reaching a central point in their working lives. They were confused, disappointed. They'd arrived at their central point to find it was not a high spot, but a dip. Maybe even a spiral. He defined this new crisis as what happened when high achievers hit middle age and feel tortured because of 'unrealized goals, lack of self-determination or physical changes'. It being the 60s, the mid-life point was assumed to be between 30 and 35, and the high achievers Jaques surveyed were men.

Though Jaques named it, and nicely, the idea of a critical moment of change at life's central age had been knocking around for quite a while. Literature loves the idea of a failing, flailing fellow in his middle years, and Carl Jung, through his work in the 1930s, believed that the midlife stage was vital to human development. 'The very frequent neurotic disturbances of adult years all have one thing in common: they want to carry the psychology of the youthful phase over the threshold of the so-called years of discretion,' wrote Jung. We want this, he said, even though it can't happen: 'We cannot live the afternoon of life according to the programme of life's morning: for what was great in the morning will be little at the evening, and what in the morning was true will at evening have become a lie.'

Jung believed there should be colleges for 40-year-olds, institutions of learning to help us get through the painful transition to full maturity. I like this idea. The Middle-aged

University. A place to study your navel, if you can still locate it, Chunky.

When I type 'midlife crisis' into the British Library search engine, I get 359 returns. Some are songs – 'Midlife Crisis Blues' by Jon Scott Cree, 'Mid Life Crisis All The Time' by the Cowboy Killers, 'Mid Life Crisis' by Faith No More. There are blogs and websites (midlifecyclist.com). There are research papers.

It's noticeable that references to midlife crisis seem to increase exponentially as the dates become more recent. There is a handful of books and publications in the 60s, a few more in the 70s and 80s. But from the 90s onwards, midlife crisis is so widely understood that it's used to apply to almost anything. Articles examine the MLC of the Bush administration, the World Health Organization, Indian technology firms, North West Syria. Even outer space: 'The Ultimate Mid-Life Crisis: Active Accretion of Gas and Dust and Planet-formation Around Old Stars'. Middle age means that once-twinkly stars get weighed down by too much stuff, by family closing in on them.

As the decades progress, not only do midlife books become more numerous, they change in tone. After 2000, they are almost always funny, extended merriment concerning trousers with elasticated waistbands and grumpiness about modern music. These books are about men, and often written by someone called Mike. There's *The Full English, Pedalling Through England, Midlife Crisis and Truly Rampant Man Flu* by Mike Carden, out in 2007. *Uneasy Rider: Travels Through A Midlife Crisis*, Mike Carter, 2008. *So You're Having a Midlife Crisis!* Mike Haskins and Clive Whichelow, 2009.

In the 70s and 80s, books about the angst of the middle years took the topic seriously. These days, the idea of midlife crisis is no longer serious at all.

*

Jung preferred 'transition' to crisis, but after Jaques, midlife crisis became the most common phrase to describe the tribulations of the middle years, and the term was quickly expanded to include women.

Female writers tackled the subject. One of the most influential books was *Passages*, by Gail Sheehy, a journalist who was moved to write about the different stages of life when she covered Bloody Sunday and a young lad was shot dead right next to her. It triggered a sort of breakdown, a 'whither life and what does it mean' epiphany – a reasonable reaction, let's face it – and she interviewed a lot of couples at different stages of their lives in order to work out a pattern for living. Much later, she wrote an updated version, a whole new book, called *New Passages*.

She wrote this version because in her original book, and other middle-ish books of the time, the assumptions around a woman's life were very different from today's. Then, marriage happened in your early twenties, kids followed soon after and you stayed at home to look after them and your husband. The midlife crisis of a woman in the 70s and 80s was assumed to happen after her children stopped needing her, and she was left to dust a lonely house for thirty to forty years.

Prime Time, by Helen Franks, which came out in 1981, looks at women between their mid-thirties and mid-fifties. In it, she describes a woman 'no longer burdened by domesticity and childrearing' who has the time 'for emotional stock-taking, a re-examining of beliefs'. She tentatively suggests that such a woman might want to take on some paid work of her own. But many of her subjects are held back from entering employment by their lack of experience, their years of wife-and-mother work. And, shockingly, by their husbands, who want to keep their wives at home, making hot meals and organizing the ornaments, even though they're out all day and the kids have left. Franks writes about a New York psychologist who held workshops for middle-aged women. Not to help them cope with their own midlife crisis but to learn how to cope with their husbands'.

Also in the 80s, Jim Conway, a US pastor, wrote several books about midlife crisis, including one on the midlife crisis of men, and another, with his wife Sally, on the female version. The books are great at pinpointing the feelings of intense inadequacy in men in their forties, the desire to jack everything in – family, work, house – and go driving across the country . . . But they are not so hot on their wives.

In *Women In Midlife Crisis*, Conway (Jim) writes this: 'When I was going through my midlife crisis, Sally was teaching school Monday through Friday. My day off was Monday. In order to be available to be with me, Sally resigned from teaching so that we could get away more frequently for the recuperation and reflection time that I needed.' Good old Sally, eh? Must have loved those jolly Mondays.

Pauline Bart made a study of 533 American women aged between 40 and 55, who were in psychiatric hospitals for depression but had no history of mental illness. Her conclusion was that the women were depressed because they 'had lost the companionship of their children, they had fewer people to shop or cook or clean for, they had been brought up to fulfil themselves through their homes and families, they had no qualifications, had gained no work experience for many years, had no confidence, low self-esteem and nothing to look forward to'. It was 1971. At that time, the greatest users of anti-anxiety drugs were women aged between 45 and 54.

I read William Bridges' *Transitions, Making Sense of Life's Changes*. In it, a man says: 'I feel as though my whole life was built on a frozen lake. We all go on with our activities. We work on the house and play golf and entertain and have our fights. I put in long hours at work and think I'm doing well. Then every once in a while I think, This is ice I'm standing on, and it's melting – or Was that a crack I heard just then? I try to forget, but I keep thinking, Damn, that ice looks thin!'

I read *The Middle Passage: From Misery to Meaning in Midlife*, by James Hollis. He writes, 'Anyone in midlife has witnessed the collapsing of projections, of hopes and expectations, and has experienced the limitations of talent, intelligence and, often, of courage itself.'

I look up funny quotes. 'Midlife is when you reach the top of the ladder and find that it was against the wrong wall': Joseph Campbell. 'The really frightening thing about middle age is that you know you'll grow out of it': Doris Day.

I think about how to write this book. I think: Wouldn't it be great if the book itself had a midlife crisis? If it collapsed in the middle, started doubting itself and the way it had gone about its life so far?

Why are there so many funny midlife books these days? Has midlife crisis become so ingrained as a cultural joke that it's hard not to mention it without us laughing? It's like saying 'farty poo bum' to a 5-year-old, or showing a picture of a dial-phone to a teenager. Ho ho, I know this one. The very concept is hilarious.

I say to people, 'I'm writing a book on midlife crisis,' to see if they laugh. They do. Some of them say, 'Hey, interview me!' Some say, 'Interview him!' and point to their friend or husband. But all of them laugh. Then they define themselves against it. They haven't bought a sports car (they've bought a fixed-wheel bike). They're not leaving their wife for the twenty-something secretary (she's in PR and she's 31).

They're not stuck in the same job they've always had (they've started teaching younger people how to do that job). They're still in love with their partner (they just don't have sex). Ha ha ha.

After a while, I realize they're trying to hide their embarrassment. We are easily shamed in the UK and middle age is so cringe-making that we have to deflect it with a joke. Not only because to admit that you care about it is to admit a reprehensible weakness of character – can't you go marching gladly into your middle years without making such a fuss? – but also because we will not accept that we have anything to do with the crisis part, that uncool state of being.

And so we all define ourselves against it. I say 'midlife crisis' to people and they point at others. Or they pick out the easy parts: the buying of gadgetry, their kids becoming obsessed with their old vinyl. They deny that the truths of middle age, the darker implications, might actually apply.

I wonder, though, if the jokes are getting in the way. They help us skim over the sadness, they mask our bewilderment, and the other option – despair – is hardly appealing. But the MLC jokes remind me of other funnies, the ancient ones, the take-my-mother-in-law gags, the anti-gay or racist one-liners. Comedy shows us where our fears lie.

I have a meeting with a TV commissioning editor. He laughs and says, 'I don't believe midlife crisis exists!' He is wearing an earring, has split up with his wife and is dating someone fifteen years younger. I should have asked him if he had a new bike.

'Have you had a midlife crisis?' I ask S, who is a bit older than me. He was married before, and has two older children, who are adults themselves now, married, settled down.

'Nah,' he says. 'I had my crisis when I was 21. When D was born. Dad said to me at the time,' (I know this story), '"Ah, the toothpaste's out of the tube now, son." You can't push a baby back inside. You bring a child into the world and your life stops being about you.'

Yes, but that's part of it, I think. The terror, and the tedium, and the sheer delight of your children. And you, knowing they will go.

I keep reading. It turns out that there are a lot of people – distinguished academics, psychotherapists – who insist that midlife crisis is not a thing. After all, unrealized goals, lack of self-determination and physical changes are not problems exclusive to forty-somethings: you can run up against them at any stage in your life. The academics point out that middle age is tricky, busy, overwhelming, but that doesn't mean there's a crisis. Nothing to see here. It's just middle age.

Also, a crisis tends to be triggered by an event: a parent dying; losing your job; a long-term relationship breaking up; having a child, or the children leaving home. Any one of these upsets can trigger a sudden shift in thinking, a shaking of the foundations of your life. Which is what happened to S, in his early twenties.

But S is becoming an anomaly. These days, more children are born to women of 35 and over than to women under 25. And most of these crisis-triggering events occur around middle age, that busy time.

And, like I say, we make jokes about midlife crisis. This is the greatest evidence for its existence. Jokes are how the British acknowledge anything fundamental. If it wasn't important, we wouldn't be laughing about it.

Somewhere inside, I seem to believe that middle age should be the pinnacle of life, the moment when all your previous efforts add up to something meaningful and you find yourself at the top of the mountain. I mention this to a friend, psychotherapist Philippa Perry, and she says: 'That's only a metaphor. Why not change it?'

For a while I try to imagine life as a long climb to the ultimate summit. But then I start noticing all the studies that indicate a different shape. Every time I find a piece of empirical research, it insists that, when it comes to our lives, happiness is U-shaped. Across several nations (Australia, Germany, the UK, others) the saddest time is in middle age. We're full of joy when very young and very old, but struggle badly with the time in the centre. We go through our forties at our lowest psychological ebb. Some of the studies pinpoint 47 as our unhappiest age; some say 44. But it's always in our forties.

Other research has found that great apes – chimpanzees and orangutans – have a similar life pattern. At the end of 2012, a global team (from Edinburgh, Arizona and Kyoto) studied 508 orangutans and chimpanzees and discovered that they suffer from middle-aged angst. As the apes live to around 55, they have their crisis in their late twenties.

Andrew J. Oswald, an economics professor from the University of Warwick, writes: 'It seems the curve of happiness should no longer be considered a social and economic phenomenon, the preserve of economists, sociologists, social psychologists, psychiatrists or mysticists. Instead, intriguingly, the U shape appears to be so deep within us that it may need a natural sciences explanation.' Not a crisis, then, a life condition.

More research. Pile it on. Let the book have its breakdown, with me. Let it look at itself and unpick what it sees. Give us the bad stats.

The average age at divorce is 45 for men, 42 for women. In 1970, most divorces happened to people aged between 25 and 29. In 2012, the number of divorces was highest among men and women aged 40 to 45; 65 per cent of divorces are instigated by women; 42 per cent of marriages will end in divorce, after, on average, 11 years.

Adults aged 45-plus are three times as likely as those under 45 to drink every day. Between 1991 and 2008, alcohol-related deaths in the 35–54 age group doubled in number. The percentage of 45–55-year-olds who take cocaine has doubled in a decade. Nearly a quarter of all drink and drug hospital admissions are of people in their forties.

Among marathon-runners, a study shows, 49-year-old men are at the greatest risk of suffering a heart attack; 93 per cent of such attacks occurred in men whose average age was 49. Other studies demonstrate that what is named as 'pure exercise dependence' is found most often in men in their forties and fifties.

Almost half of the long-term unemployed (47.2 per cent) are over 50.

There are two age spikes in male suicides in the UK: when men are in their early twenties and early forties. There has been quite a lot of notice taken of those in the younger group, but less support is offered to potentially suicidal middle-aged men. Because, you know, they're middle-aged men. They're the powerful ones, surely.

The bad stats. The dip to sadness.

We all want to be happy. But middle age, the time of money problems, of work responsibilities and looming insecurities, of boredom and frustration and a lack of self-realization, of caring for those younger and older than ourselves, of diminishing fitness, energy and relevance: that doesn't always seem like such a happy place.

6. Jealous

I bring up the question of middle age with almost everyone I meet. People tell me odd, illuminating stories that help.

One man I talk to says he had a 'massive' crisis a few years ago, when he was in his early forties. It was a nervous breakdown, really, triggered by him splitting up from a long-term girlfriend, but it manifested itself in extreme, searing envy. Of people he didn't know; of people he knew well. He had to give up seeing several of his oldest friends for a time because, in his eyes, they had everything and he had nothing and he couldn't hang out with them any more because it was making him so unhappy.

What is unusual about his story was that he was a millionaire. But his cash didn't help his crisis. This man wanted what his friends had – what I have: a partner and kids. Money made no difference to his situation.

I enjoy this story (the man is no longer in pain), not because it reveals that what everyone wants is to be loved but because I'm down to my last couple of hundred. It affirms what I pretend are my choices: to be married, to have kids, not to have thousands of pounds hanging around in my bank account. Ha! I think. I knew money didn't bring you happiness! All my favourite books and films told me this. Religion too: Jesus turning over the rich men's tables in the temple. They all insisted that being not-rich equates with being good. So the reason I haven't earned millions is because I'm a morally superior person. It has nothing to do with me not having the requisite talent to earn a huge amount, or not caring enough to barter down prices, or not being able to keep hold of money when I have it instead of spending it in the wrong places.

Of course, if I didn't care about money, I wouldn't be thinking like this.

Money is part of life, and it should be thought about, as should jealousy. The story is about the man being jealous of his friends' lives, and also about me being jealous of his.

A story about money.

In my late thirties, I was offered a chunk of cash by a publisher to write a book about Madonna, in honour of her turning 50. Very, very occasionally, S will remind me of this, our non-existent 'Madonna patio money'. If I'd been able to work out how to write the book, we would be living in a house with a patio, possibly a small area of grass, maybe even – I know, I know – decking.

But I couldn't bring myself to write 120,000 words about a famous person without some form of cooperation from that person, and Madonna was never going to give me any. I got in touch with a few people she'd worked with, set up some interviews, but when I approached her official representatives, the answer was no. So how would I write the book? Would I need to go through her bins? Did she even have bins? I'd have to follow her around as she got on with her impenetrable life, as she zipped across the world on prearranged schedules I would never be party to. I'd talk to security guards and fans and people who went to the same school as she did forty years ago, to anyone but the inner circle, and what would be the point? I would hate myself and it wouldn't be the book the publishers wanted.

P was only a baby and I didn't want to go away for weeks on end, and I didn't want to write about someone who didn't want me to write about them.

I gave back the advance. The book didn't happen. Life went on.

My attitude to money has changed. In my teens and twenties, money was a means to an end. I would work hard for a bit, earn enough to do what I wanted, and then I would stop working to go and do it. Mostly, this involved going away. You don't need much cash to do that.

Once I had the flight or the ferry ticket, once I jumped on the bus, everything else was fine. If I didn't have anywhere to stay, I met people who knew a place to crash, or I slept in doorways, or stations (legs inside sleeping bag, money in socks, head on bag, arm crooked through the strap), or on abandoned pallets, or a beach, or I used a tent or crept into abandoned storage containers. I've crashed out in the railway station at Milan (after 2 a.m., the police moved us outside the station, to sleep on the pavement in the doorway). Under a bench in a public park in Zürich. On a rock on Lampedusa (all the beaches were sand-less, covered with jagged volcanic outcrops). All fine, because I had somewhere to stretch out and I was usually with a friend.

When I went away then, a lot of time was spent on the basics: where we were going to sleep, what we would eat, how we would get to the next place. No matter who I was with, we would somehow spend all the money we had in the first three days, then survive for weeks. Not having money made us resourceful: we would scour markets as they shut, pick up wonky vegetables, snaffle stale bread. We'd talk our way into nightclubs and then nick drinks, eat free tapas and nibbles put out on bars. We would find hash, smoke some of it and swap the rest for food. We would jump trains on scuffed-up, rewritten tickets. We would accept evenings out from men we knew probably wanted to sleep with us, just to get fed, and then we would run away. We would get by on charm and noisiness. We were young.

At the moment, I have to stop myself getting agitated about where we live. I blame TV property shows, stimulating a long-dormant home-improvement gene. Also: envy. My middle-aged emptiness, my inside absence, has become epitomized by another absence, the lack of a small patch of concrete in which we could shove some mouldy pot plants and P could practise his football skills. The Madonna patio. We can't afford to buy a house with a garden in the area where we live because we live in London, and since the bank and I bought our flat in 1999, house prices have soared like someone's spinning numbers on a roulette wheel. We would have to borrow twice as much as I borrowed for the flat in the first place, and the bank won't give us that, because we're freelance and we don't earn enough money per year. Also, we're too old. Add twenty-five years to my age and you're way past retirement.

S says: 'I don't want a garden. Living in a flat is much safer – you don't get robbed. Anyway, even if we had a garden, you kill every plant you've ever touched. You're shrubbery's Dr Mengele.'

I say: 'I only want a Madonna.'

He says: 'You should have written that book, then. We live in London. It pisses down for ten months of the year. There's a park round the corner. If you're looking for sympathy, it's in the dictionary between shit and syphilis.'

How did the people I know make money? What did they do? We seemed to be doing much the same things for a while, and then I looked away and looked back and they were earning six-figure salaries, living in multi-levelled houses with glass-encased kitchens on the back and gardens big enough to host a shed and a Wendy house and a patch of meadow grass. Maybe I shouldn't have spent all that time going away. Maybe I should have learnt DIY, added value to our delightful residence. But every time I think of doing up the sitting room, I think, Oh, God, I'd rather go out.

I talk to Philippa Perry again. She says: 'Even though we use the words interchangeably, there is a difference between jealousy and envy. Jealousy is not good: it's about holding on to stuff you have, being possessive over what's yours, such as your partner. Jealousy means you get angry because you think someone is trying to get hold of your precious things. But envy – covetousness – can be useful. If we're envious of something a friend has, or what a famous person is doing, that envy can show us where our ambitions lie.'

I say: 'Maybe I should buy a lottery ticket.'

Philippa tells me it's more important to use envy as a motivator. If you're envious of someone's wealth, then why not start budgeting properly, or work to get a job where you're likely to be paid better, or sell stuff on eBay, or move to a cheaper area? Why don't you? Why don't I?

S and I go to a birthday event of some rich friends. It's at a private members' club and there are a lot of people there: film actors and pop stars and writers and directors and artists. There is lovely food and wine. What's strange when you hang with really well-off people is that you never pay, even if you want to. Lots of rich people are generous, and there is not much you can do to say thank you (you can't do the washing-up, or proffer a bottle of wine or buy them anything they don't already have). You can be un-boring and kind. You can refrain from insisting that they perform when they don't want to. You can assume that they are as fun and as funny as your not-rich friends and act accordingly.

Many of the rich people I know are proper fun. Some are wild-hilarious-nutso, because they were born rich and it divorced them from polite convention, like the 93-year-old S met in Ireland who owns a stately home and goes clubbing regularly. He likes house music, but only the hard stuff – the 'boom-boom-boom', he calls it. The nutso-rich open their houses to anyone; they host festivals somewhere on their rolling lawns, or parties on an island that their children remembered they owned. They are divorced from the world in a fantastical way, free from conventional worries, tied down by family and manners but not much else.

Some rich people are artists who got lucky, who created something that other people are willing to pay a lot to own. They are full of ideas and schemes and jokes and excitement; they are fantastic company because, despite everything, they are not motivated by money.

Money doesn't kill joy. Nor does respect for money. The love of money does something odd to the tender parts of your heart but, in the end, money just enhances what you are. If you were boring before you had money, you are irredeemably tedious once you're rich.

So. I appear to be envious of people with money. Locating the source of that envy is all very well but, in middle age, the truly unsettling aspect of coveting your neighbour's assets is that you may be too late to get them. They have disappeared. If you are past the age of conception, you will not be able to have your own child. If you have stayed at a certain career level for some years, it will be hard to advance. If you are too old to get a mortgage, you cannot buy a property. Envy might indicate what you would like to do, but age will disqualify you.

Facing the limits of your talent, hitting the permanent fence that surrounds your world, is hard. You're too old to play for United. You can't win the Turner Prize past 50. You haven't put in the 10,000 hours of practice on the guitar and now you won't be in a rock band and, anyway, how could you spare the time?

It's depressing, this restriction of available achievement, I find. What's the point in bashing away at life when you're too old to achieve what you wanted? You might as well just grumble from the side-lines, be bitter about those who are organized or talented enough to achieve. It reminds me of a type of man I used to meet a lot, a particular sort of music fan, who liked to snipe at my taste and belief in pop music. Why was I wasting my time writing about such trivial pap? Why wasn't I searching out the real deal? These men would tell me they would never lower themselves to work for *Smash Hits* or the Murdoch press, or to consider Top 40 bands. They'd corner me to list increasingly obscure artists, and when I eventually said I didn't know what or who they were talking about, their triumph was absolute. But, despite their mad knowledge, they weren't involved in music in any way at all, except as consumers. They weren't even writing about it.

'People fear failure more than they desire success,' says Philippa. 'And that gets us pretty stuck sometimes. We stay where we are rather than dare to risk failing at something.'

I think this is true. But also success depends on circumstance, on luck and somehow saying the right thing to the right person and someone with power being kind to you. Often, on support: someone to look after the kids, parents who loved you and taught you self-sufficiency. Also: being able to concentrate for long enough to get the job done, not getting distracted by your seemingly vital social life, and having the skill – the knack – of hearing what important people are really asking you to do. Of understanding when opportunity knocks.

Like Philippa said, it depends on not being frightened, and we are all frightened at some point. When I started working at *Smash Hits*, it took me a week to get up the gumption to tell my editor he'd got my name wrong on the masthead. He'd got confused with my nickname and the surname of a famous actress and instead of Miranda Sawyer, the first time I saw my name in print it said: Bunny Richardson. (I did tell him, and he did change it. I'm proud of this: I know of someone who had to drop his subject at university because his tutor called him the wrong name and he never had the courage to tell him the right one.)

Somewhere deep inside us, we know that there are exceptionally gifted, determined, clever people who deserve all the accolades and success that they get. But we also know there are many more people – just as clever, just as gifted – who didn't get the breaks. Envy loves that knowledge.

Envy is hard to admit to. It is nasty, it is shameful. It is first-world problems; unforgivable, really. It's hard to think of it in positive terms, to see envy as motivation, rather than bitterness.

But the thing about middle age is that it requires you to understand your situation. To think about where you are. And how do you know where you are? You compare your life to the one you think you should have. The one you thought you would have, the life you imagined when you were younger. Where did it go, that life you were designed for?

Your lost life filters through the life you have now, casting too-bright light over your daily existence. It makes your real life seem tawdry and small. You feel not 'I could have been a contender', but 'I am still a contender.' If only all these other fuckers could see it.

Or perhaps you've hidden your lost life in memory boxes stuck in the attic. You catch your lost life, sometimes, when you flick through old photos, or stumble across TV broadcasts of vintage pop performances. And your heart wants to burst out of your chest, as though you were the same age as when you first saw those gods, those alien beings who sang your feelings and changed your life into something special and meaningful. There are TV channels specifically designed to engender this reaction.

The pain of knowing you are now too old to beat sporting records, too out-of-date for your talent to make any impression on the young people who are driving culture, that pain might be ridiculous, but it is still pain. Magical thinking, when it doesn't conjure up the magic, can leave you sour. You are not the Great and Wondrous Oz. You are a small grey-haired man pretending to have spectacular gifts you don't possess.

And, of course, we live in an envious society. Capitalism has built entire industries around envy. I look at the young models with their long, slim limbs and I wonder how much it would cost to get that skin, those legs. Even though I know those particular assets don't exist for anyone over 25. Even though I couldn't afford them anyway.

One of the things I notice now is that in conversations with other people there's almost always a status element. It's disguised, but it's there. So if someone says they're so busy they can't cope, they're really saying, 'I'm important because I'm indispensable.' If they tell you they're alone but managing? Read: 'I'm strong and capable, despite being abandoned by the person I built my life around.' Going out to gigs, getting hammered? Still relevant, not old. Know what's going on locally? In touch with authentic experience. Kids picked for a sports team? Great parenting, plus talent passing down the generations.

We are all trying to tell other people something important about ourselves, and that important thing is how well we're doing, according to how we want to be defined. We're staking our claim – 'Standing on our own piece of carpet,' says Philippa – affirming our status, and there's nothing wrong with that. It's information offered, it's an attempt to make friends, to help us all understand each other better.

Status, we love it. On Facebook, when we write about what we're doing, we're offering a Status Update. And we edit what we post, consciously, unconsciously, because status is wrapped around our identity. We all compare.

Status Update: if you compare yourself to people you've known for some time – school friends, clubbing mates, old work friends – you will be somewhere in the middle. (In almost every aspect of life, we are somewhere in the middle.) A very few of those friends will be properly successful.

I have friends who are very successful, whose status has risen as though it were shot up into the air, exploding across the sky, like a beautiful firework. I still see many of them, but not all. A properly successful person is very busy and new friends may fit in better with their new life: people of similar status or with similar jobs, who are married to someone who works in the business, whether that business is making movies or selling fridges. Also, if someone becomes well known, you stop being able to do some of the stuff you used to do together. You can't go out for a meal, unless you want to eat in two-minute shifts. You have to stop conversations for fans to get their selfies. You find yourself acting as your friend's minder, moving people along in a brusque manner. And your friend never comes over to your house because theirs is so much more comfortable, with better things to do. So why not go over there? It's nicer.

I have friends who have left me behind and, though I don't mean to, I have left some friends behind too. But I have other friends I didn't know so well a while back, whose lives have morphed and warped and have ended up somehow slotting in close to mine; they have hooked up with a partner who I think is brilliant; they enjoy the company of my husband and kids. Old friends get left behind, by all of us, and new ones swim into focus.

Philippa says, 'The biggest mistake we make is to compare our inner selves with other people's outer selves.' How we feel has nothing to do with how we appear. The thriving millionaire was a broken wreck inside.

Still, we like to do this. It's how we've always done things. We read other people's exterior signals to check what's going on underneath. And, luckily for us, there are many modern methods to aid us in our pointless comparisons. There is the media generally, and now there is social media. Instagram and Facebook let you know exactly how well you're doing, because you can see how well everyone else is doing. Your peer group parades their superior exteriors, their happy lives and, if you're not feeling great, you compare your inner world to their outer version of theirs.

Envy will ooze from these comparisons, the rotten stuff: it leaks, oozes. It's an inevitable side effect. Like your teeth falling out if you become addicted to meth.

I know that I'm rich – I'm healthy, I love and am loved, I enjoy my work – but my all-the-medals, utterly privileged, completely wonderful existence doesn't stop me sometimes envying other people and their seemingly more amazing lives.

I don't need much to survive on. I spend my money on my kids.

('Are we rich?' asks P.

'Yes,' I say, because we are.

'Well, can I have a Swegway then?' he says. 'Tyler has one and he's a year younger than me.'

'No,' I say.)

I drive through Dulwich and the houses are vast, with gardens, close to the park. They are owned by bankers, by multi-millionaires. We will never own one of those houses.

I see other middle-aged people looking in estate agents' windows, at the pictures of the houses in the area. They are yearning, even as they point and laugh at the prices.

I go to a festival and, on the Saturday afternoon, a man dressed from head to toe in gold-patterned Lycra comes to sit with us. He is 30, a hedge-funder. Festivals are where he lets off steam, he says, by dressing from head to toe in gold-patterned Lycra, and also by taking MDMA, which he has. He's pretty bonced. He's called Henry.

Henry has hit a where-is-my-life-going moment and wants to know what we think. He doesn't really like his job, but he can't give it up because he wants to buy a flat. I say, 'Well, you work for a hedge fund, you must earn enough to be able to buy a flat.'

He says, 'Yes, but I want a two-bedroomed flat in Knightsbridge. I'm going to need a million. As a deposit.'

'Knightsbridge is horrible,' says my friend. She's not lying. It really is.

I'm not jealous of the 30-year-old hedge-funder, not in the slightest. He is ridiculous. Also sexist (he kept banging on about wanting to marry a woman he wouldn't be ashamed of when they were walking the dog together aged 50). So, despite my envies, it clearly isn't money or youth I desire. Or even MDMA. Maybe I just want a patio.

Meeting Henry the hedge-funder makes me think of envy as another kind of indicator. Our fairy stories tell us that having too much money is bad – morally bad – because we know that most money is made by exploiting other people. Our fairy stories highlight the human desire for a certain amount of redistribution of wealth. It is ridiculous that an idiot in gold Lycra can earn enough, through playing with other people's money, to contemplate spending millions of pounds on a flat.

Envy and individualism go hand in hand. Living in an individualistic, consumerist society makes us feel we can solve our painful jealousies on our own, by shopping our way out of them. Buy a flat in Knightsbridge, or a patio, and you will feel better about yourself. You will not feel less than everyone else.

But what if, instead of worrying about our own small world, we think of a larger section of people than just ourselves? Then envy becomes a bit strange. How can you be envious of a single person's success if you're contained within a community that is more than just you and your family? It would be like being envious of your own kids.

Individualism is enticing, but it is small and mean. Also, often, impractical. It might be quicker to sort out most of your own problems yourself, but the bigger questions in life will probably require input from others. People who know more than you do, simply by having had a different life from you.

When you're happy, you're happy that other people are too. When you're not, then you're resentful. If we can get happy in middle age, our envy will go and we'll be able to live in our own lives.

7. Sex

I'm walking home after dropping P at school when another parent catches me up. She has some gossip, she says. And she tells me about a mother we both know, who has suddenly left her husband and children, run off to live with another man, and he's left his kids behind, too. Five young children are involved. Or not involved, depending on your perspective.

We say the conventional things. Both of us are taken aback that a seemingly happy family was, in fact, so miserable that a grown-up felt forced to abandon it. Both of us are surprised that the mum has left her kids behind. She'll come back for them, we think.

But what really flabbergasts us both is that she actually had the time to have an affair.

'I'm too busy to shit,' says my friend. 'Let alone have sex with someone who isn't within two feet of me after the kids have gone to sleep.'

Have we reached the Divorce Years? Are we here already? The sad final scenes, the bitter unravellings of those swift and joyful months when friends found the one they couldn't move past . . . It doesn't seem so long ago that every summer contained a wedding to go to. I used to bitch about them: the expense, the travel, the stupid sentiment. Now, I really want another wedding.

I talk to someone I care about and she mentions, lightly, that she and her husband don't agree about anything any more and that their marriage is completely over. But they can't separate: not just because of the children – though they are definitely a factor – but because they can't afford it. 'I can't pay the rent on my own,' she says. 'Neither can he. We're stuck.' Pricey houses and static wages act like old-fashioned convention, putting on the pressure to keep marriages together, no matter how unhappy.

Another time, I go to a do and I wonder where my friend's wife is and he tells me that they're splitting up, so she didn't come. And I laugh, because I know he's joking, and he's laughing too, but he isn't joking, and he tells me that it's for the best because their daughter is still a toddler so she'll never know any different.

And then I drop the kids at a party and find myself in the road hugging a mum I know only slightly because she tells me that her husband has been having an affair. That he is leaving. And she is being funny and strong, making jokes about hooking up with old boyfriends, and hopping on to her yoga teacher – but then she describes how confused their twins are about the whole thing and her eyes fill with furious tears. The white heat of her anger. It makes me want to back away. But I can't, so I watch her burn in front of me.

'The worst thing is,' she says, 'that I still love him. I still fancy him, for fuck's sake. But now I have to stop. I'm being forced to give up on something that I still believe in.'

Those bad stats again. Between 2002 and 2008, the Office for National Statistics reports that the number of divorced women over 45 went up by a third.

As Louis CK says, all divorces should be celebrated because they mean the end of a bad marriage.

*

But celebration seems impossible. Part of the horror is the cliché. We all made a promise, when we were young, that we would be different. We would never resort to those tired roles, never behave like those awful, obvious adults. But here are our friends, shouting along with the soap script, playing their parts as the vindictive husband, the philandering wife. It's so hammy! But it's real. This is Year Zero for their children's therapy. We're all fuck-ups and we fucked everything up.

And, God, the cliché is so much more painful, so much more destructive than we ever imagined. I watch friends disintegrate, their faces and voices change, as though their atoms are being melted from the inside. A couple, each of them charming, whose marriage went so wrong that he grabbed her round the throat and spat in her face. Another couple split and afterwards he proclaims himself happier than he's ever been, while she cries and worries about his self-medication. Think about yourself! I want to shout, but don't.

The depths of the confusion. The fall-out. The embarrassment. A parent brings along his new partner to watch his kids perform in a show, and we smile as we are introduced to her. (She's not even twice the age of his children, who dance grimly before her.) Does she want to be here? Can he feel his kids' distress? Is this why manners were invented, so we can all gloss over the pain? Skate swiftly over the surface or everyone will fall through the cracks.

Also: is divorce catching? What was so bad about the relationships that have ended? They didn't seem so different from ours, from everyone else's. Funny, attractive, loving people in funny, attractive, loving marriages.

I have no idea what happens within someone else's marriage. Who has? Mostly, you don't know what's going on in yours. You're too busy living inside it, shouting up the stairs about a mislaid item of sports clothing or texting questions about who can take one child to a party or are we actually going to that thing on Thursday, I forgot? So much of marriage is arrangements, division of labour, checking of details. It's hard to inject romance into a husband–wife exchange when the essence of that exchange is to establish which one of you was meant to buy toilet roll.

I think our marriage muddles along okay. But maybe I'm complacent. On the same day that my friend tells me about the runaway mother, S shows me an item of clothing he's found in his office, which doubles as our spare room. He dangles it in front of me. It is a white lacy thong.

'Yours,' I say. 'Or my dad's.' Definitely not mine: I hate no-cheek knickers.

We do the only sane thing to do with a thong – which is to put it on your head and make big googly eyes through the leg-holes – and then I sling it in the bin.

I don't feel any paranoia about the thong. I presume it was left behind by one of our friends who stayed the night. It was a bit dusty: I feel more paranoid about how dirty our flat is.

Although I can definitely feel jealous, I've never spent too much time worrying about whether S might leave me for someone else (who wears small pants). If he decides to cheat on me, then really, truly, what can I do about it? He fell in love with me because he thought I was great. If he no longer loves that great person, or no longer fancies me, or no longer respects me enough not to have sex with someone else, then complicated new knickers are not going to make him change his mind.

But I know, too, that sex is a vital, life-changing force. And I've read enough books and watched enough films and have enough broken-hearted friends to know that the strongest of marriages can unravel when its thread is snagged by the thrill of someone new. It doesn't take much to step out of the protective circle of a long-term relationship. You just have to convince yourself that your eternity ring is a shackle.

Perhaps I should be more worried about the thong. But, you know, it's a thong. 'Thong' is such a stupid word. Thong thong thong. If I called it a G-string, would I take it more seriously?

Some conversations about middle-aged sex.

'He can't keep it up for long,' she says. 'It's okay, really, I don't mind all that much, I can finish myself off easy enough. The problem is that when it goes wrong, it makes sex feel like another thing that I have to do. Something else I started with good intentions but didn't manage to finish. Like when you order Christmas presents online and you choose everything really carefully and put it in the basket and get all excited – but there's something wrong with the payment page, so you can't pay, and you've spent all that time getting excited for no reason. You know you'll have to do it all over again, another evening. Like that.

'Oh and then, one morning after a not very successful night before, I went in to wake up X (her teenage son) and he wouldn't move, so I pulled the duvet off him and he had a stonking hard-on. That was a very weird moment, for lots of reasons.'

A different night, a different speaker: 'We haven't shagged in two and a half weeks. I don't know if it bothers him. I suppose he has a wank, that's what men do. But it's so far down my priorities at the moment, I don't actually care. He thinks that what I want is a date night and a massage – he keeps suggesting it. What I really want is for him to do the online supermarket shopping or supervise the kids' homework and get them to go to bed. That would be more likely to get him a jump.'

A man: 'I look at women on the tube. And I think, God, she's bloody gorgeous . . . And so's she . . . And then I think, Well, do I want to shag her? And I kind óf do but I'm married, so obviously I don't. Also, I'd have to get her to agree.

'But also there's a doubt in my mind that things have moved on, that I'll be an old driver in a fast new car and I wouldn't be able to cope, I wouldn't know the new moves . . . Basically, I think, Well, even if I got her into bed, then, oh, fuck, I'd come too fast, or I'd lose my hard-on. All it takes is for your body to let you down once or twice when it comes to sex and you wonder, Is this the beginning of the end? Am I becoming a dirty old man now?'

A male friend: 'All you want is to know that you're still desired, that she still fancies you.'

Another one (married): 'I haven't had a blow job in a decade.'

I remember, years ago, when a good friend was having trouble with her then-boyfriend. They were in their early thirties and she was worrying about whether they should stay together, should they move their relationship to another level, what was happening with them? She talked and talked about it with me and another girlfriend, discussing what she should say to him, how she should phrase difficult questions.

Then one of us said: 'You do know that you shouldn't say any of this until you've had sex? That's the most important tactic for negotiation.'

This was not a joke. Having sex means that some arguments just don't start.

Divorce isn't always about sex, not at all. Even if the tipping point is one partner sleeping with someone else, sex is the symptom, not the problem. You don't shag someone new if everything's okay at home.

And if it's not okay? Relate is one of the places where partners can look for help when things are going wrong. I talk to Denise Knowles from Relate.

She says, 'Men aged between 40 and 55 can be working their rocks off, literally. Tiredness is the great libido leveller. Our lifestyle today lowers testosterone and increases cortisol. That can have a physiological effect, and men can withdraw from sex because they don't feel they can trust themselves to sustain an erection.'

She also says that what most women want is time. They want someone to help with the childcare, with the day-to-day chores, especially if they work too.

'If the man helps, that frees up the woman's time and shows support, which means she's much more likely to feel like joining in with his idea of a date night. If she feels like a housekeeper, she doesn't feel valued, and it's hard for a woman to have sex with someone she doesn't like very much.'

I go to an awards ceremony for work and sit next to a man who has a young face but is, I think, around my age. A singer who was very successful in the 90s is performing. He says to the audience, 'You're the reason why I have four or five houses, so thanks for that,' then makes jokes about his songs not getting on the Radio 1 playlist any more, unless he does a duet with someone younger and cooler. He is 39. 'That's not something I think about much,' he quips.

I make jokes about the singer with the man sitting next to me. I tell him that I'm writing a book on midlife crisis.

The man says, 'When you lie awake at night in the dark, wondering what you're doing with your life? When your kids find your favourite skateboarding T-shirts and nick them because they're cool, and it makes you wonder if you're too old to wear them any more?'

He has been married for sixteen years. He and his family live in an expensive property outside London; his children go to private school. He's keen to tell me how well he's done, but self-deprecating about it too: a bit like the singer.

I say, because I bet he has, 'I bet you've got a fancy bike.'

He has. He and a group of male friends go mountain biking – they call it training – on a weekday evening, then install themselves in the pub until past closing time. No wives allowed. I tease him about this. He takes it well.

He says, 'We got a dog. After sixteen years of marriage, at least there's still someone who wants to sniff my balls.'

This is a joke he's made before. By telling it to me, he's being friendly. Perhaps a bit flirty. But, still, it brings me up short.

This stranger is telling me he doesn't have sex with his wife any more. He doesn't have sex with her any more because she doesn't want to, and he feels awful about it.

An American author called M. Gary Neumann reports that only eight per cent of cheating men give sexual dissatisfaction as the reason for infidelity. Forty-eight per cent of them say that emotional dissatisfaction is the primary reason.

The men say they feel unappreciated, and wish their partner could recognize that they're trying to be good husbands. But they don't talk to their partner about this, because they worry that talking will cause more anger and rejection. Also, that if they start a discussion about issues in their marriage, their wives won't ever stop talking.

Other fears and worries? They see their partner's defensiveness as anger, rather than a cover for her feeling rejected. They blame their partner for boring sex but won't talk about ways of making things more exciting. They feel self-conscious about their own performance. They want to protect themselves, their partner and their marriage and they do that with silence.

I talk to Philippa, and she says, 'Sex actually gets more scary and more important the longer you're with someone.'

In a new relationship, where nothing much is invested, it's fairly easy to say to someone exactly what you want during sex. After all, you're often playing a part when you first meet someone you fancy, or at least trying out a character. Your relationship hasn't been defined, your roles haven't settled, so you can mess about with who you are. If it goes wrong, so what?

But if you're in a relationship that has lasted a long time, if you're asking for something new in bed, you're risking much more. You're risking being ridiculous. You're risking being refused. What if your lover laughs at you? Then you're being laughed at by the most important person in your life.

'Yes,' says Philippa. 'It can seem like you're risking your entire world.'

Philippa and I sit in her kitchen drinking tea and chatting about bollock-sniffing. She says that, for some people, 'It feels easier to have an affair, get found out and leave the wife, than it does to tell your wife that you're at her mercy. If you're unable to say, "I feel sad, vulnerable and unlovely because you're not interested in my testicles," to your wife, then you might well end up having an affair.'

I think that many men would find that particular phrase hard to say – and there can't be many women who would put their partner's testes high on their list of fascinating interests – but I see what she means.

Philippa tells me that if Mr Bollock Sniffer had an affair, it would be a 'conflict-phobic' affair – an affair that happens because you can't talk about your desires with your partner in case it causes conflict.

There are other reasons for affairs, she says. Some people are nuts for conflict. They make contact through conflict: they have an affair, get caught, and hope that their husband or wife will also have an affair so that the battle, which is their true connection, will escalate. Others are sex addicts, shagging whoever whenever they get the chance. Some compartmentalize, so they genuinely believe that the affair is separate from their married life. Others have a side-shag because they feel too vulnerable being intimate with one person alone.

And then there's the 'exit affair', which is pretty much how all relationships ended when I was young. One of you started sleeping with someone else, the other one found out; a few weeks of weeping and drinking and pity-shags, *fin*.

I say, 'A lot of midlife marriages end because the man has an affair with a younger woman. Why is it always a younger woman?'

'Middle-aged men feel sexier than their wives,' says Philippa, 'because a wife is probably at her sexiest when she's got a gloss of maturity but is still nubile – when she's around 25. Whereas for men, because they have power in our society, the more money they have, the more powerful and sexy they become. So a 53-year-old rich man feels equal to a 25-year-old nubile woman. But he's also insecure about it, so he needs the reassurance of the trophy. He needs to have her.'

I've never been keen on unpicking the mechanics of sex because, as with anything truly ecstatic, a lot of the joy disappears once you think too hard about how it's done. But outside who puts what where and how, I think some of the relevant mechanical factors in midlife sex could be: tiredness; hormones; unspoken resentments.

I speak to academic and therapist Josh Cohen. We talk about many things and then he says this: 'Sex can be a very convenient place to park all your resentments about your relationship, precisely because you don't have to talk about it. It can be a very nice little repository of silent rage and resentment. It simmers away. It's a quiet, malignant contract.'

He says, 'There is only one paradigm and it's youth, and we can have youthful sex, and that's it. After that, we're meant to bitterly wean ourselves off our investment in sex and pretend we're interested in other things. Or we can carry on as though we're still 19. There's no curiosity about what it might mean to have a sexuality beyond youth.'

I say that talking to middle-aged people about sex has made me realize that some couples struggle with something they never expected to happen when they were young. Not that they both might not want to have as much sex, but that one person might want more than the other.

'They have to think about what that means,' says Josh. 'What does it mean if their wife or husband isn't always up for it, in one way or the other? If what excited your spouse about themselves and about you is no longer the same as it was . . . Why not be curious about that? Curiosity generates excitement and it seems to me we've lost our curiosity and our capacity for excitement about what being in middle age could actually bring us.'

'I have seen couples,' says Philippa, 'who are terrified that they're drifting apart because they no longer fancy each other. They've got everything in common, they know each other's histories, they know what a glance across the room means, they've got amazing communication, but they're still worried. It's almost as though the world has intruded on their coupling, saying, "Tut tut, you should be having it off. And if you're not having it off, you don't love each other."'

Who died and made Russell Brand our Sex Monitor?

'If you prioritize sex, then you're going to have a new partner every two or three years,' says Philippa. 'I think it's more important, perhaps, to imagine who you would want around your deathbed than who you would want to jump into bed with.'

I know of a few middle-aged men who will state, flatly, that their sexual nature is stuck in adolescence. That they still fancy young, sexy people and they can still do the business with them. They define themselves as having a high sex drive. As though a doctor gave them a note. Is it genetic? Saying you have a high sex drive allows you to turn it into a fact of life. But if it really is built into your biology, then what are you going to do about it?

Defining your sexual appetite as high – as youthful – is the ultimate way of ignoring how old you are. There is something heroic, in all senses of the word, in telling the world to ignore your wrinkles, your grey hairs and gippy back, and instead define you by your shagging age. Go on, you Peter Stringfellow you!

Also: what is that shagging age? Is it your own youthful shagging age? Or the youthful age of the men or women who turn you on?

A female friend who has been married for well over fifteen years, confesses that she lusts after young men. Cycle couriers, in particular. She extols their thighs, glistening in oil-slick leggings.

Another says, 'I get really strange crushes. They're so strong, as though I'm properly in love, or I'm in love like I was when I was in my teens, lots of lust and soppy romance. I want to run away with him, away from everyone else. I obsess about his strong arms and his twinkly blue eyes. And it's really disconcerting, because one day I wake up and the crush has

gone and he's just my son's sports teacher again or the postman or whoever he really is.'

Sometimes I look at people in their twenties and I cannot
believe how beautiful they are. I don't fancy them – smooth,
bland beauty doesn't turn me on – but I can understand
how, if it did, their looks could dazzle you into getting things
wrong. When I was in my teens, I would hear about a friend's
dad making inappropriate conversation with the babysitter –
with the daughter of his mate! – and we would all make sick
noises and call him a dirty old man. Now, as well as thinking
he's a dirty old man, I think, Oh dear.

'I can imagine,' says one of my male friends, 'getting
so confused, so het up about what becoming an older man
means, that one day I might be on the commute and I might
just stick out my hand and touch a woman's breast. I worry
that I might do it. And then everything would be over.'

'Like tit Tourettes?' I say.

'Sort of,' he says.

'I don't think anyone takes into account how your hormones
change,' says my friend. 'I'm going into the menopause and
mine are all over place. Some days I'm really horny and some
days, if he tries it on, I don't want to, it's the last thing on my
mind. I feel bad because I don't want to, but also a bit irritated.

'And then, on top of that, there are some days I want to
actually kill him. I lie there counting the reasons I should do
it. I'm quite glad that the bedside lamp is fixed to the wall
because if I could lift it up, I'd brain him.'

I'm watching *Enchanted* with P and F. 'Do they have to do the
kissy thing in every film?' says P, frustrated. 'It's so annoying.'

Afterwards, F insists that he dance with her. They hold
hands and twirl bumpily around. Then she pushes him next
to the mantelpiece. 'You stand there,' she says. 'And I do the

walking.' From the other side of the room, she walks carefully over to him, on tiptoe, holding out her skirt. When she gets to him, she stops. Throws her arms around his middle. 'Now we cuddle.' He corrects her grip. 'You put your arms up here.' She does so, and says, 'We married now.'

We got married in a wood by a campsite. We walked through the trees, holding hands, to our friends who were waiting for us. We did not arrive separately. I did not hold out my skirt. There is a picture of us on the fridge: S is kicking his leg out, I am swinging off his arm. His suit is pink, my dress is blue.

For a time, whenever she saw the picture, it made F cry. It was the colours of our outfits. Incorrectly gendered.

8. Fitness

From the age of 7 until I was 21, 22, I practised gymnastics at least twice a week. I don't have to try too hard to recall every detail of the school hall where my gymnastics club trained. The ladder of wooden bars on the wall, the hidden netball court taped on the varnished wooden floor. The slumpy weight of the crash mats as we pulled them out, on their sides, from the back storeroom; how the floor area Velcroed together; the feel of the beam under my feet, hard wood beneath the thin yellow covering; the French chalk fluffing into the air as I rubbed it onto the asymmetric bars.

I could walk you through my floor routine, even now. Three corner-to-corner tumbles, one that ended with a strange twisting backflip that landed in a piked position on the mat. Feet landing first, then, *whump!*, the bum. Leaps, jumps, including one full 360°. Dance 'elements'. British Amateur Gymnastics Association regulations stated that floor routines should be between one and one and half minutes long. I would perform to a carefully edited Music for Pleasure version of 'Ruby Tuesday'. Later, to a cut-down, easy-listening 'Pink Panther'.

For all of my youth, gymnastics invaded my dreams, occupied much of my spare time. I would practise on any available surface: grass, pavements, indoors, outdoors; handstands, handsprings, Arab springs, Baranis. I was always tucking my school skirt into my knickers and chucking myself upside down. I went to gymnastics holiday clubs during the summer, on my own. I enjoyed them. It was easy to make friends with other girls in their early teens, if Nadia Comâneci was a mutual goddess.

I was so enamoured of gymnastics that I would almost kill myself doing it. I was short-sighted, but this didn't stop me running as fast as I could for twenty-five metres, towards a vaulting horse that only swam into focus when I hit the springboard and threw myself up and over its top. Outdoors, I would happily launch my body into the air with just a scratchy piece of scrub to land on. Concrete was my crash mat: like a skater without a skateboard, I would balance on every metal stair rail, every narrow wall, then flip off the end, slap onto paving slabs.

In the 70s gymnastics for girls was like football for boys: almost every girl in the country had a go at some point in her life. Which meant there was a lot of competition to represent your school, your club, your county. Despite my dedication, I was only ever an averagely talented gymnast. My stomach muscles weren't strong enough. I never really mastered a lay-out float. My flexibility left a lot to be desired: I could only do splits one way, as opposed to three.

Still, I was a neat performer. I was strong. I had great balance. I listened. I helped the younger ones. I turned up, week after week after week, for years. My parents were one of my sporting strengths.

Gymnastics is a sport that is hard to keep up into your middle years. You can't do it casually, you can't work it into your everyday life. There's no maintaining those muscles by doing handsprings all the way to work instead of taking the bus, or meeting friends for a friendly vaulting competition in the park. Anyway, it's unseemly as a sport once you're past 25:

too close to narcissism and check-my-sexy-splits party tricks. Better to find other ways of enjoying your body and what it can do.

In 1910, the *Family Doctor* magazine warned its readers of the folly of the middle-aged continuing to enjoy their youthful sporting activities: 'Youth will play tennis all afternoon and evening; middle age is quite content with one set.' In the 40s, a Lancashire office worker wrote to a newspaper about the alarming case of a 'middle-aged man who took up bowls, and is now in hospital for an internal operation'. In the 70s, a primary-school headmaster from Wolverhampton believed it would be best for him to give up refereeing his pupils' football matches once he got to 40.

All these examples are from a book called *Prime Time: A History of the Middle Aged in Twentieth Century Britain* by John Benson. They say, more or less: give up sport past 40. But in the second half of the twentieth century, these attitudes changed. Gradually, it became desirable for middle-aged people to stay youthful through keeping fit.

In *Chasing the Hawk*, Andy Sheehan writes about his father, Dr George Sheehan, who began running at the age of 45. This was in 1963, a time when grown-ups did not exercise in public. When Dr Sheehan ventured out from his backyard to jog around the local streets, he did so 'despite the honking horns and the sounds of laughter from the cars that passed him . . . "Why does your father run around town in his underwear?" we children were asked.'

In 1981, James Fixx brought out the bestseller *The Complete Book of Running*. It would be remiss of me not to note that Fixx died of a heart attack at 52, while jogging.

When I was 37, I snapped my Achilles tendon, playing tennis. I'm not very good at tennis, and I try to make up for my lack of skill by running around a lot. I sprinted for a drop shot and – *blam*! – my Achilles snapped. It felt like I'd been shot.

I had an operation to sew the two parts of the tendon back together, and used crutches for six months. Sometimes my friends would push me around in a wheelchair. Once, we went for a drink and a man I didn't know, who was joining our group, shoved my wheelchair into a different spot without asking me if I wanted to move. Actually, he did it without talking to me at all. I shouted at him. It's interesting to discover how some people look at you when they think you're disabled in some way.

(But we are not disabled! We are not hunched and shuffling! We can keep up! We are younger than you think!)

About a year and a half after I snapped my Achilles, I gave birth to P. And then I had F, five years after that. During that time, I did very little exercise. My body changed. My life changed. I found it hard to locate the person I was before I was a parent. I could see that person, but she was a long way away, waving at me from behind thick glass.

When F was around a year old, though, I felt as if some of my old self had returned and I decided to take up running. I wanted to be outdoors, I wanted to be alone, I wanted my head to empty, and my body to stretch. I did some exercises to strengthen my tired muscles and then, after a few months, I went running. The first time I did, I wore jeans. I ran a little way, then walked a little way, over and over, for twenty minutes. And when I got home, the serotonin rush was so strong, my head felt as though it was hosting a firework display.

I wrote down how I felt: 'I want to go up to strangers and lick their faces'; 'I have sparks coming out of my arse'; 'I am Jesus in trainers.' God, I was so high.

Because of this, it occurred to me that I've had a fundamental fact about my life completely wrong. All the years that I spent going to nightclubs, I thought I was out of my head due to the effect of the music and the people and the stimulants. And, actually, I was out of it because of the exercise. Dancing all night: that was the rush.

Somehow, I'm annoying everyone in the family.

'Go for a run,' says S. 'Put your trainers on. Go away.'

'I'll run with you,' offers P.

I say no. P is too fast for me. He was too fast for me when he was 8. I can't keep up.

B is a friend I haven't spoken to for a while. He likes to work out.

'Oh, yes,' he says. 'I used to spend all my time popping pills and now all I do is bench press and boxing training.'

It happened when he decided to give up smoking. Every time he wanted a cigarette, he did ten press-ups. Ten turned into fifty turned into a hundred. And then he took up boxing.

'Boxing is definitely full of people who like the rush,' he says. 'I mean, you can say it's about getting fit, boxing, but it isn't. It's an unnatural thing to want to do. It's about violence. They like fighting and violence. You get a massive rush from violence.'

When boxers aren't training, he says, they're monsters. 'Excessive personalities. Massive boozers, drug-takers, womanizers, disgustingly huge sex drive, like they're almost sex pests. They're the worst people to hang out with, but also the best,' he says, and I know what he means. Those characters are always around when you go out. The ones who take everything too far, who end up getting threatened by gangsters or in the back of a police van because they don't know when to shut up. They don't know when to stop. They're a pain in the arse; they can be dangerous. But the party wouldn't start without them.

Anyway, B doesn't take drugs any more. 'I was on ten Es a night,' he says. 'It had got to the point where someone would offer me a handful of pills and I'd neck 'em and only ask what they were half an hour later.' He adds: 'I think people disapprove of drugs because it's unearned pleasure. You bought that pleasure, it's cheating.'

B understands the culture that builds up around people's choice of relaxation. He describes the gyms he goes to. Not the vanilla Fitness Firsts, the civilian Virgin Actives. He goes to private gyms, one-offs. He tells me that he is unusual in those gyms because he doesn't take drugs. Steroids are preferred by most serious fitness freaks, though they do take other drugs. He tells me about a particular private gym that he goes to, cheap, with basic furnishings. The place is full of pumped-up men (mostly men). 'In the male changing rooms, there's one shower for everyone, a big communal shower.' There are many Eastern European guys, who soap themselves down merrily with a hypodermic stuck in their bum, topping up their steroid intake. Others hoover up a line of coke – quite publicly, without hiding it – before bench-pressing 200 pounds.

(This reminds me, somehow, of President Putin, with his cauliflower chest and his smooth brow; his topless, gun-toting virility. He thinks those who don't pump iron and bang Botox are pussies. He looks at our politicians and laughs, while arm-wrestling a grizzly bear.)

'I'm definitely addicted to exercise,' says B. 'Because I know all the rules and I break them anyway. If you're serious about working out, then you take one day off for complete rest a week. Or a whole week every six weeks, or at least one week every twelve. But I can't do that. I can't get through the day if I don't exercise.'

This isn't a negative thing, he insists. B sleeps well and feels great. He doesn't get the Fear, because he's not drinking or taking drugs; his high lasts for four to five hours and is fully natural. B is happy. He talks about his other friends, who like to drink.

'They tease me because I won't drink spirits,' he says. '"Oh, B, you're so *boooooring* . . ." I like a few beers. But if you said to me, "You have to choose between giving up beer or exercise", the beer would go, no question.'

A study in 1987 found that pure exercise dependence – being addicted to exercise – is found most often in men in their forties and fifties. There are theories as to why. Perhaps the dependent men are addicted to the endorphins – that rush again – caused by sport. Or perhaps they're avoiding something. Exercise can be a way of dealing with stressful feelings, and without exercise, the feelings come flooding back. Not the pursuit of pleasure, but the avoidance of pain.

I find another report that says, if you feel you lack control in your life, then the exercise you seek out tends to be high intensity and tough. You may feel that pushing yourself in this way will empower you. Or that you need to be punished for behaving badly, and you'd like to alleviate some of your guilt. Or you may want to show your friends on social media that you're fit enough and have enough time to be able to push your body to its reducing limit.

If you're still searching for the rush, you can find it. You can carry on taking drugs. You can carry on chasing sex. You can start doing both of these activities. I know people who waited until their forties to branch out sexually, to try gay sex and brothels and orgies, generally to catch up on what they felt they might have been missing out on. I know of others who started going to big raves, staying up all night on E, jumping up onto podiums to celebrate their new delight, their just-found joy in community and music and dancing.

Those I know who have done this did it when their children reached early adolescence; right at the moment when their kids were leaving the bright sunshine of childhood to move towards the night, with all its dark pleasures. This timing might be significant. But it might be coincidence.

Anyhow, a lot more of my friends, the ones who did all their mad sex and drugs and going out years ago, getting all of that out of their system, those ones, are swapping hedonism for fitness. This was not always the case. Not so long ago, they were suspicious of the gym, of anything that seemed corporate and expensive and vain. If your identity has been even partly inspired by youth culture, by drug philosophy and the futile romance of an outsider, then the careful maintenance of your corporeal being can seem boring and conventional. Plus the music in gyms was beyond appalling, utterly unacceptable.

But now I know very few people who don't do some form of exercise. There are the gym bunnies, who finish work and drive to rooms full of complicated matt-black torture machines to get busy with the equipment. The women tie their hair back into ponytails and set off on a long run on the treadmill, headphones on, not wanting to socialize. The men look at themselves in the mirror as they hold their hand-weights. They stare at themselves, and they lift the weights up and say, 'Hnnnnnnnhgh!' at their reflections.

There are the outdoor runners, more serious about it than I am, who share their personal bests on Facebook or post up pictures of themselves at finishing lines with their arms around their running mates. There are those who flail at boxing pads held aloft by bored personal trainers; others who are yelled at in the rain by bald men in army gear with rucksacks on their back. There are the yoga ladies, whether tired baggy-trousered mum or perky Ibiza babe, twisting and stretching and longing for the moment when they get to lie down flat.

My friend L, already sporty enough to run marathons and go on long-distance cycle rides, turns 43, decides she's going to get properly fit, and employs a personal trainer. Another friend does the same, after her long-term relationship breaks up. As a side benefit, this friend has sex with her trainer. She is far from the only woman in her forties who does this. A young friend, who is married to a good-looking PT in his twenties, tells me that her husband has had to give up coaching middle-aged women because they always try to get him into bed. 'He just trains men now,' she says. 'It's less complicated.'

'Look, you can't get away with doing nothing once you're 40,' says a friend. 'You have to do some type of exercise or it all goes wrong. If you don't exercise, your back stops working. It starts to go all rigid. You seize up. All of you. Your mind, too.'

You need a different type of energy to get you through your forties. That old-school fizzed-up mania only takes you so far. It only gets you out of the front door; it doesn't get you through the day. What's required is an enduring, patient, low-level momentum that can withstand the relentless trivia of adulthood, that can push you through the hours of sitting on hold to the phone company, of waiting in line to post a present, of going over the same point again and again with your children or with someone else who refuses to understand something that – honestly, no, really – is fundamentally quite simple.

In the end, fitness – health – is about that energy, I think. About increasing it, lengthening its span, catching it from other people and new experiences, feeling it surge into you through music, drawing it into your heart from a walk on a cold day. You get tired more quickly in middle age, we know that. And there is nothing more elderly than listlessness and fear.

*

If middle age is about understanding there is less time left to go, then we have health adjustments that need to be made.

There are the cyclists, of course. The call of the bike is strong in the middle years. I know a man who cycled from London to Valencia when he was 47. I have another friend, who lives in a smallish house with his wife and two kids; he owns seven bikes. S has four, along with my son's (one), my daughter's (one, plus a scooter) and mine (one). Oh, and he's just bought a fold-up model. We live in a first-floor flat. We've had to take out the second toilet so we can hang the bikes in there.

There are cycle shops in every urban centre, selling bikes and biking gear, but also coffee and cakes, little notebooks and posters that display sayings like 'When I see an adult on a bicycle I do not despair for the future of the human race' (H. G. Wells. We have it on a postcard in our kitchen).

In 2010, a report by Mintel coined the term MAMILS; it entered the *Oxford English Dictionary* four years later – and offered research to show that a growth in bike sales was being propelled by 35–45-year-old men with families. (Despite the recession, the MAMILs, rich men all, with health insurance and financial allowances from work for fitness activities, were buying bikes that cost at least £2000.) Since Bradley Wiggins won the Tour de France in 2012, fifty thousand more people have become members of British Cycling. In October 2014, membership reached a hundred thousand for the first time. The average age of a member is 40.

For those who take cycling seriously, its appeal lies in its combination of individualism and clubbiness. You can practise on your own, on your route to work, and then you can hang out with fellow cycle types in the pub on a week night. It can get technical, if you want: there is expensive gadgetry to be researched and bought, apps to be uploaded and consulted, nutrition to be considered, training tweaked for specific events.

Also, if a husband says to his wife that on Sunday he is going to sit on the sofa and ignore the family for half the day, while she rushes around ticking off duties from the never-ending duty list, he will be given the shortest of shrifts. If he says he's going cycle training or – even better – on a race, that is allowed. Cycling is the new golf: a rich chap's way of getting out of the house and away from his family for six hours every weekend.

I speak to Mike Shallcross, who works at *Men's Health* magazine. He tells me that more men are getting fit in their forties and fifties. More people are getting fit, full stop. In the UK between 2006/7 and 2012/13 there was an increase of 1.4 million adults who took part in some form of sport for at least thirty minutes per week. The increase was most marked among the 45–54-year-old age group, where it increased from 30 to 34.3 per cent.

Mike and I talk about triathlons. Mike says: 'Triathlons used to be for nutters. Now they're for everyone from their mid-thirties onwards. It's like triathlons are on their bucket list.' You start extreme exercise because you become aware that you're going to die. Mike also says that most men who get in touch with the magazine about getting fit in their forties do so because 'They realize they can't get away with their lifestyle any more.' They don't want to change how they have fun, so they need what Mike calls 'corrective steers' to keep on being able to behave as they like.

I wonder if they worry about having a heart attack. Doing drink and drugs and competing in triathlons don't seem the best fit to me, though I seem to recall that a (female, hungover) friend got round the NYC marathon years ago by stopping every hour to bump some cocaine. She was in her twenties, though.

By middle age, most people have developed some underlying early-stage vessel disease – which means that plaque is building in their coronary arteries. I read an article in which Kade Davison, a clinical exercise-science teacher, says this: 'If anyone is going to have a cardiac event, they're far more likely to have one during exercise.' By 'anyone', Davison means anyone middle-aged. It is normal in intensive training to experience pain and you're told to work through it. But if you're a middle-aged man, this can mean you're ignoring the warning signs of a heart attack.

I go running, round the park, twice a week. I wear my Lycra trousers and my trainers and I run very slowly, not much faster than most people walk. I try not to get frantic about my speed because I worry that getting competitive with anything or anyone – including myself – is a shortcut to some kind of seizure.

Sometimes I run with P, but rarely: running, for me, is solitary. I have taken part in one race, a 10K, because I was asked to by an editor. I was challenged to find apps that would enable me to run a race. So I tried out a few, and hated most of them. They kept wanting me to share my running efforts with my online friends, as though they'd care. With social media, when it comes to running, if there isn't a medal involved, you might as well be posting pictures of your dinner.

I ran the 10K at a very slow speed (afterwards, when I checked my results, I discovered that I was in the slowest five per cent of runners). I didn't stop, which I was very proud of, and I walked for a long way afterwards, trying to find a bus to get home.

*

I interview comedian and actor Eddie Izzard about his marathon running. His mad marathon-a-day effort was for Comic Relief and was not a midlife crisis, he says, though he admits to a 'wobble' when he turned 40. He says his true life-crunch happened earlier: when he was 23 and came out as a transvestite.

'The running of the marathons at 47 – that's a continuation of me doing gigs in French, or playing in America,' he says. 'They're all challenges, they're all building blocks. Any life crisis is essentially someone saying: "Shit – I've got to restructure everything." I did that in my twenties and since then, I've just been building, without any crisis. I've been running since I was 43, and it might be catching up in one massive go, but it's not "Oh, my God, I've got to change." My running has adventure built into it. It's just adding things to my life.'

Eddie was sporty as a kid. He played a lot of football, but when he was 13 he went to a boys' school that didn't allow the pupils to play football. 'So the word "athlete" wouldn't have been in my head, because it was the word of someone else, a sporty person.'

Now, he considers himself an athlete, who must go training.

'I want to be a marathon runner. I want to be able to knock off a marathon, match fit, at any time. Training, like an athlete, and big distances. I feel the idea that we run or get fit as a hobby is not good. It's got to be part of your life. It was always our life. When we came out of the trees, two million years ago, we didn't come out unfit . . . We weren't in the trees just eating coconuts or a bumper pack of bark, we were leaping around, fit as fiddles. All wild animals are fit! Every single one. One hundred per cent. Not even ninety-nine. From squirrels to tigers, they're all fantastically fit, and that's what we should be. We're supposed to move about! We're not supposed to sit there, eat a bun and watch telly.'

'You need to have three things to be a footballer,' P tells me. 'Skill, strength and speed. I've got the skills, but not the other two so much. I'm maybe one and a half out of three.'

Football gives P pleasure, not just because he loves to play, but because he relishes its organisation. The order of the teams in the leagues. Player formations – who should play where, according to carefully assessed ability, mostly from numbers on Match Attax cards and FIFA computer games. Stats: games played, attempts on goals, goals scored, goals missed, successful passes. He evaluates experience in numerical terms, then slots it into its place. It is a type of truth for him. When I pick him up from school, he asks me, 'What was your day out of 10?'

But this methodical honesty runs counter to another of his traits: his belief that he is the most important person in the world. When P tells stories about his life, he reworks them so that he is the star. He says: 'I was the only person who didn't have lunch today, Mum, all the food was gone and the dinner-ladies wouldn't even give me a tiny piece of bread the size of a dot. And so I had to eat a piece of paper from a toilet roll.' He says: 'Messi passes to Ronaldo who does a dummy and chips it to P who does an amazing over-head kick and IT'S IN!! WHAT A GOAL!!'

And so, despite his own precise assessment of his abilities – one and a half out of three – he is definitely going to be a professional footballer when he is grown up. He will play on the wing for Manchester United, like Best, like Beckham, like Ronaldo. There is no doubt about this.

A friend who went through the midlife horrors found that he couldn't follow football, though he'd always loved it. Not even his favourite team.

'I couldn't watch the players run out onto the pitch,' he says. 'I was so jealous of them. They were in their twenties, at the top of their game. And what was I doing, in my forties? I felt like I'd wasted my life.'

When P plays matches, I stand with the other parents. We are friends now, a team ourselves. We shout, but we've learned only to give encouragement, not to get nasty or specific.

Most other parents do the same. But not all. I've seen adults bellow at their kids when they get it wrong, really yell at them, screaming insults from the side-line. The children look over, anxious, and play on; but after the game you see their faces close down, their expressions slump into neutral. They are 7, 8, 9 years old. Their parents know that they're pushing their child away, but they can't help themselves, they can't stop the onslaught. It is vital for them that their child succeeds at this, their chosen sport. Their child is living their sporting life, now that they can't.

These are P's stats (and every one of his friends). Chance of becoming a professional footballer: around 0.1 per cent.

These are mine (and every one of the parents). Chance of becoming a professional footballer: nil.

There is a Saturday-night programme that we all watch together. It involves ordinary people performing extraordinary acts of fitness, attempting to get through a course that makes me tired just to look at it. They jump from rope to rope, they sprint across wobbly surfaces, they yank themselves up tall structures using only their arms. They run up walls.

P is convinced that S and I should enter the competition. He thinks we'd win. We say, 'Sure!' and look at each other behind his back.

P wants to join a child gym, but we won't let him. We're old-fashioned, I think. I remember *It's a Knockout*, how amateur and bumbling everyone was who took part. How unfit. Fitness and competition are serious now, even for us non-athletes, sitting on the sofa on a Saturday night. Watching ordinary people perform like they're in the Olympics.

There are some sports that bring you back into your body, that naturally pull you into the feeling of how you were when you were young. Running is one. I watch P and F and they run for no real reason: they pick up speed, lengthen their stride, set off fast, just because. (Toddlers, who can walk but not really talk, run after each other in circles, round and round and round.) Running, after a while, becomes a shortcut to your previous self. You are inside your body and your body is working, just as it did when you were 9, 19, 29.

Swimming and cycling do this too: perhaps more than running, because they don't make your joints grind and gripe in the same way. The water is doing some of the work, the wheels go round for you. When you push yourself in these solitary activities, these solo efforts, the freedom you feel is familiar. It's your own. Physical movement makes you remember who you were and who you are.

I think that if you played football when you were young, then football has the same effect, though you must be playing a game, against another team, so that you are engaged in the whole event. Kicking a can doesn't give you enough of a high: it's not physical enough.

You are inside time, your body is working, your mind is wherever it goes when your body is working, you are in and of yourself, you are no age and every age all at once.

I run because I'm too old for gymnastics. Nice and steady, careful as she goes. Stick to the paths, you don't want to trip.

But what I really want to do is to veer off and go pelting across the grass, to stretch my hands up and reach forward and down and twist my body into a round-off, a back flip and then a back somersault. To throw myself up, tuck my legs up to my chest, drop my head back and watch my feet land.

Or to thrust my arms across my torso, flick my legs over my head in a free cartwheel. To point my toes and feel the whole of my body pull itself into line. To hurl myself into the air like crumpled paper and arrive on the ground like a falling leaf. I know how that feels. I remember.

When I was young, I had a recurring dream about being chased by some malevolent force. I would be running scared for a while, and then, not. Because, my dream self would suddenly remember, I had an amazing get-out. All I had to do was to speed up a little, run as fast as I could, put my arms flat and outstretched . . . and I would fly. Soar up and off into the sky. I would fly. It was easy.

My flying dreams happened a lot, and I remember that sensation of launch and glide, of wheeling into the air, diving above the houses. It's completely familiar. I can recall it as clearly as I can recall the sensation of landing with feet together, knees bent, arms straight and close to the ears, after a handspring vault.

And yet, they are both dreams now. I will never do a handspring vault again. I will never do a back somersault again, not even a walkover. I will never feel that sensation. The tensing and flexing of muscles, the twist and spin in the air. The dancing beauty of it. That feeling of your body doing exactly what you ask of it. The most astonishing, outrageous, utterly natural thing. Gone now.

9. Looks

I am having a facial, my second ever. I am trying to act my age.

The first time I had one was for a magazine article, many years ago, and I hated it. For some reason, I had to take my clothes off and wear a dressing-gown. (This completely threw me, but I think it was to stop oils dripping on to my top.) I lay, nervously, on a massage table. To me, massage tables never seem that different from operating tables, no matter how soothingly pan-pipey the surrounding environment. They're too narrow and high. I always think I'm going to fall off. One sudden coughing fit and you're on the floor, nose spread like jam over the Italian slate.

Anyhow, my first ever facial. The lady doing it seemed okay, though I wasn't that keen on how close she got to my face. She commented that I had 'some congestion' on my cheeks (she meant blackheads. I had a traffic jam of blackheads) and asked me if I wanted extraction. Unfortunately, I thought she said extracts, and assumed she meant a few more floral oils. I said yes. But that's not what extraction means. She bent her face even closer to mine and started squeezing my spots. It was awful. I had to shut my eyes to stop her seeing my tears.

There are many things I enjoy about being a woman, but being made to cry through embarrassment and pain is not one. Especially when it's happening in the name of beauty. Why put yourself through such humiliation? Why pay for the privilege?

I am not a huge beautifier. Until I was 40, I rarely wore foundation. I washed my face with water and used no other products on it. I took my eye make-up off with a bit of soap on a wet flannel. I was a bit mucky, I suppose.

However, middle age means you have to change your habits when it comes to beauty. This is true of men and women, though women seem to take this more seriously. A 2012 study across 15 countries, including the UK, found that 76 per cent of respondents believed that using the right beauty products can make you look younger for longer; in 2015, the over 50s became the biggest buyers of beauty products in the UK. Everyone seems to have learnt that if you are 39 plus, it is vital to cleanse and moisturize. (The middle action, tone, important during my teenage years, appears to have fallen out of fashion, like rabies.) Although I'm not sure what happens to your skin if you don't.

There are umpteen enticingly packaged cosmetic products for older women out there, plus some cheaper grey ones for men, and – luckily for ignoramuses like me – there are reliable beauty columns to help us work out what to buy. So now I use an expensive grime-removing product with a hot cloth on my face at night, and in the mornings, when I remember, I put on serum. (I don't use the grime-removing product in the morning, though. It's too expensive. How dirty can you get when you're asleep?) And I wear make-up when I feel it's needed. Which is actually not as often as you might expect.

Looks are looks are looks. When I tell someone my age and they say, 'Oh, you don't look it,' I say, 'Thank you, that's nice' (it is). But it isn't really the point. I am my age. This is what my age looks like on me.

What *is* the point, and is more interesting, is what's happening to me, and to you. The old me is disappearing.

Another me is emerging, pushing through. As we age, we shed our skin and a new person reveals itself to the world.

Something happens to your body in your forties. It happens too slowly for you to notice and too quickly for you to do anything about it. This is what happens, if you're interested. It is interesting.

You start to smell different: stronger, more pungent. Your underarms get stale more quickly. Your breath needs monitoring. ('Stop breeeeathing, Mummy,' says F.) Your teeth appear stained, no matter how hard you brush. Your bum starts sagging, your stomach expands, your hair changes texture and colour and begins to recede or fall out. Your thighs increase in size and change consistency, and so do your arms, which become like lovely hams, and this all happens *pfff!* Like that, a magic spell. *Pfff!* You have been transformed. Hello, new you.

Your flesh is fleshier. You consider putting your biceps between two pieces of bread and chowing down.

Your body becomes less efficient. You can't shake off a hangover, a bag of sweets gives you night palpitations. Drugs? Eating a starter, main course and pudding makes you feel like you might die. At social events, in darkened rooms, with wine and no dancing, you observe that some of your friends are fading at 10 o'clock; drooping eyes, lolling heads. A younger person might assume they're drunk. You know they're sleepy. A cab, which used to be a place for arguing or snogging or trying to get the driver to turn the music up, has become a bed on wheels.

Or are they your friends? You stop knowing who anyone is. I bump into someone running down the street and he shouts, 'Hi,' as he rushes past, and I think: Who *is* that tramp? Then I realize I had a passionate fling with him about twenty years ago and he just hasn't had a shave.

It is strange. Disconcerting. Not only do you stop recognizing other people, you stop recognizing yourself. In your twenties and thirties, you look at photos of yourself and think, Ha ha! That's because you'd have your arms around two of your mates, or you'd be doing a handstand and showing your knickers by mistake. Sometimes, you'd think, Ugh, bad hair, or, Those shorts were a mistake. But mostly you laughed, because you looked as though you were having a good time. You *were* having a good time.

But in your forties, someone will take a photo of you and it will genuinely take you aback. Something has happened to your face. It has turned fluffy, and dropped at the same time. Your eyes have receded and become round. There is redness, though you aren't drunk. You have lines – that's OK, you expected that – but you also have strange flesh pouches, on either side of your mouth. And the lines don't go where you expect: they're vertical, or they shoot off like a mad tributary towards your ears. Plus, what is happening with your hair?

If you're a man, your hair goes – either it goes coarse and grey, or it just goes. If you're a woman, the colour you always dyed your hair starts looking brassy or witchy or weird, like a wig. Or the style doesn't do what you want it to do: it doesn't look artfully undone, it looks like you haven't washed it in a decade. Make-up stops working. Your skin is different, your concealer can't conceal it. Your eyelids change – your eyelids! – they get looser, and hooded, so that when you put on eyeliner it won't make a straight, cool sweep out and up, but puckers and wobbles, even when you pull your skin taut.

The way you look is not the same. How you are seen by the world is utterly different from before. And now you can see it too. What to do about that? For someone who just used to get up and go, who would sleep for as long as possible before lurching from bed and running out of the door, the faff of having to make yourself presentable in your forties is quite a thing to get your head around. If I put on what I want to (jeans, sweatshirt, trainers, a practical jacket) and I don't do anything to my face, I look knackered, incapable, as crumpled and useless as a discarded tissue. But I'm not knackered and I am capable. Does it matter if I don't look that way?

My vanity still exists. I can feel it twitching; it seems embarrassingly misplaced. On smartphone videos, the children singing, jumping over each other to hog the camera, I catch sight of myself in the background. Laughing, hair askew, in a dressing-gown. And, even though it doesn't matter, even though who cares, even though . . . Oh, God, honestly? I look like absolute shit.

Unexpected physical changes I have noticed since turning 40

- Feet. Like a dried-out river bed, creviced, parched. They flake and peel. I watch TV and pull strips of skin from my big toes. Every so often, my heels develop cracks so deep that I store the fluff from my socks inside.

- Eyebrows. I never plucked my eyebrows before I was 42. Perhaps this is why they're now like an unkempt hedge, with gaps in their foliage and stray twigs that jut out. I pluck them haphazardly and fill in the line with a pencil or eyebrow gel. I enjoy this. I like how I can make myself look more certain of my opinions. I can make myself look cross.

- Knees. Never where I expect to find them. Always lower than seems anatomically correct.

- Hair. Gone exploring. Taking root, tough and long, in previously unmapped areas, e.g., breast, toe, thigh, forehead.

- Pores. Perfect (if they were a bar). Always open.

- Speed. Slower, more deliberate, due to the necessity of carrying more bulk. This bulk is harder on the feet (see 1).

Tracey Emin has a show at White Cube called 'The Last Great Adventure Is You'. It has many pieces in it – tapestries, bronzes, drawings – most of which are based around her own body. She does some interviews to promote it, and in one she says this.

'I'm trying to work out why my body has changed so much. I've gone from being a really thin girl – even when I was 40 I was thin – to becoming matronly and womanly. I'm trying to come to terms with the physical changes. There's a big difference between being 35 and 50. Massive. And that's what I'm trying to understand. Where does that girl go? Where does that youth go? That thing that has been lost, where has it gone?'

All of my female friends do something to alter their appearance. Mostly, they alter their hair: dye it, or get it straightened or relaxed. I have dyed my hair some form of blonde since I was 14. That's well over thirty years of bleach, some home-applied, most not, slapped on top of rubber hats, or folded inside small pieces of tin foil. I am so familiar with hair bleach now that I can tell, by smell alone, if the hairdresser has mixed it to the correct consistency.

Some of my friends go to beauticians to have their other hair – underarm, leg, pubic – pulled out, stripped off, zapped, banished. Others make a point of a regular facial. Most go to the nail bar, some to have gels on their fingernails, others just for their toes. Several have had their teeth whitened, or replaced with more regular-shaped crowns (each real, living tooth individually filed down to a sliver, then the new, ceramic tooth glued on top). A few ignore the cancer concerns and use a sunbed; more get fake tan applied professionally, or slather it on themselves.

All of us wear make-up, at least some of the time. All of us have creams we apply, cleansers and moisturizers and glistening liquid serums. Gel containing grains of sand that we rub on our faces to grind away our skin, reveal the youth beneath.

These adjustments to our appearance, no matter how small, are a habit, formed in our teens and twenties, and it is disconcerting when the habit is not enough. When it doesn't give the results it used to.

A few of my friends have had minor cosmetic surgery. Liposuction, to remove their post-baby tummy. Botox, fillers, a nose job. I have, too, I suppose: a couple of years ago, I had my eyes lasered so that now I can see without contact lenses. No more fiddling around with solutions, no more glasses that made my eyes small and far away. Before, I was so short-sighted that I couldn't put on my mascara without my lenses in. Now, I see like God. The detail! I'm not always sure that this is an advantage.

F is doing my make-up. She applies mascara to my cheeks, smears eye shadow on my forehead. Then she brings out the face-paints. After she is done, I look like a Frank Auerbach painting, smudged and thick with colour. My face is not there any more. This is fine by me.

As you age, not only does your face change, it stops match-ing the way you feel. This is annoying. If people keep ask-ing you if you're okay, then even if you're great, on tip-top form, you start to question yourself. Somehow, your face isn't conveying your mood, and the world assumes you're grumpy, or ill, or not interested in contemporary pop music, when you're just living.

Although it's strange how those who know you well don't seem to see your looks. A friend's mum has a facelift. She looks exactly the same as before. A friend of mine has ten knackered teeth replaced with shiny superstar versions. People keep ask-ing him if he's been on holiday. The first time I saw anyone with Botox was at a tabloid Christmas party. A female editor stopped me and said, 'Look at my forehead!' I looked. It seemed normal. 'YES!' she shouted. 'I've had Botox, isn't it great?' I made the right congratulatory noises, but, to me, she hadn't changed a bit. She was still mad.

Which makes me wonder why I'm bothering with my second ever facial. So far, it has been quite nice – except for having to put on a dressing-gown again – though I'm still a little nervous about the table. I lie quietly and surreptitiously hold on to the sides.

The woman who is giving me the facial is from South Korea, and says that her home country is about ten years ahead of Britain when it comes to beauty products and techniques. She also tells me that different nationalities want different things from their facials. Russian women want to look as young and glamorous as possible, no matter what the price or technique. The French don't like surgery or putting anything unnatural on their skin. Americans know what they want when they arrive, usually a new wonder product. And British women only come in to solve a problem, such as skin damage from sunbathing, or acne scars.

We spend a happy hour talking about her career, me lying on my back, she rubbing stuff into my skin, pinching my neck gently, giving me a head massage. I fall asleep for a little bit.

When I wake up, it's time for the final flourish. She puts some more cool lotion on my skin.

'This,' she says reverently, 'is the famous placenta cream.'

Placenta cream! I feel like Cruella de Vil. I feel like being sick. I am having foetus cells massaged into my face. I might as well be tempting small children into my gingerbread house and fattening them up to eat.

*

So, yes: my second – and, so far, my last – facial. There isn't much point in facials unless you go regularly, and they're time-consuming and expensive. And if the climax is sheep's placenta, then, really, I'd rather spend my money elsewhere.

Before I leave, though, I speak to the head of the spa, Esther McVeigh, a firecracker of a woman I like very much. EF MediSpa is Esther's business, and a very successful one it is. She has three award-winning, highly successful shops (in Kensington, Chelsea and St John's Wood) that offer a full range of beauty treatments, from non-invasive – facials, massage, consultations, creams – to various forms of cosmetic surgery. Esther is 57. She doesn't look her age, but she doesn't look young. She looks fun, saucy and rich.

Esther says, as I knew she would: 'It's all about what's happening on the inside, not what's on the outside.' But she follows it up with: 'An orgasm a day will keep the miseries at bay.

'That's what women need. You want to look better, be sure you make time for it. Use your husband or do it yourself. It will give you radiance.'

I laugh. I think but don't say: Another thing on the to-do list.

Esther thinks middle age doesn't happen these days until you're in your fifties, though she admits she's talking about rich London, the London that comes to her salons. She says: 'I see the most gorgeous women, who are worried about how they appear and I think, What the hell are you going on about? But, then, I spend a fortune on my health. I work out three days a week, I do yoga once a week. If I'm down I'll do Chinese medicine. I'm always looking to keep myself up there. I work so hard and for such long hours, it's a difficult balance. Women are never satisfied . . .'

As we talk, another woman comes in to show Esther her face. The woman is beautiful: in her early twenties, long-legged, with a Louise Brooks bob and a lovely face. Well: a once-lovely face. She appears to have just been involved in a car accident. Her face is all red and inflamed, speckled with blood, little cuts all over it, and her skin is mottling with bruises.

Panicked, I wonder for a moment if we should call an ambulance. But no: the cuts, apparently, are from a treatment – PRP, 'platelet rich plasma', treatment – and she seems very happy with the result. 'My skin will be amazing in a couple of days,' she assures me.

I am horrified. Esther laughs at me, but not nastily. She teases me for being vanilla, for reacting like a novice. Once you're properly into beauty treatments, PRP seems utterly normal. After all, it isn't permanent. And women are never satisfied.

I bump into a friend I haven't seen in a long time. She's a couple of years younger than me, an outdoor type, who's good at camping and snowboarding and walking for a long time in adverse weather conditions. She doesn't wear make-up very often. She's American.

She tells me she's had Botox in her forehead and filler in the lines around her mouth. I'm so surprised – shocked, really – that I gape at her. She looks normal, like a middle-aged woman.

She says: 'I want my looks not to be an issue. I don't want to look younger, I just don't want my looks to be in the equation at all. I don't mind being middle-aged. I just mind it showing too much. I don't want to look like I'm 25, or even 35. I want to hover at 40 for the next twenty years. I'm liberal, I'm a feminist, I don't think women should have to do these things. But I'm a pragmatist, too, and people do look at your face and they make judgements.'

She makes me think of when I was younger and used to worry that people were judging me because of how I looked or behaved. When, of course, they were just thinking about themselves and whether anyone was judging them.

'Oh, I hated my thighs up until about eight years ago,' she says. 'All the energy I put into self-loathing!'

I say: 'But thighs are fine. You can just wear opaque tights.'

'Yes,' she says. 'I do. So now I just transfer my self-loathing to my face . . . I didn't tell my husband about the Botox. I told him about the filler, but not the Botox. He was surprised, but then he said, "It's your face."'

But is it, now? Is it your face if you pay to have it changed? Is it your face if, when you look at it, you don't recognize yourself? What about if, when you look at it, you see your mother instead?

I talk to another friend, a journalist who has written a lot about beauty treatments. She says: 'You don't have to go for that frozen look if you don't want it. You don't have to do anything at all. But this stuff is out there, and you should know about it.' I feel as though everyone is in a club except me. Perhaps I could join. But I'm still unsure of the club rules, and the club seems a bit like Fight Club: you're not allowed to talk about it. Plus, you get bruises.

Both of my friends tell me it's impossible to discuss having Botox or fillers with people they know because everyone immediately judges and shouts. 'If you have a nose job, that's kind of okay,' says the journalist. 'But you cannot be honest about any maintenance procedures. Expensive unguents are kind of okay. But not *too* expensive. People get really angry.'

I read an article that says there is evidence that having Botox changes your mood. If you stop yourself frowning, you feel less frowny. If everyone in the club had it, they'd stop getting cross with each other.

'Getting Botox is a sackable offence,' says S. 'If you got Botox, I'd divorce you.'

I say: 'You wouldn't notice.' But I don't get it done.

After talking to my beauty-conscious friends, I start looking at television presenters differently. I start to spot when they've had a bit of work: there are no deep lines around their mouths, or frown grooves between their eyebrows, or puffiness around their eyes. They don't look young, exactly. They look blank, neutral. Screen-friendly.

There is a book by David Bainbridge, a clinical veterinary anatomist, called *Middle Age: A Natural History*. In it, he argues that middle age is a specific biological stage in human life. He points out that there is a controlling force at work in our middle years that allows a few bits of our bodies to fail, while keeping other parts in good condition.

Sight is one of the things that is allowed to degenerate. Few 35-year-olds need to hold a menu at arm's length to read it, but by 50, most people have age-related long-sightedness. The same is true of skin. No 50-something has the wrinkle-free skin or tight pores of a 35-year-old: skin's elasticity reduces in middle age, whatever you do to it. (Also, though Bainbridge doesn't mention this, female fertility. Most 35-year-old women are fertile, most 50-year-olds are not.)

Perfect eyesight, perfect skin and being able to produce babies, if you're a woman: none of this is deemed vital by our benign dictator, the body. Once we get past 40, there is nothing we can do to keep those particular parts of us working in a youthful manner. Your body is diverting its energy into other areas: it's busy keeping other parts of you functioning.

You may not agree with your body's decision. But if you want your redundant bits to stay young, you have to resort to deliberate, invasive methods. IVF. Egg donation. Contact lenses. Laser treatment. Botox. Fillers. Face-lift.

Cindy Crawford is 48 and does a photo shoot on a beach. Some of the pictures are released, supposedly before they're touched up for publishing, and they cause a sensation. This is because the pictures show what are deemed to be the defects in Cindy's body: the cellulite and minor sagging on her thighs and stomach.

I have worked on style magazines. I look at the pictures and think: What a good model Cindy Crawford is. Her body is making an interesting shape: one that is strong and sex-ual and sells the few clothes she's wearing. I also notice the light in the picture. The sunlight is very bright and reflects off the sand and the water, and I wonder why the photographer chose to take the picture at that time. He must have wanted defined shadows, a deliberate contrast between dark and light, as opposed to the blurry, warm luminescence you get at dawn or dusk. The super-brightness is why Cindy's cellulite is easy to spot.

Cindy is called brave for letting the outside world see her defects. And then it's revealed that the pictures are fake. The cellulite was added, as opposed to being taken away.

To me, this says how little her skin matters. Profession-ally, its texture is a teeny-tiny part of what is going on in the picture. And one that is easily dealt with – smoothed or made rough – through Photoshop. Her skin is not the point.

I've interviewed a few models in my time, including Kate Moss before she took a vow of silence. Kate was funny and charis-matic and she looked like a skinny lioness – all tawny, her eyes and cheeks and hair a toning shade of gold. Her skin was stretched smooth over her bones, a canvas ready for paint. She reminded me of *Badlands*-era Sissy Spacek.

I've interviewed Naomi Campbell, too. Nothing she said made any sense at all, but it didn't matter. I'd just seen her walk down a catwalk. Naomi Campbell walks like nobody else: she strides, she struts, she flounces, she prowls. She is sex on legs. Plus, wherever she goes, she brings an atmosphere of chaos. You look at her and think, Uh-oh, something's about to happen . . . She reminded me of Liam Gallagher.

And once, through an odd set of circumstances, I went to Eva Herzigova's birthday party. The party was small. We sat on leather banquettes. Eva was there with her husband. Small, brown and compact, he looked like a smiley baked potato. Eva herself was amazing, all sparkly, her straight limbs and perfect bosom barely covered by a shimmering wisp of a dress.

There was sushi on a side table. I went to get some with the band I was interviewing: INXS. Lead singer Michael Hutchence was the reason we got into the party. No one else joined us. I sat and ate and looked at the models. They looked thin, obviously, but also un-normal. Their heads were small in relation to the rest of their bodies (unlike most famous people, who are teeny-tiny, but with big heads). The lines of their faces sloped and curved, carved shadows out of the half-light. Their skin seemed sheer, almost see-through. They were fascinating to look at: will-o'-the-wisps, translucent, wafting, ribbon-limbed. Not sexual: alien. And silent.

Someone brought out Eva's birthday cake and paraded it around the room as we sang 'Happy Birthday'. And then, it disappeared back into the kitchen, as though its calories might stick to us if we looked at it too long. It did not come out again.

In a corner, I saw Helena Christensen. She had been Michael Hutchence's girlfriend for a long time; he'd just finished with her to go out with Paula Yates. Christensen didn't look like the other models in the room: her head wasn't small, her body was fuller. She looked fantastic, a wonderful, sexual woman.

Helena Christensen was not looking at me. She was looking at Michael Hutchence. After a while, he went over to her and they sat together, at a table, their heads close, talking intently. Helena seemed as though she might cry.

And I understood three things. First, that unless you're a model, you'll never look like a model. You can make an effort, scrub up nicely, but you cannot make your limbs longer, the planes of your face sit in an ever-fascinating angle. It's not what you're here for.

Second, even if you are a model, if you don't have charisma, you don't make an impression.

And third, as Elvis Costello's seventeenth album has it: *All This Useless Beauty*. None of it helps. Even if you are as stone-cold wondrous as Helena Christensen, when your heart breaks, you feel it the same way as everyone else.

I am not entirely relaxed about my looks changing, but I feel sadder about my body becoming less fit than I do about my face becoming less pretty. I work harder to keep fit than I do to keep pretty.

At a party, a woman younger than me tells me that she doesn't like getting older because men don't fancy her as much. 'I used to like that feeling,' she says. 'That I could have them. Now I'm starting to feel they don't notice me as much.'

In my experience, there are men out there who would be happy to shag any woman of legal age, up to and including 90 years old. Really, I can't bring myself to care if men fancy me or not. In fact, if they're not S, I'd rather they didn't. Like most women my age, I've had years of being shouted at, leered over, told where I rank in a sexual preference table. I've been groped and flashed at and wanked at and followed. I've been patronized and flirted with and remarked upon. And when I've protested, things have got worse.

When you're young, such sexualized bullying happens a lot. It's a running commentary. It affects your confidence, it wastes your time. When you're older, it doesn't happen as much and, honestly, this is a relief. I like sex but I don't want someone's low-level sexual radar to get in the way of me having an interesting day.

When Kristin Scott Thomas was 53, she said: 'I'm not talking about in a private setting, at a dinner party or anything. But when you're walking down the street, you get bumped into, people slam doors in your face – they just don't notice you. Somehow, you vanish. It's a cliché, but men grow in gravitas as they get older, while women disappear.'

This sounds fine, to me. In many situations, I don't want to be noticed at all. I like looking at other people, watching what they're up to. I enjoy eating in cafés by myself. It's nice to talk to strangers, and then it's nice to leave. Checking out art galleries, going for a run, watching art-house films . . . often better alone. But if you are beautiful, this doesn't happen. Your looks have their own life, separate to yours. You have to deal with the people your looks attract. You have to spend a lot of time managing others' expectations (telling them to fuck off). It must be like having a tiger as a pet.

My brother is fantastically beautiful. He's gorgeous now he's in his forties, but he was so handsome in his youth that when he walked into a room he could have had his choice of anyone, male or female. I think he found it fun. I found it fun, if I'm honest: walking in behind him was like watching a love bomb going off. Bodies everywhere. Still, I think it's easier to be a specialist taste. If someone fancies you, you know, anyway.

And as we age, we might want people to take different things from our looks, not merely whether we're fanciable. Being fanciable isn't enough. It's boring. You might want people to think you look efficient. Or not to be messed with. Or rich. Or fashionable. Or artistic. You might not think about any of this at all, and just want to wear clothes that cover you up, make-up that makes you feel better.

If I'm honest, I want people to think I look cool or clever or interesting. In order to achieve this, I dress down at formal events to show I don't care. I wear a lot of black (ditto). I do care, obviously, or I wouldn't think about it.

I go to Frieze art fair, the best place in London for Botox-spotting. If you manage to get in early enough, to see the VIPs and the art buyers (mostly male) and the ladies accompanying them (who often know about the art they're buying), the ladies' handbags look too heavy for their pipe-cleaner arms. They stroll through on their amazing shoes, sipping just the one glass of champagne. The ladies at Frieze have a certain look. Their faces have been treated so that they appear a particular way. It's ageless: they don't look young and they don't look old. They look rich. Rich is a look.

In the camera's still moment, in the moment's glance in the mirror, Botox and fillers make your face look beatific. It's only in real life, when your face has to move, that you look odd. You speak, but the top of your mouth is rigid. It just sits there, sticking out like a roof above a pizza oven. You smile, but there are no shadowy dips beneath your eyes. Instead your eyes rest on top of freshly plumped pillows, children peeking out from under a duvet. You're angry, but your eyebrows are too far apart to register rage, and the top of your nose has flattened and spread until you look like a cat. A benevolent, not-angry cat.

Still, in photos you look lovely, and everyone is a photographer, these days. Every moment documented and put up on Instagram, phone memories clogged with pictorial 'moments'.

Running to stand still. Hair, nails, make-up, clothes, surgery: just to look 'normal', meaning not old. The beauty business for the over-forties is going through a boom time. Beauty often does well in a recession, but also there are more working women over 40 than ever before, and in order to stay working, they believe they need to invest in how they look. It's economics.

I still feel young. Not in a beauty-advert way: I don't mean my skin has a dewy glow, or I like wearing ball gowns in the rain, or that I actually believe the maxim 'You're only as old as you feel inside.' I mean young as in inexperienced, over-emotional, anti-establishment. But I don't look like I feel, these days.

P has a face that is always mobile, his feelings flitting across his features like clouds scudding across the sky. It is never still. And it's not just his expression: he's so young that his physicality is changing too, his nose lengthening, his cheeks slimming down, his teeth pushing and pulling, rising and falling in his mouth, higgledy-piggledy. His legs are getting longer, his stomach is hardening from all the sport he plays. His eyes are almond-shaped, sometimes. Sometimes they're round and wondering. It's impossible to take a photo of him that looks like who he is.

We watch our children change and we accept those changes because we have it in our minds that they're growing. But we are grown. We do not change. Here we are! We have reached our destination, at 38, or 43. We do not accept our changing, no matter how interesting it may be.

*

When you meet someone you haven't seen for thirty years, at a reunion or big birthday event, what always strikes you is how different they are from how you remember. He's got so fat! And bald! What's with that scrappy grey beard? She's gone for a new hair colour, not sure if it suits her, and she has that flushed look all across her cheeks and nose . . . I don't know if I'd have recognized them if they hadn't said hello.

And then you stop to talk for a few moments and you realize that the bits that have changed are not the vital ones. Because the way they move is still the same, how they stand, kind of twisted with their weight all over on one side; and the voice and the humour and that endearing habit of laughing in the middle, rather than at the end, of a joke, as though the anticipation is more enjoyable than the climax. The fundamentals remain.

No matter how much effort you put into maintenance, the parts of you that are not needed in older age will morph and slump and deteriorate. Your outside will become something different and unfamiliar. You will look old, and, to you, that will be new. But the vital elements, the true essentials, the stubborn heart and the keep-on drive, the love of puns and pop music, the actual identifying characteristics . . . That stuff remains.

You walk away, and you say to yourself: 'It's amazing. They haven't changed a bit.'

10. Routine

I was 36 when, all of a sudden, I realized I wanted to have a child. It took a long time for me to get pregnant. At one point I thought I should start taking my temperature to find out when I was ovulating. But the thermometer instructions said I had to do so at the same time every day. This wasn't easy. I got up at 5.30 a.m., 10.30 a.m., midday, 2 p.m. I stayed in my flat, in his flat, I crashed on a blow-up mattress at a mate's, dozed on my brother's sofa on a Sunday afternoon. I forgot to put the thermometer in my bag when I went out.

The instructions said that if I plotted my temperature, the resulting line would be flat and consistent. Ovulation occurred when my temperature changed suddenly, when the line jumped up a step.

But my line looked like a mountain range, all peaks and troughs, sharp spikes. No identifiable pattern, no regularity. No routine.

After a few months, I said, very seriously, to a friend: 'I think I don't actually ovulate.'

She said: 'You're not the first woman ever who menstruates but doesn't ovulate. You're not a freak of nature. You're an idiot.'

Now I am an idiot with a routine. On the back of the kitchen cupboard there is a piece of paper with the days of the week written on it. Under each day is listed what P has to take to school, what F needs for her day (it just says: bag. She is proud of her bag). Also what time each of them needs picking up, what's happening after school and where, what's needed for whatever they're doing (kit, instrument, money, water bottle). If you look at the piece of paper, you know what has to be done. I may have said that sentence before, in a louder voice.

So. Alarm at 6.45 a.m. Clean teeth, have shower, write/ do emails, wake kids/prise them from electronic device, sort breakfast, eat breakfast. Help daughter to dress while son kicks socks around pretending to put on his uniform. Dress self while they wash and do their teeth, check list on cupboard door, check bags. Have argument about how long it takes to put on a pair of shoes and where is your PE kit did you actually bring it back from school and what do you mean you should be bringing in a structure made from plastic bottles and no you can't take your Cinderella carriage to nursery and not your Lego either. Leave flat at 8.30 to walk the five minutes to school.

Work.

Have lunch.

Work.

My working mostly day ends at whatever time gets me back to do the school pick-up at 3.10 p.m. On two days a week, the kids go to afterschool care and I pick them up at 5 p.m. On other days there is: football, swimming, gymnastics. (Advice to parents of sporty children: get them interested in an indoor activity. Watching small boys play football throughout a series of cold, dead British winters has almost killed me.)

The routine is not mine. It is theirs, kind of. We're all tethered to their timetable, which is a school one. School regulates parents as much as children. It requires us to believe that the schedule is non-negotiable, offering threats and rewards as inducements. Meetings with the head if your child gets too many late marks; 100 per cent attendance badges for the kids who never get ill; fines for taking your children away during term-time. It's the same with out-of-school clubs: children get a certificate if they turn up every week; they're dropped from the team if they're late or don't attend.

Even if your own timetable is one that you devise yourself, your time is contained within the big routine of where the kids need to be and when . . . and that big routine promotes frantic-ness. It wants you busy. It wants you to fill in your non-child hours with more low-brain, high-paced 'productive' activity: meetings, phone calls, lunches, face-to-face contact with people who might give you work sometime if you tell them what you're really passionate about (finding a cheap Furby?). Not to forget: paying bills, buying presents, organizing parking permits, replying to emails, making jokes on Twitter, making sure there's food for tea. Busy busy busy.

It's hard to write inside all this activity. Writing needs a brain clear of domestics, free from arrangements. Often, my head is full of noise. If I have too many phone calls to make, or messages to answer, or someone wants to go for a coffee to talk about an idea, as though drinking coffee isn't an activity that should be done absolutely alone while staring hard at a computer screen – if my day requires much of that sort of human interaction, work doesn't really happen.

Poor me, huh? Play the tiniest violin. I don't leave the house at 6 a.m. and get back thirteen hours later. I don't have to go to the same place every day, to sit at the same desk surrounded by the same people I hate and who hate me. I am lucky. Much of my routine is enviably freestyle. Which means it is created, every day, by me. This can be tiring and lonely. It can be great, but it is relentless.

Actually, if I were a more successful, more highly motivated person, my routine would be tougher. It would be my own. I would rise at 5 a.m.; I would drink a glass of water immediately; I would exercise and meditate at the same hour every day; I would ignore emails until 10.30 a.m. and only check them once afterwards. My routine would free me from worry and unnecessary procrastination. I would 'check in' with loved ones, as opposed to physically wrestling them into their vests. And I would therefore earn more money, so I would be able to drop everything and do a live radio interview with only a few minutes' notice, because I would be paying someone else to be present in the early morning to supervise the kids.

I would follow up on all the ideas I have for articles, books, documentaries, podcasts. I would answer my phone. I would engage the services of an affordable builder who would actually turn up as arranged and get on with solving the never-ending problems of a crumbling hundred-year-old flat without ever bothering me again with questions about tiles or paint. Or parking permits.

Also, the idea of reorganizing anything about the established routine would not make me want to run really fast head-first into a brick wall.

The prospect of attending a work event between 5 and 8 p.m. would not make my mind melt.

Persuading afterschool club to take P when it's always really full, finding another parent to do the football run, getting P to their house from afterschool club, asking the child-minder to look after F, finding a babysitter to pick her up from the child-minder's, bring her home and put her to bed, making sure the babysitter has keys so they can do that, remembering to put some form of meal in the fridge for P to eat after football, ensuring that the adults concerned have each other's phone numbers. Paying them.

All this to speak at an event that will earn me £80 after all the childcare has been paid for. Or that won't earn me anything. The three-dimensional hassle of it.

Also, my kids are more fun than almost all of those events. So I stay in.

'Not nursery, not nursery AGAIN,' wails F. Look at the paper, know the routine. Is it immature to resist doing the same thing each week? Is it childish to want to live according to a non-specific timetable, not to know what you'll be doing every Thursday at 3.30 p.m., every Saturday at 10 a.m.? I have a column that I file weekly, which doesn't make me feel too trapped, but, then, I can write it anywhere I like. I don't have to be physically present, standing in a specific place, at a certain time. I don't have to be physically present but irrelevant to the action. A bystander, a deliverer, a taxi-driver, a bore.

When I ask the kids if they want to give up their out-of-school sports, they get really upset. And what else would I be doing that's so amazing anyway?

Maybe . . . seeing another city, reading a book all the way through in one go, meeting people a bit like me but different enough to be interesting. Changing, instead of remaining. I find that when I get out there and talk to people I like, but don't know that well, my head opens up. To want fresh experiences doesn't always mean you're tragic, or embarrassing. You're not a disco nan if you want to hear new music that makes you dance. It's all just stimulation, your fur rubbed the wrong way for a change, different things to talk about when you return to have a familiar meal in a familiar place with a familiar person.

The routine is fine. Really, it is. It's the deal, with kids. As the children get older, the routine will loosen and become truly theirs, rather than mine, and other sorts of daily crises will crash-land and dominate. I understand.

Still, it's going to last in some form for many years, so it's best to try to embrace it. Routine is my friend! Except it will keep changing at the last minute. Routine is not very routine. A text from school saying that afterschool club is cancelled, that there's band practice tomorrow first thing (he's in the band?) so can you bring your child to school twenty minutes early. Or that there's a curriculum meeting on Wednesday at 9.30 a.m. or 2.30 p.m. (9.30 or 2.30! Does nobody have a job?) Can you bring some cakes for the cake sale? Can your child bring money for the cake sale? Your child-minder is sick, can you come now? Your child is sick, can you come now?

When a friend calls and asks me what I've been up to, often I can only think of the routine. Which is boring, so I say: 'Oh, you know. Just ticking over. Nothing unusual.' The finickity-ness of scheduling and rescheduling is not erased by the relief of having sorted out whatever minor problem needed solving. Instead, it is so front and centre in my brain that I forget to say, 'I was part of an interesting onstage discussion about whether we want our celebrities to be mad'; 'I hosted an AGM where anti-BP protesters tried to take over the meeting'; 'I interviewed Paul McCartney.' (I did!) My head is full of the routine, plus add-ons. Has he done his homework? Have I written something convincing in her reading notebook? If that parent can't bring him home after football, who can?

Also, the routine never lasts for long enough. A few weeks of school and it's the holidays again. Which would be fun if I could solve the problem of when I can work. I really need to organize the kids into a routine.

In some ways, doing the same thing, at the same time, every day can open up a new world. A world where other people are doing their same thing, at their same time, every day. After a while you recognize this, you acknowledge each other, strike up conversation. Regular interaction with people you sort of know can be heartening. You make jokes with the postman, with the woman in the corner shop. You pass moments with other parents, talking deep or light, crying if you want (who cares? Crying is normal. We're drowning in our children's tears). You can dart away in the middle of a chat because the littlest one has worked out how to use her mittens as nun-chucks. No one minds. They get it.

These people see more of you than your siblings, than your oldest friends. You miss them when the routine changes, when your children move from one playground to another, or get picked for a different team, or leave the school. You miss them, even though you don't really know each other. There should be a word for this missing, the odd ache that comes from the loss of regular, cheerful, low-maintenance acquaintance. It's a feeling that can come out sideways. You spot the lollipop lady, the one the school had to let go because they couldn't afford to pay her, at the shops and fall on her with too much enthusiasm. You see a man who used to work at the second-hand furniture shop and you talk at him manically before falling into silence, and you realize you don't even know his name. And it's not that you've forgotten it – though you would have forgotten it – it's that you never knew it.

A year ago, our days were a little different. F and I would meet D, her child-minder, after we'd dropped my son at school. We would meet on the corner of a road, or at a church hall. There was a different, parallel routine, built around the opening days of various toddler playgroups.

One time, when we were waiting for D, I saw an elderly woman. I knew her by sight. She attends church every day for the 9.30 a.m. service. She has white hair and a beige coat and a stick and she's kind to the children who buzz unsteadily around the lobby while we wait for the hall to be opened.

On this day, the lady was walking to church, as was her routine. What was different from usual was how she looked.

Her forehead was all wrong. It was hanging off. A large, deep flap of skin had come away from her skull and had flipped down, like a ramp. The hole where it had been was open to the air, and you could see inside the lady's head, you could see blood and white bone and even a glimpse of brain (can that be right? Is that what I saw?). There was blood dripping, in rivulets, down the contours of her face.

She had fallen, but she would not accept any help. She didn't believe us when we told her she was injured. I had to physically restrain her, put my arms around her and steer her inside the church to a chair. She kept saying, 'Leave me alone! I'm fine! Don't fuss! Nothing's wrong!' She tried to bap me with her stick, which F thought was funny. (F said, curious, 'Who's her? Why is her head falling down?') The priest found the first-aid box. We sat the lady down. Her head was wrapped, the horrible flap tucked up and away. We called an ambulance.

When they took her away in the ambulance, I cried. It was the shock of it. The sight of her was so graphic, so horror-movie. It was awful. And it was especially awful because it happened in the middle of an everyday routine, one that she liked and wanted to preserve: 'Nothing's wrong!'

The routine seems to protect you from harm, but it doesn't. It actually makes you too confident, as though nothing out of the ordinary could ever happen.

When I think of my parents, I think of their little ways. How my dad plays the piano, how he doesn't clip his nails so they click-click on the keys, personal percussion accompaniment. I think of the chair that he used to sit in to do the crossword, to listen to the football scores. The sofa that he sits in now – placed in the same spot as his old chair – to do the crossword, to listen to the football scores. I think of my mum standing in the living-room doorway, her fists on her hips, an angry martyr because none of us responded to her call to come and have tea. Driving the car, the way she changed gear: slowly, deliberately, always leading with the heel of her hand. That habit ended up with her having an operation, to cut through and free up muscles in her palm that had stratified through the same use, over and over.

I'm not sure that routine does much for adults other than keep them in one place. It takes a lot of energy to complete and repeat, over and over. To maintain. All that power: sparking, short-circuiting. All that revving on the spot.

And at some point, your energy lessens, but the routines stay. They become habits. Habits are more permanent. Once they become settled, second nature, they become how you live your actual life. How you live your life is the person you are.

You have to be careful with routine as you get older. Not enough and your life falls apart. Too much and you become rigid. You freeze-frame while everything around you speeds up, dances around you and moves on.

Chekhov said: 'Any idiot can face a crisis. It's this day-to-day living that wears you out.'

You know these pleasures are fleeting. They are disappearing, as your children grow and their gaze turns from adoration into assessment, as they drop your hand and run to catch up with their friends. They don't look back. They are disappearing, along with whatever remains of your youth and patience, and you'd like to hold on. Even as you scream at them about not listening, or not clearing up, or not finishing whatever needs finishing the night before rather than just before we leave the house . . . whatever seems worthy of screaming about. Still, you want to hold on.

Because these are the good times. I love my children and their particular ways, how she curls her mouth into a sneer when she wonders where water comes from, how he can't stop himself moving when he's talking, jittering on the spot, fingers fiddling with a button, a plastic toy, anything within reach. The way they demand you give them your serious attention – not a smirk, not a raised eyebrow – when they perform their own versions of 'Shut Down' or 'Let It Go'. Not habits, just who they are, who they're becoming.

It's possible to be grateful and frustrated at the same time. You can love your life while resenting its irritating habit of punching you in the guts at regular intervals. (It's the regularity, not the punching.) The tick-tock-tick-tock of kids' lives and the routine they live by means that your time together speeds up. Months, years, decades pass. Time grabs you by the shoulders and marches you forward. Life flows behind you, a plane-trail in the clouds, blossom on the breeze. Your children will leave you soon, as they must, as they should.

11. Out of It

P and F are playing a complicated game. There are high kicks and mad jumps from sofas, wild somersaults, complicated dance moves. They beat each other up with cushions to the head and then, when one is on the ground, moaning, in some sort of agony, the other makes a dramatic rescue attempt. P shouts, 'It's gonna be okay!' then drags F along the floor, pulls her upright, tries to get her to stand up. She's resistant and floppy.

I watch them. Their actions are familiar. I bonded with many of my friends in a similar fashion, through the hare-brained adventures of going out and getting smashed.

I sometimes think that the biggest change between my youth and my middle age isn't having kids or getting married or needing more sleep or worrying about gardens or any of that. It's that I don't get wasted any more. I've pulled out of that habit.

Because, back then, we were all united when it came to booze and drugs. All up for a good time, all on the same trip. We were open-minded, we got messy but, by our standards, we weren't completely ruined. We had codes around our drinking and drug-taking, subtleties of behaviour that seem ludicrous to me now. Heroin was disliked, but smoking it was just about acceptable; injecting it was not (using needles for any drug was grim). Cocaine in a joint was okay; crack was disapproved of, though people tried it. Weed, ecstasy, speed, coke, acid, poppers, mushrooms, DMT and ketamine were all fine. Nicotine: of course. And all forms of alcohol, including absinthe, and vodka bongs.

We were excited by drugs in our twenties. (We were excited by everything that didn't bore us.) Weed was standard, a constant bonding experience. Mushrooms were hilarious: look at the funny clouds! Keep looking, for eight hours! Speed meant you could paint your room really quickly. And ecstasy was a breakthrough, a gateway to a new way of living and being. It was communal, loving, exhilarating. It was easy: no banging needles, no chopping lines, no rolling joints. We felt as though the world made sense, as though people would come over to our new way of being.

But someone will always go harder and darker. Crack and heroin arrive suddenly – overnight, it seems – and once those are in your orbit, everything changes. Even in our twenties, people started falling through the loops. Friends would alter. They became belligerent, incoherent, a pain in the neck. Their eyes went strange, the person you knew was no longer in there, no matter where or when you saw them. You realized that you never saw them straight. They would disappear. You'd think: What happened? And someone would say, They were sectioned after staying up for five days. They left London because they'd been kicked out of their flat or they owed money to the wrong people or they robbed their girlfriend. They hanged themselves, they took an overdose, they had a car crash, they choked on their own vomit.

And those of us who made it? Are we kidding ourselves as to how strong we are, how experienced? I stopped smoking weed when it wasn't a laugh, when the conversation train seemed to leave without me and I wasn't convinced that I'd made it to the station, let alone got in the same carriage.

I stopped taking stimulants because the fun bit got small and, instead, I'd zoom instantly to irritation and paranoia. I stopped because the Fear started arriving, not the next day, not even during the night, but while I was actually supposedly having a good time. That wasn't the rush I wanted.

Madness is doing the same thing over and over, expecting different results. Your reaction to drink and drugs changes as you age. Getting wasted when you're 25 is completely different from when you're 45. Especially the aftermath. The hangovers arrive like a hostile alien invasion. They swarm you, you cannot fight. You are pinned down, poisoned, from head to heart to soul.

A lot of fiftieth birthday parties seem to get very messy. We like to say that the drugs have got stronger, which is true. But also we are weaker.

An old friend of mine gave up drinking when he was 45. He says: 'I decided I was going to divide my adult life into two halves. Twenty-five years' boozing. And twenty-five years without booze.'

He gave up after a many-week bender that took him to New York, then Manchester – partying 'with a bunch of doctors and judges, everyone off their tits' – then out to the countryside and a New Year's Eve on the Jim Beam and the JD and the charlie: 'I was totally out of it for a month.' He woke up on New Year's Day and couldn't get out of bed until 6 p.m. His kids were worried about him, he was three stone overweight and he was in agony. 'I thought: This is going to finish me off, if I carry on like this. Don't get me wrong, as a swan song, that month was brilliant. But I had to stop.'

So he did. No drink, no drugs. His social life had to change, obviously, but he gave himself some rules. Now, if he's going out with friends, there has to be a purpose to the evening – 'a third-party stimulus' – like a meal, or a comedy night, or a film. If he's going to a party, he will stay only two hours: '9.30 till 11.30. And then I leave. It's fine. Nobody cares.'

We're having coffee. He finds he has a lot of extra time on his hands. He fills it by reading ('There are loads of fascinating books out there, written by really clever people. And they have more to say than the twats down the Dog and Duck'). And he goes running, five or six times a week. It has some of the same de-stressing effect on him that his drinking used to have. He tends to run after work, which was when he used to drink a bottle of wine.

He says: 'There's nothing so good as a night out on the piss. And I'll always have the Pub Years. But I'd like to live the life I'm living until I'm 70, to be active and thoughtful, to work and engage with things. You get less sharp as you get older and I don't want to do anything to make that any worse.'

We talk about the difference between drinking in your twenties and early thirties and drinking when you're older. His forty-something boozing resulted in him getting into some proper scrapes. The drinking kept him behaving as though he were younger, as though he were the same age as when he'd first started properly drinking. It helped him ignore the fact that his life had changed, that it involved other people: wife, kids, workmates. It made him continue to take risks, to believe himself hilarious and invincible. To suppress his psychological baggage by never confronting it. To drag his angst around, through being drunk or hungover all the time.

'And then,' he says, 'I stopped drinking and discovered I was far less complex than I thought. My main problem was I was a pisshead.

'Also, why pretend you're young? You're less interesting when you're young. At uni, what are you going to talk about after you've banged on about your parents and your course? You have to drink to hide your inadequacies. But at our age, if you can't find something interesting to talk about with someone for two hours, with all the shit you've done and all the stuff you know, then that is pathetic, really. Middle-aged people have a lot to say, and it can be really fascinating. You don't need drink to get you through that.'

I am interviewing a British film director, a woman who's around the same age as me, who grew up in the suburbs of Manchester, as I did. Her name is Carol Morley and her first film, *The Alcohol Years*, told the story of her life as a teenager in the early to mid-80s. Carol talked to people who'd known her when she was young. They looked into the camera lens and said that, back then, she was a mess, a drunken sexual embarrassment.

In 2001, when I interviewed Carol about *The Alcohol Years*, we both got very drunk. Now, over a decade later, I'm talking to her about her new film, *The Falling*. We don't get drunk. We sip cappucinos and freshly squeezed fruit juice and discuss *The Falling*'s themes, which include the inability of teenage girls to imagine that middle-aged women ever had a youth that included sex or pleasure.

Towards the end of the interview, we try to remember what happened the first time we met.

'I still have that coffee pot!' says Carol. I don't remember us having coffee, let alone her stealing the pot. 'We went to Pizza Express, don't you remember?' No.

As far as I'm concerned, we did the interview at Blacks, in Soho, then blagged our way into the Groucho Club, though neither of us was a member. I don't remember food. I do remember Carol making me laugh by pretending to chat up some lecherous old blokes (they were probably in their early forties).

Carol gives me a look. 'I blacked out after Pizza Express,' she says.

During the 90s and into the 00s, my interviewing technique (if you could call it that) often involved getting plastered, either during or – if I was being professional – after the interview. Somehow a forty-five-minute chat about a new album or art project would fast forward into me and the interviewee being utterly hammered somewhere inappropriate: an important stranger's expensive house, a VIP gathering at a private drinking club. Later, we'd be in scuzzier dives: all-night drinking holes, located at the top or the bottom of treacherous stairs somewhere in Soho, Brixton, the East End. That was if I was in London. If the interview was abroad, I would change my return flight, stay on for a few days, crash in someone else's hotel room, meet new people, get smashed with them, too. I didn't seem to know how or when to go home.

It didn't matter. In those pre-mobile-phone days, when you had to be in a particular place to press a particular button to rewind a tape to hear your answerphone messages, friends and family didn't worry where you were. If you weren't at home, you were somewhere else. You were fine. Who was checking, really?

I used to be so good at drinking. I was excellent on vodka and tonic, a delight on fizzy wine, an all-night-all-day trouper on white rum or tequila. It was part of the job to be able to handle your drink and drugs. There are few successful musicians in their twenties and thirties who are able to live their demanding, babyish life without uppers and downers to smooth everything out. And when you're asked if you want a line of coke by someone you've just interviewed, it can be seen as bad form – rude, really – to say no. I did say no, after a while, because drugs started to get on my nerves when I hit my early thirties. But I rarely refused to drink.

When I got pregnant with P, I had a quick tally-up of what I had been doing in the previous days and weeks. I'd flown long-haul and short-haul, I'd got massively, room-bendingly drunk in New York, as well as New Orleans and Miami. I became worried about the unborn embryo twirling inside me, its cells dividing and multiplying, spinning in a sea of vodka, flung about on aeroplanes. Friends said: 'Oh, how would anyone get pregnant without booze?' I read up on embryonic development and obsessed about foetal alcohol syndrome. I stopped drinking. It was easy.

I hardly drink at all now. When the future is upon you, a day in bed, smothered in hangover, seems a terrible waste of time. Plus the horrors got too much.

I'm not teetotal. I still like a cocktail, still have the lazy days, drinking cider or prosecco on the grass while the kids chuck a ball about, ordering takeaway, eating it on a picnic blanket. All fine, even though all-day tippling turns into a never-ending headache quite quickly for me. I don't get hammered any more, though. So what I no longer get is the rush, the jolt, the hit. The euphoric acceleration, the shortcut to joy. Sometimes I miss it.

I miss the technicolour snapshot of a moment in time, the background rushing towards me until the landscape flattens, becomes detailed, sharper and harder than real life. I miss the sudden flinging of myself outside myself. I search for that. But outside drink and drugs, where can it be found? In exercise, in sex, in sudden weather changes . . . In an open-top car on an opened-out road. In dancing to a song that makes your soul explode. In the sun bursting through as you run alongside a small child that wobbles, then glides on a bike . . .

The familiar tough beauty, the chemical heart-lift thrill. As though my eyes are sparkling marbles and the world is an unbreakable jewel.

F careers down the hill, legs pedalling crazily, shrieking in fear and delight. A rush and a push. The land is ours.

I hear about an acquaintance who smashed up his house because he was drunk, who woke up his wife to tell her he was going to crash his car into a wall to kill himself. She had to get their teenage sons to restrain him. In the morning, he didn't recall a thing.

Another story concerns G, who gets pissed and gets off with a work colleague – nothing meaningful, just a spot of gropy snogging at a Christmas do – but, afterwards, the colleague sends him a text about it, and her husband finds her phone, her text and comes round to G's house and confronts G's wife. G says, to everyone concerned, that it only happened because he was drunk. But that doesn't seem to help the situation.

And then there's the friend who woke up from a night out to find himself on the sofa, with his toddler son shaking him, because 'You are blooded, Daddy.' He was, too. He'd bled all over the cushions. His nose was broken. And he had no idea how it had happened. He had to phone his friends. But they couldn't remember either.

We can drink ourselves to death and we can do it quicker than we think. Between 1991 and 2008, alcohol-related deaths in the 35–54 age group doubled in number.

Now, adults aged 45 and over are three times as likely as the under-45s to drink every day. I read a quote from Eric Appleby, CEO of Alcohol Concern. He says, 'Many over-45s drink daily, and those from professional or managerial households drink more, especially women. While drinking is decreasing among younger age groups, the middle-aged middle classes are taking unnoticed risks with their health.'

The bad stats are there; they are easy to find. From 2006 to 2013, the number of young men (25–44) who drank at least five nights a week halved, from 18 per cent to nine per cent. The number of middle-aged men (45–65) who drank five nights a week went down too. But it is still 20 per cent of that age group. Twice as many.

The percentage of 45–55-year-olds who take cocaine has doubled in a decade. The data suggest that it is the result of 'continued use among an ageing user cohort' – those who started taking coke when they were young and forgot to stop. The proportion of all illegal drug-users who are middle-aged has nearly doubled, from seven per cent of all users to 13 per cent.

From 2010 to 2013, more than half a million people were admitted to hospital for substance misuse; of those, 120,000 (24 per cent) were in their forties. In fact, admissions peaked in the 40–49 age group. I have to read that again. Nearly a quarter of all drink and drugs hospital admissions are people in their forties.

I talk to Tony Reo, a psychiatrist. He works with older people to manage their drug and alcohol use. Tony says there is a spike in drink and drug use in people in their late forties and early fifties, and he thinks that 'We haven't seen the peak of this generation's drug and alcohol use.' He uses the words 'this generation' a lot. It isn't his generation. It's mine.

'This generation grew up with a liberalized attitude towards alcohol,' says Tony. 'There were lots of fun, cool adverts for alcohol when they were young – Campari, Babycham, Heineken – and the attitude towards drink-driving was very different then.'

He describes people who don't want to become like their own parents or grandparents as they age but want, instead, to be seen as young and fun. Alcohol and drugs – 'going out and getting smashed' – are a way of achieving this, says Tony. 'Among this generation, alcohol is treated as a bit of a joke,' he says. 'You only have to read online comments to news stories about alcohol misuse to see that. People in their forties and fifties are cynical about the harm alcohol can cause.'

Tony can remember a time during the 90s when even doctors weren't very bothered about drinking. If a pharmaceutical company sponsored a lunch, everyone would get smashed.

I think: If you're in your forties, you've formed your own peer group. You hang around with people who do the same as you do. So, if that peer group is based about drinking, there is nobody who will say to you that you might want to cut back. Plus, you have more money than you did in your twenties so, you know, get a round in.

Tony has found that people only really believe that their drinking might be a problem when they suffer severe physical symptoms, 'such as liver disease, or a stroke'. He points out that such symptoms are the extreme end of addictive drinking. He sees a lot of alcohol-related brain damage. He's concerned with psychiatric effects, so he points to blackouts caused by alcohol – 'If you can't remember what you did last night, that is a strong predictor of dependence and addiction' – and also to disordered thinking: an inability to plan ahead, poor financial judgement.

If you can't remember what you did last night. If you can't plan ahead. Poor financial judgement. Also: feeling more than sad. 'Clinical depression is strongly linked to alcohol use,' he says. 'We don't quite know how, but excessive alcohol use appears to trigger something in the brain that leads to depression.'

I keep reading. Here is what I read about age and the effects of alcohol. Older people metabolize alcohol just as effectively as younger ones; and the speed that alcohol is eliminated from the body isn't affected by age, either. But changes in our bodies – such as having less muscle – means that the same dose of alcohol leads to higher peak alcohol concentration. Also, older people show greater alcohol-related impairment in reaction time and intellectual function. Kidney function declines by around 30 per cent between the ages of 30 and 50.

A middle-aged drunk person gets drunker and acts drunker than a younger one on the same amount of alcohol.

There are plenty of people who carry on getting leathered into their forties and beyond. Most of us are happy to continue our relationship with alcohol all the way through our lives. (That cliché: if you give up smoking and drinking, you don't live longer, it just seems as though you do.)

Some things change: maybe you stop going to the pub but start frequenting bars. Or you only drink wine, with a meal, or you decide to learn about wine, or get a 'how to make cocktails' book for Christmas, or have an actual drinks cabinet, and leave alcohol in it for extended periods of time, in order to make grown-up drinks. Maybe you start getting fiddly and snobby about drinks in the same way you used to be about drugs.

Maybe you look at the future – or the present – and think: I don't want to face that sober.

Someone told me that when alcoholics give up drinking, they're advised to up their sugar intake, eat fruit and sweets and chocolate in their first few days of abstinence. The vast amounts of sugar they were getting from alcohol: that sudden loss can be hard for their tired, overstressed bodies to take.

I do not have an addictive personality. However, sometimes I go mad and eat a whole bag of Haribo in one go. The high I get is strong enough to stop me sleeping. Still no rush, though.

Perhaps the answer is to allow yourself the time to behave like you used to. I talk to N, who is in his early forties and has two small children. A few years ago, he and his friends decided to go to Ibiza on a mad one for a week. 'One Foot in the Rave, my wife called it,' says N. 'We called it Fat Dads on Pills.' A proper occasion, with a proper title. Now Fat Dads is an annual event.

Fat Dads started when N had a few of his male friends round one night and they got a bit pissed. He put on Modeselektor and the six of them started raving in his living room. 'And we thought, We could do this again! Why not? We should all go to Ibiza!'

So they did. One week in August, no partners, no kids. Fun! Except that, for some reason, N decided to take all of his drugs in one go: 'I don't know why,' he says. 'I'm usually the sheepdog, herding everyone together, making sure they're okay. But I was the one going, Can I lean on your shoulder for a bit, mate? I became an utterly useless raver.'

We've all done it, I say.

He says: 'You know, I couldn't cope with all the setting stuff up, the schedule. Like, "We've gotta meet this guy at 4 o'clock and then we have to be here at 6 o'clock to get the tickets and we have to be somewhere else at such and such a time." And when we got to wherever we were going, a lot of places felt functional and reductive, bouncers shoving people, everyone out of their heads, like zombies.'

(Where were the pillow fights? The high kicks? The somersaults?) After a while, he didn't know why he was there. He hasn't been back on the Fat Dads week, though his friends have.

'When I was younger and went raving, I hadn't arrived at a point in my life where anything defined me,' he says. 'But now I'm a father, a husband, I run my own business. I can't be anything I want to be. I can't go on a flight of fancy with you because I'm not that up for where you're meant to go. Also, if I go for an evening out, these days I demand a level of comfort and customer service that isn't provided by Amnesia.'

N used to like the way that going out was a bit of an ordeal. The way you'd all go through something epic and then, in the morning, you'd be at someone's house, watching the sun come up, looking at your friends, the survivors, thinking, We've all been on an intense trip but we all got home safe. It made him happy.

Me too, I say.

'Yes, but what I realized when I was in Ibiza is that I'm actually happy already,' he says. 'I really like having kids, I like my life. So the drugs and the raving aren't going to make me that much happier.'

You can keep doing the same thing, but if you're not honest about how it affects you – how different the intoxication is from what it was when you were young – then you're kidding yourself.

I remember a friend joining AA towards the end of the 90s, and I didn't understand why. He wasn't George Best. He wasn't drinking vodka when he woke up in the morning (well, not every day), he wasn't lying in a gutter with no home to go to (he lay in a gutter with a home to go to). So, he blacked out and woke up with no idea where he was. Wasn't that the sign of a good night out?

Now, I know that I have no idea about other people's addiction problems. You can be addicted to sugar or glue or legal highs or the foam part of asthma inhalers, let alone coke or heroin or alcohol. It took me ten years, on and off, to give up cigarettes. Now I think, If you reckon you have an addiction, you probably have.

Drink and drugs can be a way of accessing the old, young, you. Of celebrating the person you once were, and how you can still be that person.

Or they can be a way of ticking off what you haven't done in life.

I speak to a man who reached 42, 43 to find his life was settled. He was in a managerial position at work and earned a big salary; he was married to a woman he loved; they had kids and lived in a nice house. 'I had a slight sort of unease all the time, but nothing serious.'

And then he went a bit mad. 'It was as simple as "Is that it? I've done everything right, so what do I do next?" And what seemed like a good idea was to indulge myself. Because why the fuck not? You feel like you're running out of road. You find yourself working for a 32-year-old hotshot and you're like, "Hang on a minute! Don't you know who I am?" That sense of "I've done that, and the world is not as lucrative or exciting as it once was." I wish I'd bought a sports car.'

His job meant that he went to a lot of awards ceremonies, and he started taking a bit of cocaine at them. And then he suddenly found he couldn't really do anything without coke, and after that, he wasn't doing anything except coke. It escalated from sitting in hotel rooms with the guys, watching porn and doing lines, to sitting by himself in hotel rooms, watching porn and doing grams. At one point, his dealer asked him if he thought he might be doing too much.

He went to Australia – the furthest place he could go – to try to get away from himself and his problems. It didn't work. He came back, travelling through Singapore airport with several grams of cocaine in the back pocket of his shorts (if he'd been caught, he'd have been hanged), and checked into the Priory. He'd got himself from a few lines to a full-blown addiction in the space of four years.

He doesn't drink alcohol or take drugs any more. He says: 'I am by far the oldest person in my workplace. But I'm fine with that. I look back now, and instead of feeling depressed that the ride is over, I accept that that part of my life has gone. It's someone else's turn. Please go ahead and enjoy yourself, because you're 24 years old.'

I ask him about the rush.

'I was absolutely addicted to that,' he says. 'I think people do get addicted to it, and our society encourages it. A lot of the music and entertainment industry is built on peaks and troughs, on excitement. But you end up restless, irritable or discontent. That was me. I was all three. And coke helped with that, and then it didn't. A lot of drinking and drugs is about punishing yourself. Feeding yourself this stuff that you know isn't good for you. A relentless self-loathing.'

I remember something that Josh Cohen, the psychoanalyst I talked to, said about drugs: 'This is a slightly glib generalization, but there seems to be something about different substances that attach to different toxic sentiments. Cocaine attaches to self-hatred in a big way.'

'Ecstasy is attached to love and youthfulness,' I say. He agrees. But later I think, Maybe I meant 'love of youthfulness'.

My friends from my twenties are still my friends. Some have carried on getting smashed, some haven't. It's a strange divide, almost arbitrary, like putting people in teams according to what coat they wear, or if they eat cheese. We all used to be on the same team. We all did the same thing. And now we don't.

Among a particular sort of person, there is a special reverence saved for ayahuasca. Those who are interested in mindfulness, in pesticide-free food, in knowing themselves, in opting out of the capitalist rat race, some of them are very excited by ayahuasca, a hallucinogen found in certain plants in South America. If you use the plant to make tea, you get a strong trip.

Ayahuasca is related to DMT. Shaun Ryder once talked to me about his DMT experiences. He said he broke through the matrix and a little green alien told him the meaning of life. Unfortunately, he couldn't remember any of what the alien said – or, indeed, anything about the alien at all – straight after he'd come down from the DMT trip. Instead, the little green alien came back to him in flashbacks, a few days later, which was a bit tricky when he was driving.

Anyway, ayahuasca is big in Ibiza, and becoming increasingly so in other places. I have a friend who had a very profound experience on it. I would never dismiss profound experiences, even if they are drug-induced. Something can shift in your mind or your heart that changes your life, and there's no reason to be snotty about it because it was kicked off by a chemical fire-starter. Also, if you're using Josh Cohen's theory that drugs are connected to the motivations of those who take them, then ayahuasca is very much associated with emotional and intellectual breakthroughs. It's for free-thinkers. And free-dayers: one trip lasts for a very full-on twelve hours, and you're meant to prepare for it and take a couple of days to recover. I'm not sure how much time that would leave for the school run.

My friend H takes ayahuasca. She is a woman who never really bothered with drugs – she didn't like cocaine, never tried E, did a bit of acid and hated it – and she wasn't a drinker, either. A bit of weed, that was her thing. But in her forties, she had a hard time for quite a while – lost her job and her house, was given a lot of shit and no money at all by the father of her child – and someone recommended ayahuasca. And as it was a tea made from a root, rather than a chemical compound, she thought, Okay.

She tells me about how she took it. It sounds thrilling. There was a ritual. A shaman from Peru. Musicians playing strange instruments. A church-like ceremony atop a mountain. Darkness.

H had one cup of tea and shut her eyes, as instructed. The effect was strong: she very quickly went into a Disney-style cartoon world, which was diverting. But there was also an element of panic and – quite quickly – nausea.

Being sick is a big part of the ayahuascan experience. You're not meant to eat much in the days coming up to taking it, so when you're sick – into specially dug holes in the ground, with Peruvian ladies there to look after you – you bring up a lot of bile. My friend felt like she was chucking up the remnants of her bad relationship, ridding her body of the poison of a man who had turned out to be toxic. She found this overwhelming, and got panicky. And then she was offered another cup.

She drank three cups and, she says, the experience completely sorted her out. During her trip, she felt as though she could see her life clearly: she considered the people in it, present and past, recognized patterns. At one highly charged moment she felt shards of ice shoot out from her heart. 'I could see them leave,' she said. 'It was amazing.'

The next morning, she left the dark place and wandered out into the sunshine. 'And everyone looked so beautiful,' she tells me. 'I loved them. We shared an experience and they were beautiful.'

This is the part of ayahuasca that appeals to me. I know that feeling. The 'people are wonderful' effect. The little fluffy clouds come-down after the great big adventure.

H has done the tea trip quite a few times now. She shows me a book of Gaudí illustrations, the cover of which is a green lattice of regular patterns. It looks like a series of holes in the ground. 'That's what it looks like,' she says.

The picture reminds me of a C. S. Lewis book in the Narnia series, *The Magician's Nephew*, where the characters have to jump into different pools in a forest – portals – to get to where they need to be. The picture also reminds me of how I used to feel about maths: as though it would help explain how the world is made. I thought that maths was linked to nature and space and time, and that life could be rationalized, if only we could find the right equation. I thought there was a real connection between patterns in the world – nature's mathematics – and our collective human emotions. Somewhere inside me, in my redundant, embarrassing hippie heart, I still feel this.

*

A friend and I go to see Beck play at the Roundhouse. I see a lot of people I used to see when I went out in the 90s. One of them is a singer, who squeezes past me and my friend. He's with another man, whom we both know well. We say hi to the second man, but the singer ignores us. This is no surprise to me, as he has ignored me for twenty years. I thought he might say hello to my mate, though.

She turns to me. 'He hates me,' we both say at the same time, and tell each other the stories of why. They are different, but they both involve a lot of drink and drugs, extreme situations in hotels and on planes and in horrible rooms overcrowded with bullying hangers-on and scary dealers. At the beginning of our stories, which are adventures, of course, the singer likes us: we are seen by him as being on his side. At the end, we have been deemed the enemy.

After Beck finishes, we hang around for a while. The singer makes direct eye contact with my friend and me. He shyly waves a bottle of water at us, and says, 'All right?' We say, 'All right,' back. He doesn't drink or take drugs any more, I think. He's changed.

Later, I think about this and I realize that, oddly, he's a sort of friend. It's those past adventures. They mean we have a lot in common: history, mates, a shared belief in music. We have the same taste, we like the same things and – more importantly – we hate the same things. We went to the same parties. We made it through to our forties without dying or going mad. We're lucky.

The rush is great and I miss it sometimes. But not as often as I thought I would. Now I'm older, the adventures are just anecdotes, memories of madness. They help you know when someone's on the same side.

12. Work

I'm talking with the taxman about poetry. Well, about writing. I've phoned HMRC to explain why I don't have the money for my tax bill and have been put through to Keith, the taxman. I've said that I've been writing a book, which takes time, and I can't do better-paid work while I'm doing it. I'm trying to convince him that writing a book, if you're a journalist, is a sort of upskilling. Like I'm getting trained to be a web design trouble-shooter, or I'm learning accountancy, or doing relevant voluntary work (that one's a bit close to the bone). Keith listens politely, but remains unconvinced.

'Can you put the amount you owe on your credit card?' he asks. I say I can't, because the amount that I owe is too big.

'A loan?' says Keith. 'We prefer you to get a loan.'

I don't say anything.

Keith sighs. 'Can you sell your car?'

I'm bracing myself for Keith to ask me to sell our flat. Keith relents. He puts me on a payback scheme, a whacking amount per month, but with minimal interest. I love Keith.

P wants to know what work people do (people other than S and me). After years of believing he's going to be a footballer, he thinks he might want to be an actor. I don't want him to be a footballer. I don't want him to be an actor, either, so I'm happy to explain alternative careers. We talk through the jobs of his friends' parents. They include a physiotherapist, a school maintenance man, a costume-maker, a PA, a few law-yers, a few musicians, a midwife, a chef. There's a firefighter, a film editor, a gardener, some teachers, some child-minders, IT experts, charity workers. They work in the theatre, they work in supermarkets, they run a pub, drive a cab.

As we talk, I realize I'm thrilled by the variety of different jobs we're discussing. All so different! And all so interesting! I begin to think less about P's potential working life and more about mine. I consider changing career. I'd be a brilliant midwife-come-cabbie-stroke-gardener.

A couple of the parents work in the City, and when P asks me what that means, I'm a bit stumped. 'They make money because they make other people money,' I say, at last.

P looks at me. '*Booooorrrriiiiiinnnng*,' he says.

When I moved to London, I remember being very surprised by people's emphasis on your work. When you met them, they introduced themselves, using their first name and surname. Then they would say something like 'I make programmes for the Beeb. Art films, really', and then, 'What do you do?' This was at the sort of parties that happened straight after work. Not the parties that started at midnight.

What do you *do*? Such an odd thing to ask. What do I do? Lots of things, Nosy. I wasn't used to the question. Nobody asked that in Manchester, no one asked it in clubs. It was too personal, a bit police-y. If you met someone for the first time, you would just give your first name – if you even said that – and then you'd try to make each other laugh. Comment on the situation you were in, talk music, or dance moves, or maybe football or DJs. Your job never came into it.

And the friends you made through those parties, bumping into them over and over, at clubs or in the tent next to yours at festivals, the ones you got to know over the years: what did they do? In real life? I didn't ask, and neither did they.

Eventually it turned out that some of them did things that could be deemed important. They were an underground DJ, or had some high-up job in broadcasting, or – this happened a couple of times – they were successful contemporary artists. In most cases, I didn't work this out for years. (I know: some journalist.)

Ages ago, I went to a party for the opening of a bar with a friend. It was a rare night out for her – she had a young child, whom she was bringing up on her own – and she was asked the what-do-you-do? question over and over. When she said, 'I don't work at the moment. I'm a stay-at-home mum', the questioner would nod vaguely, look over her shoulder and excuse himself. And, yes, it was always a him.

The clubbing revolution of the late 80s and early 90s had an unexpected knock-on effect on work. Somehow the unity that people found on the dance floor – the liberation, the love – led them to believe that long hours in a crappy job wasn't the way they should go. They gave up working in admin, they dropped out of college, they sacked themselves from management consultancy (*boooorrrrriiiiinnng*), they walked away from their job in the biscuit factory and they never went back. Shoom, one of the first ever acid-house clubs, had a newsletter. A few months after the club opened, Jenny Rampling, wife of DJ Danny, wrote an article in the newsletter pleading with Shoom regulars not to quit their jobs.

But they did. So did clubbers in the Hacienda, in the fields around London, at Back to Basics, at Cream. There was something about the newness of house music – the way it confused the police and upset the establishment – that made clubbers feel they could overcome the way things had always been, revolutionize their lives, opt out of dead-end jobs and make their own way of living. So they did; or at least they tried. Some just went to clubs, couldn't find the time or mind space for anything else (maybe a bit of dealing). But others became clothes makers, or graphic designers, got into journalism. Many turned DJ, loads joined bands, others made music solo, in their bedrooms, got a track pressed and took the white label to record shops. They started filming gigs, or filming friends, or making funny animations or being funny themselves, on stage. They set up magazines or record labels, became actors or managers or PRs or models.

And . . . it worked. The creative industries in the 1990s grew and got noticed, until they became part of the way that the UK sold itself to the world. It's called soft power now – the atmosphere of a place, its ethics and style and socializing opportunities, its unique charm – though back then, some people worried that it was soft Thatcherism. Could ethical entrepreneurialism really exist? Wasn't any job outside the public sector just Tory-lite? Many of us could still remember the manufacturing industries, especially in the north. We were suspicious of private enterprise. Until we realized that it might mean us, with our ideas, and our friends, doing stuff we liked and getting paid for it.

So that was what we did. At the time it meant freedom, and excitement, and some money. Our creativity and our ideas and our vigour were our employment solution. How strange – dislocating, disheartening – to look around and see that those solutions don't seem to work any more. At least, not for you.

Do we need a bad guy? Perhaps we do. Enter, twirling his dastardly moustache, the internet. Since 2000, the internet has changed everything. It has devastated the music business, wrecked print journalism, scythed its way through books and film and comedy, even fashion. The only creative industry it hasn't torpedoed is fine art, and that is because art's value is in its uniqueness, the fact that a single creation is the only one that's out there. Most of the other fun stuff depends on reproduction, and on the copyright of whatever it is that's being reproduced. But Bad Guy Internet had a fist-fight with Copyright and smeared Copyright all over the walls. Then he gave away all the reproductions for free. And those factors, combined with the way that everyone now wants to be a creative (that new noun, that misplaced adjective) – even the sons and daughters of bankers, even the children of politicians – means that the work is not what it used to be.

I think of my friends now, trogging up the motorway on a Saturday night to play the graveyard slot at a student union bop. Entertaining drunken hen and stag parties in a comedy venue that turns into a nightclub after 10.30 p.m. Writing reams of copy for half the rate we got when we started out. Being passed over for remixes because there's a newer, cheaper DJ, who lists them as a hero. Being asked, once again, to work for free, because of the 'exposure', when the bank doggedly refuses to cash those exposure cheques.

And sometimes I wonder why we never bothered with a pension, or 'investments', whatever they are. And spending time away from the family gets harder each time you leave. When staying up all night becomes a physical impossibility, unless it's to worry about how you'll pay the next set of bills . . . but you have to stay up, because the only way to pay the mortgage is to work through until morning. When you take on lots of badly paid small jobs because you can't land a contract for regular work any more.

Every job is a bit job. Nothing is secure. Shift work, parttime, a contract for a month or so. Companies prefer not to pay retainers, merely a few weeks' salary for work that would once have taken half a year. And unlike the 70s and 80s, women are in the marketplace now. We make up 49 per cent of the work force. There are seven million extra people out there who want to work as much as you do.

*

Michael Goldfarb is about ten years older than me, an experienced journalist, excellent on the radio and in print. Online, I find an interesting article by him on the difference between work and employment. In full-time employment from 1992, he lost his job in 2005 and went freelance.

He writes that he works as hard as he did when he was employed by someone else, but for much less money. I call him up.

'I get about 20 per cent of the money for 100 per cent of the output,' says Michael. Officially, he's self-employed, but he calls himself under-employed.

Michael started out as an actor, and only came into journalism in his thirties: 'So I was very fired up,' he says. 'I was a typical pushy American.' He hustled and blagged and got his jobs; in NPR, at the BBC. Throughout his forties, he was employed, he won awards for his work. And when he was 50, he got a great job at WBUR, a radio station in Boston, Massachusetts.

He had five years there, before a cash crisis led to him being laid off. When his bosses brought him in to tell him, he had so little idea of what was about to happen, he thought they might be giving him a rise.

Now, Michael thinks of his story as a cautionary tale, as a harbinger; he believes that most journalism will go this way, with publications closing, or laying off older writers and photographers to solve a temporary money problem that isn't their fault. Employees over 50, with their experience and their knowledge of how much they're worth, cost more to employ than those in their twenties.

Back then, though jobless, he wasn't worried. He was one of America's best-known foreign correspondents; he'd just get another job.

'And . . . I couldn't,' he says. 'I've never had another job. I'm back to exactly where I was when I arrived here thirty years ago. I'm scuffling, I'm literally begging, just to stay in the game.'

Michael is freelance. He works a lot, but he says that his work isn't the same as it was when he was employed. Employment implies commitment, from employer and employee, and it means stability. It's existed, he points out, since feudal times.

'You were a serf tied to the land, you knew what you were supposed to do, you knew who your lord was, your children grew up in it. Famines happened, wars happened, but in terms of what you did to clothe and feed your family and provide shelter, you were stable. Because your employment was stable.'

Not like now.

My parents had the same jobs for almost all of their lives. My mum took time off, then worked part-time when my brother and I were young. But she was back working full-time when I was 7, and after that, she changed jobs once, from a geography teacher to head of geography, staying as head of department until she retired. My dad got his job when he was 30 and stayed in it until he was 65. Then he stopped.

And they weren't the only ones. They were the middle-class version of the factory worker, the docker, the shop assistant. They hadn't the desire to advance themselves, to shoot up the career ladder; they weren't ambitious like that. It wasn't how they thought. They wanted to do their jobs well, and be paid for them, then go home to their family.

If you grow up surrounded by that, it shapes what you think work is. You have an expectation of full employment, of a steady, looked-after, attached job until retirement. This exists, somewhere deep inside me, because I saw it when I was young. Even though I've never – not once – had a job that falls into that category. Is this the strange predicament of people my age? An unconscious desire for stability within a working world we know as wobbly?

I speak to John Philpott, an economist who specializes in the labour market and employment trends. He runs a website called the Jobs Economist. He talks like an economist: quietly and precisely.

He says: 'The classic job for life, by which I mean the jobs that employed men from the age of 16 until they were 65, there are relatively few of these any more.'

'Are there more people working freelance, these days?' I ask. 'More self-employed people?'

John says it's more complicated than that. 'If you compare employment between now and before the most recent recession [in 2008], there has been a shift towards more part-time work, more temporary work, more contract work and more self-employment. This can range from the freelancer with knowledge skills down to an Uber driver. Certainly, there are more people employed in temporary or contract jobs than there used to be.

'But that way of working is perhaps considered to be more prevalent because the current trends in contracting work hit the media early. And this has led to a slightly skewed public perception, because the media wrote about it, and the stories have a lot of weight.'

Us media moaners have brought it on early for everyone, really.

Michael Goldfarb is talking about Germany and Holland, places where, he says, the 'natural fractiousness' between employers and unions is less than in the UK. He describes a different approach to work from that of the UK. More cooperation between employers and workers, with workers represented at board level; lower average wages but more help provided by the state; strong regional government.

In Germany, he says, when large industrial employers, such as the Port of Hamburg and Airbus, were going through modernization, bringing in machines to do jobs that used to be manual, the employers and unions came up with deals to ease the impact on workers. The venture almost became co-operative, with the unions agreeing to a shorter working week for many months. They deemed it better for most workers to take a pay cut than for some to lose their jobs and others keep them. 'In that way,' says Michael, 'the trauma of being made redundant was minimized.'

John Philpott tells me about similar situations in the UK. In the early 80s and early 90s, after those recessions, he tells me, there was a tendency for employment rates to fall completely after the age of 50, to 'drop off a cliff'. This was because there were, essentially, two options when you were made redundant. If you were a blue-collar worker, employed in manufacturing or mining, when the industrial industries went through restructuring (like the Port of Hamburg, like Airbus), you lost your job. If you were over 50 when you lost your job, you knew you couldn't get another. You weren't trained for anything else, and no firm wanted to hire a fifty-something. So you went on sickness benefit. If you were white collar, and the same thing happened, you took early retirement.

In both cases, your life completely changed. One day you were working, the next you were unemployed, and you would remain unemployed for the rest of your days.

Now, says John, things are different. 'There has been a gradual tightening of the benefit system and pension provision is less generous,' he says. 'So the over-fifties need to carry on working, and if they can stay in work they will. But if you lose your job over 50, the likelihood is you will find it hard to get another job with an employer. So they shift down to fewer hours, if they can. They become part-time workers. Or they will draw on their pension or their savings and top that up with contract work. The better-off rely on their house gaining value.'

There has been much trumpeting of the older worker, how many more of us are continuing to work into our fifties and sixties, even seventies. This is presented as a triumph (and it probably is). There are more older people who work. They just don't have full-time jobs. 'There is not the cliff edge that there used to be in employment,' says John. But there is a fall, a definite declining slope, after 50.

'The main point that I wanted to make,' says Michael, 'is this. It takes people so long to get into regular work now, it's very tough for young people to get any job at all. And then, after 50, you're on borrowed time. If you've been working steadily at something and then you're laid off in your fifties, you will never work steadily at that job again. You will never earn any-thing like that salary again. So . . . this is the point. You've got twenty years of working life, and that's it.'

Twenty years instead of forty. A half-life of work.

There is a woman who gets in touch with me via social media. She has a bee in her bonnet. She insists that married women who stay at home to bring up their kids will never get work after the children leave home. She says that there is no employment for them, especially after 50; that the job market offers nothing.

The woman makes me think of Helen Franks, encouraging middle-aged women in the 80s to consider getting a job once the kids had left. Free to work! Except now, there is no work out there for them to do.

*

John is continuing to explain things to me, in his measured, careful way: 'Working for an employer for a long time might look stable from the outside, but within the job, there may well have been a lot of changes, to do with technology, terms and conditions. So, from the outside your job is stable, but individually you might be thinking, Oh, what's happening? This is exacerbated in a recession, because the insecurity that people feel goes up even more.'

He thinks that people a little younger than him might be better equipped for the future. 'The creative people of the 90s generation are in a better situation now than the men who were made redundant in the 80s, because they're flexible enough to do something else. That something else might not be the nirvana they were expecting, it might not be that glamorous. It's an increasingly competitive job market. But they can work.

'The question is whether people are psychologically equipped for that uncertainty, that insecurity. There will be some who are fine with it, but others, who aren't, who will find it psychologically affecting.'

Michael says: 'I find myself strangulated with anxiety. My father was a doctor, my mother was a housewife . . . the steadiness of what we had. I sometimes just don't know how to cope. I try to project that "not to worry" thing to my child, and she's not quite cottoned on yet, but everything is extremely precarious. And totally predicated on two things. One, my brain functioning, and two, maintaining enough good relationships with people.'

I say this to John, and expect him to respond with something like 'Well, all jobs are requisite on your brain functioning and on good relationships.'

But he doesn't. He says: 'For various reasons, I left a good stable job a few years ago. And now, having set up by myself, I don't find the work difficult – it's the networking, the getting the contracts in, that I find hard. When you have an employer, all those extraneous parts of the job were dealt with and you just got on with the job you had to do. You were a passive recipient of work.'

John is 58. I joke that perhaps he needs a networking group, a place for men over 50 to hang out with each other, josh about the old days and exchange contact details. John says he has joined LinkedIn. 'Recently, I got a lot of congratulations from friends on a new job, but I didn't actually have one. I can see how this might create status anxiety,' he says.

Age discrimination is illegal. So if you're turned down for a job, you don't know if it's because of your age, or because your skills are of an older vintage and you haven't updated them as much.

'Yes,' says John. 'We're in a psychological bind. Traditionally employers don't invest in people over a certain age, because they think they will retire. But that doesn't apply now. People want to work and also technology changes all the time, so everyone – older and younger – needs to update their skills. A large part of the business community work as though it's the 1970s.'

He makes another point. 'I can see how this new way of working has an effect on the rise in inequality in this country,' he says. 'With stable employment, when many people were employed in one place for a long time, the relationships between people were marshalled by firms. And no matter where their talents lay, everyone ended up with similar average rewards.

'But in an insecure world it is only the people who are attuned to that life, who can make contacts and sell themselves, who do really well. And the rest struggle on.'

*

I read a study that says if you change your job in your thirties, you are far happier in your work when you reach your forties and fifties. S did this. I did not.

I read an article in *Salon* about Generation X hitting midlife. There is a sense in the article that this generation can deal with job insecurity better than it can deal with emotional insecurity. It is hinted that this might be something to do with the 70s – when Gen X-ers were children – a time when the US divorce rate nearly doubled. Also, that this is something to do with the 90s, when the X-ers were first employed, a time of employment ups and downs.

I remember the recession of the early 90s, the economic tightening of the early 2000s, the banking collapse in 2008. I remember Generation X being called slackers.

The conclusion is that they (we?) don't mind being financially insecure – we're used to that ('At every major milestone there's been an economic collapse,' points out writer Susan Gregory Thomas) – but we can't cope with an unstable home life. We know our kids can't be richer than us, but we want them to be happier.

Both Michael and John say that the circumstances in which we are operating are unique – due to the internet, due to the housing crisis. Michael gives me examples of employers reducing the amount they pay, contacting journalists to tell them that their word rate has gone down. Meanwhile, house prices rise, and the chance of buying one is beyond us all.

John says: 'We're all affected by the glories or misfortunes of life, according to that moment.'

Some of my friends have changed career; some have been sacked or made redundant and have retrained. PRs have become media trainers; journalists have become PRs. Some supplement their income through eBay or Airbnb or teaching. More have sold their house, if they had one, moved to a cheaper area; a few have downsized to two smaller properties, so they can rent one out. Lots have left their original profession and studied to become counsellors and therapists: 'One of the few jobs where age is an advantage,' says one to me.

A friend who worked in the music business in the 90s, made his fortune, then moved on, says: 'It's a problem if your dream becomes your career. Because you can't summon the motivation to do anything more mundane later in your life, just because it's your job. You can't find the self-discipline and commitment. You're too used to following your bliss.'

I bump into someone who works in a record company. I think of him as vital to the company's success, but he's worried about his future. He says: 'If it all goes tits up, I'm going back to hairdressing. The one job that you can't get done online.'

If it takes 10,000 hours' experience to master a job, and I devote two full days a week, forty-seven weeks a year to whatever career I decide to diversify into, it would take me fifteen years to be any good at it. I do not have fifteen years going spare.

In the US, it is estimated that 40 per cent of the work force will be freelance by 2020. In the UK today, there are almost 5 million self-employed people working across all sectors; this is 45 per cent up on 2001–02. In February 2017, Adam Corlett, Economic Analyst at the Resolution Foundation said this: 'Rising self-employment has been the biggest jobs story of the last decade.' Freelancing is now seen as an attractive career option by 87 per cent of students studying for a degree (pragmatism, I'd say). This, despite the fact that freelancers are not well paid. In 1994–95, the average self-employed wage in the UK was £300 a week; in 2014–15, it was £240. In the UK, 15 per cent of senior managers are self-employed; 13 per cent of IT professionals; 12 per cent of engineers; 40 per cent of professionals in design and media; and 56 per cent of skilled tradespeople in construction. In the EU labour market, freelance numbers went up from just under 6.2 million in 2004 to 8.9 million in 2013, an increase of 45 per cent.

I am thinking about someone I recently interviewed, a talented and successful woman who works at the stuffier end of the BBC. She asked me not to put her age in the article. 'They're getting really funny about people over 50,' she said.

I have been freelance for all of my working life, apart from two years' employment at *Smash Hits*. Every time I finish a piece of writing, I'm redundant again.

13. Anger vs. Dismay

'Feelings aren't facts,' says S to me again. I'm telling him a story – about a teacher, about a kid – and my attitude towards what has happened overwhelms my telling of it. I am sad. I am furious. I can't untangle the emotion from the problem.

'Oh, love,' I say to P, when he gets so frustrated over a computer game that he cries and chucks the controller to the floor. 'If it makes you upset, stop playing it. It's only a game.'

He puts his hood up over his head, pulls it down below his eyes. 'Leave me alone,' he says.

F won't get dressed. She hurls herself on to the bed. I say: 'You don't have a choice about going to school. But you do have a choice about how you feel about it. So you might as well change your mood to happy. Look!' I make a sad face and put my hand in front of my chin. I move my hand up my face and, as I do, I change my expression behind it, so that when it gets to my forehead, I am smiling. If I smile in a really manic way, it makes her laugh.

I lie in bed, rigid with tension about work, or small, complicated arrangements. I say to myself: 'You can't change the situation, you can only change how you feel about it.' Or, 'If it makes you upset, stop playing the game.' Or, 'Feelings aren't facts.' Then I smile, in a really manic way. In the dark.

Sometimes this helps. Sometimes it doesn't. I think this is because sometimes the real story isn't the facts of what happened, but the emotions around it. The feelings *are* the story. They are the facts.

What are the emotions of midlife? Regret? Disappointment? Frustration? Rage?

'I don't think there is anyone as angry as a middle-aged woman,' says the middle-aged woman, a person I've always thought of as charming and composed.

I don't think of myself as angry, but recently I've been moving really swiftly from mildly irritated calm to focused wrath. I could blame the kids, I suppose.

'Oh, I lose it with my kids at least twice a week,' says a friend. 'Today, we got to the tube and we were running late because they took ages to decide which socks to wear, so I was already a bit stressed. And then my oldest says, "I haven't printed out my homework", even though I asked her several times before we left the house if she had. And then she cries and wants to go back home to print it and I have to get to work and it's fucking 7.30 in the morning. So I lose it.'

Families are often the trigger. Who we are within them and what that means we have to do.

'My mum sent me an email and I was too busy to answer it,' says another friend. 'I spent the whole day fire-fighting problems, I had a meeting after work where I got bollocked for something that wasn't my fault. I eventually get home, I'm about to have dinner and my mum calls. I answer and she says, "Is there something wrong?" I'm like, "No, other than I'm completely starving because I only ate a packet of Monster Munch all day, why?" And she says, "Well, you didn't answer my email. I've been worrying." I had to put the phone down on the worktop and walk away.'

'My dad doesn't shout,' says a friend of P's. 'He brings a bad feeling into our house and then it stays there for days.'

*

I hear a radio programme about anger. The experts on the programme find anger hard to define. A neurological clinician talks about hot, instinctive rage, the kind that comes quickly, involuntarily. He lists nine triggers, including 'momma bear' rage. Such anger can be switched off, he says, by tampering with certain areas of the brain. A psychiatrist talks about longer-term emotions. Resentment. Seething. Unspoken infuriation that manifests as disdain. These are only dismantled by therapy and by practising alternatives to anger. Punching a wall is not recommended.

Some time ago, S and I went to Thailand. We lost each other in a multi-storey department store, and, when we eventually found each other again, we had a row. Not a massive row, just an irritable, not-my-fault-you-dick-your-fault-you-dick-stop-being-such-a-dick one. We stopped quite quickly, when we realized there was a small crowd was gathering.

Nobody shouts in Thailand. It is a huge deal to have a public argument in a country where arguing is done in private. We might as well have been caught having a quickie atop the display of cute-nosed soft toys. And though many of the watchers were hiding their faces behind their hands, through embarrassment, I recognized their expression. Appalled, yet mocking. It was the same look that people had at one particular Glastonbury, years ago, when they saw a naked woman masturbating in the middle of the festival. (In a pile of litter, by a bandstand on the main drag.) (No, it wasn't me.)

In China, on the same trip, we saw a tiny old woman scream at a young man. She was upset about a parking space, and she got up close to him, right in his face, in a manner that few people would accept in the UK. I kept thinking: Don't do that! He'll hit you! But he didn't. He shouted right back, put his face even closer to hers and yelled without restraint. It was frightening. We stopped and watched, hearts pounding, with the mixed-up look on our faces.

Our anger levels are culturally monitored. Our nationality and society tell us how angry we are allowed to get. When you live in a mongrel place, like London, you have to adjust and readjust accordingly.

I walk to the shops near my home. The pavement is crowded with people. They're waiting for the bus, bustling to cross the road, standing stock still to tell the world about Jesus Our Risen Lord, or roots and culture, or to hand out a free paper, or sell incense sticks. I try to walk through quickly, but I have to pause on and off, because the woman in front of me is old, dragging a trolley-bag, and I can't move around her.

I feel a whack on my calf. A pushchair. I look round at the woman pushing it, but don't say anything. It happens again. I turn round and say, 'Stop banging me! I can't go any faster! Hold up!'

The woman is Jamaican. She likes a row. We shout at each other for two minutes – while walking and stopping and starting – and then we get on with our days.

When I was in my teens and twenties, I regularly lost my temper, but only with particular people. My family. My boyfriend. Anyone I believed was wielding authority when to do so was unreasonable and unfair. I got a lot of parking fines.

After I had children, I understood why patience might be important. I deliberately tried to increase mine. My patience didn't become infinite, but it got stretchy and strong. Patience wraps up rage in a comfy duvet, strokes its hair and soothes. Sometimes I shove my head into a pile of washing and shout into that, then use a different voice when I walk back into the room.

With the kids, I try to be patient. But still my anger comes. It comes quickly, hot and full of adrenalin. It feels like rage, that subconscious uncontrollable instinct. It takes me by surprise.

Hormones can change how you feel so profoundly that they seem to alter who you are. I read up about the hormonal changes in menopause and how they can affect you ('the early warning signs'). There are thirty-four symptoms, says one website, including migraines, hot flushes, itchy crawly skin, inability to sleep and – unsurprising, given all the other symptoms – irritability.

The menopause can make you angry. It can turn you into an angry person. As can having periods, of course. You'd think we'd be used to it. Being pregnant can send you doolally. And then you have the baby and you are, perhaps, depressed. The menopause can make you depressed.

I am not menopausal, not yet. There is a strong possibility that I am peri-menopausal. That's a term you start hearing a lot when you hit your forties. It means you're unlikely to get pregnant, but your periods haven't stopped. It means you're on the way to menopause. Not long now! Nearly there!

There are sixty-six symptoms of peri-menopause, apparently, and many of them appear to be the same for the menopause. There are some others, though. Decreased motor coordination. Urinary incontinence. Menstrual 'flooding'. In the peri-menopausal stage, which can last years, your anxiety levels may increase, especially during the night. You may get hot, especially during the night. You may not sleep well. You may want to sleep all the time ('crushing, crashing fatigue'). Your libido may drop. You may feel down in the dumps. You may feel rage.

I've found anger to be catching, though I've built up my resistance to it over the years. I don't get het up about politics any more. My road rage is rare. I don't shout on the phone at people who are trying to help me, even when their efforts aren't helpful at all.

When P gets angry, which he does more and more as he approaches adolescence, I try not to shout back. (I do shout back, sometimes.) His anger is a reaction to frustration, to his sensitivity to unfairness or disrespect, or what he thinks is unfair or disrespectful. What makes him angry is not always what I think is going on. There are the uncertain matters of intention, of flippancy, of how repetitive, irritating action can wear you down.

Anyhow, I like angry people. Not those who lose it, who hit things and people, who smash stuff (though I did all of those things when I was young). But those who retain enough fire to speak up and question what they're told.

I talk to Suzanne Moore, newspaper columnist.

She says: 'I don't see anger and rage as bad things, I see them as necessary fuel to get through certain times. What's the opposite? Resignation? That's closely associated with depression. Suppressed anger can manifest itself as depression.'

What have we got to be angry about, though?

'We have a fantasy that there's going to be a calm time,' says Suzanne. 'We imagine that, at some point, we will be sorted. Like when you have young kids, you think things will get easier when they're more independent, but they don't. If you're in your mid- to late forties, you may well be the mother of a teenager, and they really need you and they really hate you at the same time. It's hard. Teenagers throw anger at you and you feel as though you're still a teenager yourself, and yet you're meant to soak it all up and be caring, not angry.'

We talk about how, in middle age, even people without kids are probably caring for their parents, or a friend, or a different family member. We talk about how caring duties tend to fall to women. And we talk hormones. Suzanne has been through the menopause.

She says: 'When I was going through it, I didn't have any really bad symptoms apart from insomnia, which was terrible. I went to the doctor and he said the solution was HRT or anti-depressants. I said, "I'm not depressed, I'm just not sleeping. I'm tired."'

Tired sometimes, angry sometimes . . . A few of my friends have been given Prozac for the menopause. It makes me think of Pauline Bart's study, way back in 1971, and how she found that the greatest users of anti-anxiety drugs were women of 45–54. After I speak to Suzanne, I find a study that took place in 2014. It found that the greatest users of anti-depressants are women aged 45–64. Culturally, we are not allowed to be depressed.

'There's an assumption that women have to be happy,' says Suzanne. 'Doctors dole out anti-depressants for the menopause like you wouldn't believe. And HRT doesn't work for every-body and is way overprescribed, too – there are patches, gels, but we don't make more informed choices because we don't know what they are. People who have money pay to go to a private doctor and get the same hormones as HRT, but they think they're more natural because they come from yams.'

Are we meant to be happy? Or, if not happy, are we meant to be stable: not sad, not angry? Is that what our culture wants? Or what we want? (I want to be happy. I have techniques to achieve this: going outside, eating in cafés, not watching the news, listening to music, watching *Doctor Who* with the kids, making S laugh.)

One of the ways we can become happy – or, at least, less unhappy – is by speaking to someone neutral about how we feel.

Suzanne says: 'I think the best part of private health is you get to talk to someone for an hour and they listen. You don't get that from a GP, you just get told, "You're peri-menopausal, it will go on for years, off you go."'

*

Anger might seem a reasonable reaction to a time in your life when you feel overwhelmed and under-supported, when you feel as though you are disappearing from view. When nobody notices your presence and nobody appears to be listening to you. Especially not your kids.

Philippa comes round for a coffee. She says that anger is 'a wonderful emotion' and she talks about impulse control.

'We all have a choice when it comes to anger,' says Philippa. 'We can turn the dial up, all the way to max, or we can turn it right down, become placatory. Or we can turn it up a few notches, our voice gets louder, we become more assertive. But we can only do this if we have learnt how to do so. If you have parents who have impulse control, it's probable that you will have it too.'

We all get angry, but some of us learn how to manage it. Those who do, learn to see themselves as though they're looking at themselves from the outside, to disassociate and control their feelings. Philippa tells me that the brain scans of those who have little impulse control show that they have fewer connections in their brains, specifically the pre-frontal cortex. Their brain hasn't developed the right mechanisms to control their anger. The pre-frontal cortex isn't thick enough. There is no dial that they can adjust, and they can fly off the handle – including getting very violent – for around forty-five minutes.

She talks about the different roles people take on with their anger. Their chosen roles. Some people are Placators. They don't like getting cross, they rarely confront problems; if someone else hasn't done what they would expect, such as the washing up, a Placator will just quietly do it themselves. So when they do lose their temper, it's a shock – for them as much as anyone else.

'The Placator hasn't got the dial,' says Philippa. 'She hasn't the wherewithal to say, "You haven't done the washing up. I'm disappointed. I don't like coming home to this. I'd like it if you cleaned up after yourself. I left a nice kitchen this morning, and that's what I'd prefer to come back to, if you don't want me to be unpleasant and angry again. Thank you." She has a particularly hard time in menopause, when she's very hormonal, because she's been brought up to be nice and kind and good. Also, she might have spent a long time treading on eggshells around her patriarchal partner, so the anger explosion is even more frightening.'

Philippa tells me about a couple more types of angry person: the Computer (always reasonable and logical, never acknowledges any emotion) and the Blamer (full of self-righteousness). The Computer, when faced with the not-done washing up, will tell the rest of the family in excruciating detail why it is always best to wash dishes immediately after you'd used them, because then the food won't dry on them and be so tricky to remove. The Blamer says, 'Oh, I'll do the washing up, then, shall I?' in such a withering, martyred tone that everyone else thinks, Fine, do it. Or the Blamer shouts and tells everyone else that they're appalling and have they noticed that the only one among them who does anything of any use ever is, yes, the Blamer?

There's also the Distractor. This is the person who, when faced with the washing up, says, 'Ooh, look, over there, a lovely squirrel!'

'I think I'm a bit of a Distractor,' says Philippa, as she tries on my new sunglasses.

This reminds me of how we use distraction to soothe very young children through their tricky emotions, their refusal to calm down and go along with what we want. If they dislike their food, we tell them it's a train, make choo-choo noises to get them to eat; if they fall down and hurt themselves, we talk about getting ambulances or tell off the object that they fell over ('Bad Lego *Frozen* castle'). We allow them their feelings for a short, finite time, then show them the bigger world.

Philippa and I talk about distraction for a bit until we remember what we're meant to be talking about.

She says: 'I notice that if women don't express their anger, they get miffed.'

I say, 'And how does their miffery express itself?'

'Well, usually,' she says, 'they keep thinking that the person closest to them – their partner – is wrong. Being miffed is a form of self-righteousness and if you have so much self-righteousness rising in you that it needs to land on someone, then the nearest person is your partner. I'm right, you're wrong: that is quite empowering.'

'It's also the essence of most arguments,' I say.

'Yes. But it's important not to fully inhabit that mindset. It's important to have an observer part of you going, Ooh, you're feeling a bit self-righteous, aren't you? You have to look at your partner and say to yourself, "Well, no, he can't mend the boiler even though I want him to, because he's not my dad. And that's good because even though my dad could mend the boiler, my dad was useless in many other ways."'

If you like to have control over your life, you might take it on yourself to try to control your partner by improving him. Or you might just want someone else to take up some of the slack.

Philippa says, 'A miffed person should try thinking about their partner like this: he's always been this limited and I knew it, so why get angry with him now? They should think, What is all this anger? Why is it here?'

What is all this anger? Why is it here? Is it the happiness U-bend again? Perhaps we should acknowledge when we're in the pit of life's despair. Frustration and fury are like remorse and sorrow: they are all signs of inner turmoil. They are as much of an outward indicator as leather trousers and Botox.

I check the internet forums where men write about their feelings in middle age. They don't sound angry. They sound disappointed and resigned. They sound sad.

Here are a few, from the NHS website.

'It's been a long time now since I had the zest for life . . . I don't sleep well . . . I guess I'm just tired of life and have no interest in tomorrow or the next week or the future . . .'

'I love my wife and my children, but we all live in a home that I knew was wrong when we moved here. They all love it, I don't. For me it means seven days a week struggling to pay for it. I have lost the one person I could share it all with, my wife. I now trawl the internet looking for help and, yes, porn . . . My problems aren't porn, they are me: OLD, FAT, BALD AND SO DEPRESSED. What can I do, who can I tell, who can be my friend as my wife was?'

'I have been out of work for over a year . . . I suffer from erectile dysfunction, something that was never a problem before. I have in general a very low opinion of myself, knowing that I have to all intents and purposes lost my life, no partner, no job and no money to speak of. I have attempted suicide twice in the last four months by overdosing and cutting my wrists.'

The posts were written months apart by different people. No one from the NHS website has responded to them.

I think of P's friend: 'My dad brings a bad mood into the house and it stays for days.'

Anger can turn inwards. The biggest killer of men – right up until their fifties – is suicide. The suicide rate of men between 45 and 59 has risen steadily since 2007. And if you add in self-sabotage, the drinking and drug-taking . . . Many men don't talk about being unhappy: they think that by not talking about their problems they're protecting themselves, their partner, their marriage. Their silence is like an invisible force field, keeping all the bad stuff at bay. Or keeping all the bad stuff in.

Some men feel elbowed out; isolated within their family, outside the tight, exclusive club that is their wife and kids. They hope to be cherished, celebrated, given the seat by the fire. But when they get to that comfy armchair, they can't stretch out. There's a load of plastic toys on the rug. The children are the family priority these days, not the man of the house.

Also, despite our greatest efforts, none of us grows younger, turns back into a baby. No matter how much we cry, how hard we stamp our little feet.

I talk to Stephen Buckley from MIND, the mental-health charity, about men in their forties. He has to talk in general terms, he says. Generally, he says, the problems that middle-aged men have are to do with jobs (redundancy, boredom, feeling trapped because they have to work to pay the bills), dissatisfaction with their 'primary relationship', divorce, the death of their parents and how their life changes after they have children. Generally, men have fewer social networks, and when they do see their friends, the meeting tends to be focused around a shared activity, whereas women connect through talking and empathizing with each other. Generally, men's self-esteem is tightly wound up in sexual prowess and their job – so if either is failing (if they're not performing as they wish), they feel bad about themselves.

Stephen says he is a great believer in talking therapies for mild to moderate depression. He mentions personal trainers. Physical and mental fitness are obviously interrelated; plus a good trainer, he says, will ask a client how his week was. (Like a private doctor, like an anger management counsellor, like a therapist.)

'And the opportunity to share how they're feeling, in a safe space, can help a great deal,' he says. 'It can be easier to say how you're feeling to someone neutral rather than someone close to you. You can let it go, speak it to the universe. If you try to talk to your partner about your awful day at work, life gets in the way – someone is making fish fingers for the kids' tea.'

The number of those who suffer from depression in the UK has remained at a similar level for the past fifteen years or so. The number of those who commit suicide fell from 2000 until 2007. Since then, there has been an upswing in suicides. This is due, Stephen thinks, to two things: the economic recession and the impact of cuts in care services. There are more suicides in prison, for instance, because there are fewer guards to put on suicide watch. Outside prison, there are many people with mental health problems who can't get access to their crisis contact because that contact is so busy.

'A and E is the new GP,' says Stephen. 'And A and E is not a place for someone in crisis.'

There is something about getting to middle age that makes you shout at the TV. It starts with muttering under your breath and ends with a full-lung bellow, a wildebeest on a downer. So, after a while you watch with your finger near the remote to mute or switch over whenever someone you hate comes on. I remember my mum running to the radio to turn down the sound whenever Margaret Thatcher or Ian Paisley said anything at all. Or, less predictably, John Cleese. She didn't like him either.

These days, the news is an emotional rollercoaster for me. Either I'm in floods over dying or abused children or I'm shouting at people in power who don't do anything about dying or abused children. I can't watch because I can't cope. Tears or anger. It's the midlife way.

Someone says to me, 'Don't get mad, get even,' and I think about that. Getting even requires more effort than getting mad. It requires action. It requires getting into the thick of whatever action is going on.

Ever since I was 14, I have been deliberately off to the side. Who wants to be mainstream? Only those it suits, those who fit right in there anyway. I'm happiest standing at the back of the hall, heckling the players onstage. Telling them they're rubbish, without having the guts to get up there myself. I don't like politicians – I've interviewed a few, and they never give a straight answer – and I certainly don't fancy hanging out with them. But if you're getting angry in your forties, and not just about your home life, then, really, shouldn't you work out the best way to use that anger?

Not so long ago, I wrote a column about a radio awards evening, about how every time a woman got onstage, no matter how talented a broadcaster she was, she was only there to hand a prize to a man. About how every time a woman got onstage (to hand a prize to a man), the awards show host made a comment about her appearance. Because of that column, I became one of the founder members of a group that lobbied for more women in audio. And the group was an instant success, and now has more than a thousand members. It runs mentoring schemes, networking evenings, training workshops for women in audio. It commissions new research; it is a voice for change.

And something happens after that. I make a decision to try to join in. I start putting my hand up, instead of scoffing in the shadows. So I speak, a lot, over and over, on panels about women in music, women in power, young women trying to make their way in the world. I am on a board to help bring people closer to amazing art, and I volunteer to be deputy chair. I become a school governor. I learn a bit about computer programming and I start a coding club for kids. I join in.

In short, I now do all the stuff I used to sneer at when I was young. Sneering is unseemly when you're middle-aged. When you're middle-aged, you should use your anger. It is an energy, as we know.

'We're all old and young at the same time,' says Philippa. 'You experience the world in the same way as an adult as you do as a child. You have the same feelings, the light comes through the window in the same way, you have the same social awkwardness sometimes, the same shyness . . . And that can make us angry in middle age, because we realize that we're not the wise person we thought we would be. We're not how we thought adults were when we were children.'

I'm still unsure about certain aspects of being an adult. When the ceiling fell down in our kitchen, I looked around to see who was going to sort it out. Then I remembered that the sorter-outer was me.

'It's a big con, the difference between children and adults,' she says. 'When you're older, it's not like you actually mature. You just have more techniques to deal with things, if you're lucky.'

And if you're not lucky? Then your tendencies become habits, and your habits become part of who you are.

'You can get away with shit when you're young,' says Philippa. 'But as you age, you stop or you alter or you go mad. It's true of drinking. And I think this might be true of anger as well. If you go, "Fuck you," at 20, you might be living an angry nightmare when you're 40 or 50 . . . You might need lithium. These modes of being take their toll on you by midlife. They become a heavy burden to carry.'

The feelings become facts, as real as the sun, as solid as the house you live in. And then the facts don't change. Not unless you do.

14. Music

Perhaps I need to recalibrate. Do I need to discard my loves, my desires, my hopes, or to consider them anew? Perhaps that is all middle age should be, a different way of going about your life. You don't lose yourself, you lose your way for a bit, so you are forced to find a new path to follow.

I don't know why this should be so hard. There must be plenty of examples of the new way (the midlife motorway?) out there. More importantly, is there a soundtrack?

S asks me what I'm doing today. I say that I'm going to talk for an hour to a TV production company, and he says: 'Let me guess . . . Madchester? Or Britpop?'

I say: 'Britpop. Britpop-ish . . . Blur and Björk.'

He says: 'Why do they want you to talk about Blur and Björk *again*?'

I say: 'I'm on a list somewhere.'

I do like Blur and Björk, and I'm very happy to talk about them. But I also like Jme and Fat White Family and Bobbie Gentry and Sly Stone and Missy Elliott and some of the strange Appalachian folk music that S plays me from time to time. I like music from now and music from way before. But I don't get asked to talk about that.

It can be tricky to move on from your youth, if your youth is what other people want to hear about. I'm mildly interested in what I did when I was young, but – like most people – I'm more interested in what I'm doing now. The life I'm living now. You can better understand what you're up to today if you can connect it to your past, if you can understand what brought you here. Yet to be asked to look back too much is disheartening. It makes you, now, seem unimportant.

We do look back, though, all the time. And it's partly because we love music. Music – our common history, our shared value – tells the same story over and over, and the story always brings us back to youth. Talent comes with wild, energetic, selfish youth. It's youth that creates. Talent leaves when bands get older, when singers settle down, when kids arrive. Time passes. Relevance fades. New albums are ignored. Reunion tours are laughed at. We don't want to hear anything except the brilliance you came out with when you were young and good.

In music, it's your twenties that are important. Reputations are made then, whether you're a musician, a DJ, if you work in A&R, you're a journalist, a fan. That's what you have to build on as you get older. That short, fast time when you didn't have to try to understand what was going on, you were in it and just knew.

I'm on a list somewhere.

I don't mind being asked to remember my twenties. It isn't exactly difficult and, often, it's fun. But it is always reductive. (Tick off the topics. The Stone Roses play Spike Island. Björk hits a reporter. Blur vs Oasis. Jarvis 'moons' during Michael Jackson's act, even though he didn't.) You are always asked to tell a story that's built around the TV highlights, the myths, a simpler story than the one you remember.

I go to see Siouxsie and the Banshees at the Royal Festival Hall. They're fantastic – exhilarating, powerful – and Siouxsie, encased in shiny white rubber, looks magnificent. She performs like the Queen of Goth, which is who she is. The audience, who are in their forties and fifties, are, for the most part, dressed exactly as you would expect, meaning exactly as if they were going to the Blitz Club in the late 70s and early 80s. They have not deviated, despite life and body changes. They have found their music, their aesthetic, and they are not letting go.

Some people find their music and stick with it. They actively want to stay in their musical tribe; moving on is not an option. There was a time when I made fun of people like that. I still think that it's better to be open-minded about music (about art, about life), to let newness surprise you. I don't think it's wise to assume that the music you loved in your teenage years is the best music ever made. But I don't make fun of those people now. Consistency and reliability seem more admirable character traits to me, these days. These fans fell in love young and they are not promiscuous. Plus, Siouxsie and the Banshees were – and are – a really brilliant band.

I've been to several of what could be called heritage gigs – reunions or unexpected reappearances of bands or performers who have been close to my heart. Grace Jones. Echo and the Bunnymen. The Stone Roses. Blur. Sometimes the gigs have moved me to tears. It's being able to watch musicians you really love play a song you really love, a song you thought you'd never hear played live again. You can't quite believe it when it happens.

I still don't want to listen to Radio 2 during the day, though. Or have a jolly night out watching 80s' one-hit wonders on a revival tour. Not even for a laugh. Because it never is a laugh, if you like music.

Our love of music pulls us all ways. If you're in your middle years and you like music, then you can kid yourself that you're still young. Keeping music close to you is one of the easiest ways to ward off elderliness, a talisman that banishes irrelevance. And it's thrilling. It's less messy than falling in love over and over, but it feels similar. You hear a track, a sound, a beat, and you feel that rush again. Your heart races, you become obsessed . . .

But if music is about the young, we find ourselves in a strange position. (And, yes, I know not all music is youthful, and many musicians create throughout their lives, but the attention they get comes from what they achieved when they were under 30. If Dylan played the gigs he does without his past or catalogue, then nobody would turn up.) We like music, which makes us young. But if we only like old music, if we carry on supporting the musicians we loved in our teens, that makes us old.

So we go searching for new music that we like. When we find it, we're young once more. Then we cast a covert look at who else likes this new music, who else is at these gigs and what trousers they're wearing . . . and we're no longer sure we're part of this gang. We're old again. Or we can't find any new music we like, so we sulk and return to our special room, the one that holds our vinyl albums, and we go to the stereo and we lift the lid and we check the needle for dust and we put on *The Queen Is Dead* or *Alphabet Street* or *Unknown Pleasures*. (Old old old.)

Still, it's music. It's our thing. We're still into it, it still gets us going. I know of several different men who decided to form bands in their forties. I know others who set up a label, who helped resurrect an old performer's career. Everyone goes to festivals, from four to 64.

We took our attitudes – our design for life – from music. How do you shake off those beliefs as you age? Tenets such as: It is better to die young than old. It is better to be hedonistic than sober. Rebel against The Man, be authentic and true, never wear a suit, never be a suit. Always judge a person by their haircut. If you are naturally stylish, especially when unkempt, then rejoice: this is a social attribute and may well lead to employment, as well as interesting sexual situations.

All hard attitudes to drop, when they've got you so far. As a friend says: 'I don't want to change my prejudices. They've got me through the past forty years.'

The question of middle-aged people and their relationship to music can be an emotional one. But it's also a discussion about formats, and economics. About how much we spend compared to younger people, and on what sort of music, and how we choose to receive our music, what we use to listen.

I ask Gennaro Castaldo at the BPI for some statistics. He sends me their latest booklet. This breaks down music consumption in many different ways and, no matter which way you look at it, it's clear that, when it comes to buying music in the UK, the middle-aged are important. In 2014, people aged between 45 and 55 bought the most physical product (22.3 per cent of total), the most albums (20.9 per cent) and, indeed, the most total music (19.4 per cent). We not only bought the most, we spent the most money on physical music, which means CDs and vinyl. Younger people spent more on digital product, meaning streaming.

We are right, then: music is still important to us and we are important to music. But we only like the sounds that we can hold. We hold on to them and we hold on to our youth.

I know of many people who spend their weekends at record fairs or in second-hand shops, flicking through old vinyl. They buy small record players for their kids and lend them their old singles. It's a lovely thing, but it's for them, really, rather than their children. I don't think there's anything wrong with that. Much of parenting is for the benefit of the parents, and collecting things is a way of engaging with the world in small, manageable doses.

I'm talking to psychiatrist Josh Cohen again. He says: 'One of my favourite cultural moments of the last few years is when David Cameron chose a Smiths' song as one of his Desert Island Discs and Johnny Marr said: "He does not like it. I forbid him to like it." (It was a tweet and Johnny said this. "David Cameron, stop saying that you like The Smiths, no you don't. I forbid you to like it.")'

Josh goes on: 'It's a great line, but it's more than that. It's making a point about cultural differentiation and how that has been lost.'

Music used to be how you defined yourself, especially how you defined yourself as opposed to other people. My youth was lived like this. We divided people into 'alternos' (us), and other people, people who liked the wrong music. Even now, most of my friends adhere to these values. David Cameron is the Other. He can't understand what The Smiths are about, so he isn't allowed to like them.

Josh says: 'Cultural differentiation has been lost, and age differentiation comes into this. Age has become this big soup in which we all swim. I'm guilty of this: I was at Latitude with my 15-year-old, because we both wanted to see Portishead.'

That's sweet, I say.

'Yes,' says Josh, 'but it shows that it has become very difficult for generations to define themselves against one another. We're no longer tuned into our own particular experience in the life cycle.' He adds: 'There is the question of relevance. There is a massive pressure on the middle-aged to feel that they still matter in all kinds of ways, almost in inverse proportion to their inner sense of how much they matter. Actually, many middle-aged people feel more and more excluded. There's something about the language, the music, the clothing of a younger generation that we don't understand. There's something about the trappings of a younger generation that we feel out of touch with . . . But, unlike our parents' generation, we don't have the option to opt out and be uncool.'

The head of Radio 1 makes a speech in which he takes the mickey out of people like me, people like Josh. Festival Dads and Festival Mums, he calls us. His argument is that we shouldn't go to festivals, we shouldn't bother finding out about new bands or films or art or culture. Instead, we should ship out and make space for the new generation. He doesn't want anyone over 35 on Radio 1. We should move *en masse* to Radio 2, I suppose.

He says this because he is required to. The BBC charter has informed him that Radio 1 must cater for young people. But I don't think this works, the idea that you like one type of music when you're young, and another when you've aged ten years. Your taste doesn't radically change throughout your life. If your taste isn't mainstream, if the idea of blockbuster films and made-for-the-charts pop makes you want to poke your eyes out and block your ears up, then you're not going to change your mind because it's your 35th birthday. You don't hit 35 and think, Thank the Lord, now I can listen to Bublé! Only people who don't like music think that your taste gets more conservative as you get older.

Anyway, the statistics show that music needs us. And festivals definitely do. We're the only ones who can afford the tickets. Festivals are expensive, tricky to get to, and they feature posh food. They're designed for the middle-aged.

When I think of people I know who work in and around music, I think of people who wouldn't fit in anywhere else. Music is a place where odd-bods can thrive, where hyperactive, cynical, emotional, anxious freaks are welcomed and, often, succeed. Not just the musicians. The promoters, the agents, the label bosses. Though some people are monsters in the music industry – exploitative, prejudiced, money-obsessed – more are not. They're romantics. They want life to be more beautiful, and music makes it so.

Once, life was quiet. You fought to hear music: cloistered yourself in your room to listen to the radio, to Annie Nightingale or a pirate radio station. You saved up for gig tickets, you queued up for clubs, you blagged into scary blues, got your mates in through the side door. This wasn't just because music was important to you: it was also because there was a time, within our lifetime, when decent music was rare. You had to search it out.

It's not like that now. Because we loved music so much, because we told everyone about how it changed our lives, about how it was actually changing our lives right then and there, other people started believing us. Brands began to sponsor gigs. Computer firms moved into music-selling. Fashion giants used musicians as models. Internet platforms gave us pop videos. Mobile phones, gyms, restaurants, the whole of the capitalist consumer world began to love music as much as we did, as we do.

And now music is everywhere. Before, good music came only if we did something to bring it: switched on the radio, bought a record, went to a club, sang to ourselves. Bad music was fairly freely available, as it always has been, but odd, eccentric music was harder to find. Now, that music is woven through everything we do. I watch a TV show about pottery and hear a Jeremy Deller-commissioned brass band playing house classics. I eat out in south London to the sounds of early Feist. I go to friends' houses and there is music playing in every room, from the kitchen to the bathroom, and the music is Kendrick Lamarr and it is old Italo house and it is Taylor Swift because the kids have got hold of the remote and it is TuneYards. I watch a football match, and beforehand they play the Chemical Brothers, and the fans sing 'Seven Nation Army', football's international anthem.

Music has become so vastly used that we expect it to be available whenever we want it. It's no longer a niche interest: not special, or scary, or owned by poor youth. Music is ubiquitous. And because it is, its value has plummeted. We have changed the nature of music, its meaning within society. It is now essential, like water or heating or wi-fi – but it's also ordinary, an amenity rather than a treat.

We have reduced the status of music. I mean, according to our criteria. To us who see music as special, who searched it out and clung to it for identity and a way through the madness, who used it as a moral guide, a compass, these days are weird. These days we made, when music is not that interesting. We put it everywhere, and it does everything. And nobody cares much any more.

P and I like different music. He can't stand acoustic music, he's not fond of The Beatles, he likes some pop/dance tunes that make me want to pull my ears off.

We come together on grime, even though we're both the wrong age for it. He is too young, and I am too old. This doesn't bother us. We quote lyrics to make each other laugh. 'No Uggs', 'Two-two chicken? Nandos.' Family stuff, shorthand, jokes. Like Josh and his son with Portishead, we are closer because we like the same music. We swim in the same cultural soup. I should be shouting at P to turn off his terrible music, but I like it.

That said, I don't approve of everything P listens to. He likes some proper rubbish. What's surprising to me is not that

I don't like it – that's the deal – but that I don't like it because it's wet, or it doesn't say anything, or the sounds it uses are derivative. I'm not scared by his music. I thought I would be, but instead I think it's boring. (Was that the case when I was young? Did my parents tell me to turn my music down because it wasn't scary *enough*?) I tell him to put his headphones on, or switch it off.

People who revere music tend to pass on their beliefs to their children. Their kids grow up in a religious household, but the religion is music. (I refuse to write, 'God is a DJ.') They share their faith as their kids grow up.

I take P with me to a grime gig because I can't think of any of my friends who will enjoy it as much. Skepta and Jme at Brixton Academy. We get tickets for the balcony. P is much the youngest there and, at first, he is overwhelmed, a bit scared. But the security staff are lovely to him, they give him earplugs, and then he sees a YouTuber he admires and gets a photo with him (I don't know who he is) and we go and watch the support act to get used to where we're sitting and, after a while, we nip out for some Pringles. And then suddenly we can hear Stormzy and P says, 'We have to go in RIGHT NOW,' and we rush in and sit right at the front of the balcony. And from then on the gig is amazing. It's a stone-cold brilliant gig. It is truly thrilling, for him and for me. When it's done, I whisk him out as quickly as I can and we half run half walk up the hill home, high as high can be.

It's a night that we still talk about. He knows, now, about music. He gets it.

I interview Dave Haslam, DJ and writer, about his most recent book. It's called *Life After Dark* and it's a short history of nightlife, about what we like to do once the pubs have shut. I've known Dave for a long time. He was a regular DJ at the Hacienda, in the pre-house era: he played on Thursday nights at the Temperance Club, which I went to. He still DJs now, on and off, in clubs all over the world.

Recently, he decided to sell his entire collection of vinyl. He had a small room, packed full of records, all lined up on floor-to-ceiling shelving, leaving just enough space for him to sit in the middle. He put up a picture of his vinyl room on the internet, explaining what he wanted to do. The picture went viral. Viral final vinyl. A DJ called Seth Troxler bought them all.

On stage, during the interview, I ask Dave why he decided to sell. He's a bit evasive. He says: 'Oh, Miranda, I'm on to my fifth midlife crisis now.' Then he tells a funny story about lugging his records to South America for a DJ-ing job, arguing with Customs about how many he was allowed to take through, pulling his arms out at the sockets just from carrying everything, only to arrive at the gig and see a fellow DJ pull out two USB sticks with every track he needed.

Dave says that his son still hasn't forgiven him for getting rid of all his records.

Shedding records is a big deal for someone of our age. It's removing yourself from your past. Also, I want to hear about his midlife crisis. So, a month or so later, I call Dave up. To my surprise, he's in Paris. He's living there for three months. It's a manifestation of his crisis. He's staying in a flat in Paris for three months, on his own, leaving his wife and kids in Manchester. He is writing, and he is going out and meeting different people. Making himself be sociable. And, mostly . . . he's enjoying it.

He says: 'I got to the same age that my mother was when she died – she was 52. And once that happens, you go into panic mode. I look back at my twenties and I feel like my life was full of potential, and then suddenly I'm waking up in the morning and thinking, Well, my life might be full of potential still in my head and my heart, but the reality is, that poten-

tial is not going to be fulfillable, because I'm running out of
time. You begin to think, What happens next? This is end
game.'

The panic in the night. The time-clutching. And what happened was, he started shedding things. Not his family, not his
friends. His possessions.

'I think the midlife thing should be about forgetting,
really,' he says. 'You're dragging all this past behind you, like
baggage, and it's piling up, and it's not propelling you forward, it's pulling you back. It weighs very heavy. It weighs
heavy on me. And partly that's because a lot of people want
to talk to me about what happened in the 1980s, so I'm constantly reminded.'

I say: 'Yes, I get that.'

Dave says: 'But actually, I'm guessing it's the same for
everybody. You're aware that you have all this past, and not
all of it is bad – a lot of it is fantastic – but it genuinely weighs
heavy.' Also, he says, his children are now older, in their late
teens and their twenties. They don't need him all the time any
more. Another trigger, another change.

'When you have kids,' he says, 'all your life decisions –
ALL of them – take into account your kids. Every single decision, from which restaurant are you going to eat in, to what
time am I going to have to get up, to where are we going on
holiday, to what books you read, where the shoes are kept . . .
Every decision. And then they grow up, and suddenly you're
faced with making decisions that haven't got that. So that's
weird too.'

He's in a flat in Paris, he says, because he's always wanted
to be in a flat in Paris. 'I wanted a big change for myself. I
wanted to jolt my life, as if somebody had put some kind of
electroconvulsive therapy into it.' And it's because he sold his
records that he's there. As part of his reassessment process, of

looking at his life and putting things into perspective, Dave realized that he'd got to a point where his records genuinely weren't that important to him. So he sold them.

He says: 'Selling the records freed up some cash, which enabled me to come to Paris. I've sold my past to rebuild my future.'

And how does that feel? I wonder.

'It feels emotional,' says Dave. 'It's not easy to rational-ize. And being a bookish person, who likes to rationalize and intellectualize everything, it's been weird to be faced with dealing with pure emotion. It's an instinct, flailing around. A hormonal-slash-spiritual change. I've lost a couple of outer shells, alpha male-isms. I'm more vulnerable.

'And it's an ongoing process. I'm not at the end of what-ever is happening. I don't know whether this is temporary or whether this is the new baggage I'm carrying around. Whether this is me as a new person.'

If music is your thing – and I don't know many people for whom it isn't – then even if you sell your records, even if your house burns down, it's still there. A constant in your life. A golden thread that winds through your own story and helps you tell it, a thread that joins your past to now and moves further on, with you until the end.

Music is the art form closest to our inner selves. It expresses the emotions that we can't, gives us the answers to questions we're not even able to articulate. A voice that soars and cracks, a guitar that judders on the spot, a weird noise that gets you *there* (the heart, the brain, the groin), a new melody that makes your eyes fill with tears, even though you're fine, hon-estly, it's just you feel you know that song already, that it tells your truth, though you've never heard it before . . . Music has space for you to curl up in, to bring whatever you want to it. It isn't a narrative, like a film or a book. There are no characters, or not fixed ones, anyway. There is no conclusion, no final act. You can make it mean whatever you like.

And old songs . . . You hear an old song and it takes you back, obviously, but it also tells you something about where you are now. If I listen to some of the songs that got me through my youth, I am there and here simultaneously.

In the middle of my life, I feel as though I might be young and old and the age I am today all at the same time, and music is one of the ways I sense this.

15. Playing to Win

Football, again. On the sidelines, with the other parents, watching a school match. School matches are usually less intense than club ones, I find, but today the opposing team's manager has ramped things up a level. He is very, very cross and he is very, very pleased and he flips back and forth between the two emotions, like he's a boomeranging internet clip. He shouts: 'NUMBER 11, WHO'S ON NUMBER 11?' and 'LOVE IT, ARCHIE'; 'SAMUEL, WHAT DID I TELL YOU? WHAT ARE YOU DOING?' and 'FACE THE BALL' and 'BE STRONG, CLOSE HIM DOWN, GET TO IT, YEEEESSSS.' It's hard to work out if he's happy in his frustration or frustrated in his happiness.

His temporary madness – it is like madness – reminds me of other matches, other adults. Once, P's team were waiting to play a cup final. The previous game, between teams of older kids, was still being played, so we sat down on the grass to watch (spring cup finals are held in June, when football is an excuse for a picnic). It was a close battle, physical and tough. A forward slid for the ball, and the opposing goalie, rushing to take it off him, slammed into him and knocked him down. Then, not so surreptitiously, the goalie gave the forward a boot in the head. Surely a red card! But the referee didn't deal with it. The forward lay on the ground, moaning. His dad ran on to the pitch to check on his son. He was angry. Then the goalie's dad ran on. This dad was also angry. Then quite a lot of other angry parents became involved.

We ate our crisps and watched the fun. After a lot of shouting and finger-prodding, the forward's dad walked his son off the pitch to his car. Some of the forward's team-mates followed, though most just looked confused and embarrassed. The adults continued to yell. The referee abandoned the final.

My friend James loves football, and sometimes acts as referee in matches his son's team plays. He reffed an Under-12s match (where the players are no older than 11 at the beginning of the season) and, during the game, a boy from the opposing side took a ball full in the face. He went down, crying. So James stopped the match to check he was OK and to give him time to recover.

'Next thing I knew,' says James, 'I was barged to the side by the kid's irate father who screamed at his crying son, "Get up, you fucking woman! We have to beat this bunch of Catford cunts!" I asked the parent to watch his language. And he told me to "Fuck off back to that gay bar you were in last night!"'

We laugh. It's funny, because it's so awful.

It's hard to understand why emotions should run so high, how grown men and women can lose their minds over an hour of children's playtime. It's ridiculous. And yet . . .

'Football is like war,' says S, firmly, and I remember playing football myself, at college. I was rubbish, but aggressive. My game technique was to run hard at the other team to scare them. There was anger involved. In fact, anger was my dominant emotion, born of adrenalin and panic.

But is football like war? Is a match like a battle? Hardly. No weapons. No plan to kill. And, anyway, you're not actually playing the match. You're too old for that. You're middle-aged. You're a spectator, you sad git.

Unless you're a hooligan, and your big day out includes a

fight before and after the game, then there isn't much that's war-like about the passive activity of watching people you don't know very well play a game of football. Still, the emotions it releases can resemble an invading force. For a few years, P and F and I would leave the room when S was watching football. His rage was too strong, too real. It expanded and marauded, too big for the space. Those us-against-them-win-at-all-costs feelings can come out freakishly large, like emotional explosions.

And that's just when you're on the sofa, with a cup of tea. They're even more intense when you're standing on the sidelines. Plenty of reasonable people lose their minds at the football. And then they wait a week, and lose their minds again.

Still. This isn't a war: it's just kids. Kids' football, not the real thing . . . Except that fact makes it worse. Not only is it football, that bottomless pit of despair, that soaring rocket of joy, it is children, too. And one of them is yours.

Your kid. The light of your life, the hope of your existence, your actual real-life midlife chance to make right all that you did wrong when you were young.

Your beautiful, wonderful, talented, determined child. Versus those other kids. Look at them. Look at that one. He's just like those big twats that used to push you around when you were at school. A nasty bit of work . . . See him bearing down upon this smaller, purer, better version of you, like a monster attacking a puppy. Your view of the match is warped, filtered: a golden aura around your own child, a black shadow blanketing the rest.

The average age of an adult fan of Premiership football in 2011 was 41. In Adrian Tempany's great book, *And The Sun Shines Now*, about the Hillsborough tragedy and its consequences for the modern game, he comments of Manchester United that 'in 1968, the average age of supporters on the Stretford End at

Old Trafford was 17; by 2008, it was over 40.' These days, fans drop out of watching live football in their late teens because it's too expensive and, partly due to all-seat stands, too boring. There are more fun things to do.

Buying a season ticket. Going to the match. Travelling to away games. Today, following football – professional football, Premiership football, the beautiful game – is a middle-aged pursuit.

Not every child plays football. My friend is talking about her daughter, who is a talented musician. Actually, she's not talking about her daughter. She's talking about the parents she has encountered through her daughter.

She says: 'When J was in primary school, I'd go to the concerts and there would always be parents who rushed to get seats in the front row. Then, when the concert started, they'd stare at their child throughout the whole thing and – get this – they would mime the part that their kid was playing while the kid was playing it. So the parent would be playing air violin or air flute or whatever, bowing or fingering the notes throughout the whole thing. Really embarrassing. And the kid would be obliged to look at them, instead of the conductor.'

She tells me about such parents' comments to the teacher. Things like: 'It's so good that you're supporting Y with their dyslexia. It must be a real challenge for them to get all the accidentals in this piece. My son always practises those bars to get them learnt by muscle memory.' Or: 'I'm surprised you've put so-and-so on first violin. They don't always hear the nuance of the piece. My daughter has always loved Telemann . . .'

Another friend. He tells me about watching his kids play tennis. He witnessed a parent at a tennis match call the umpire 'a fucking cretin' when he (correctly) called a shot out.

My friend says: 'The tennis parents are the worst. Then, the football parents. The cricket ones are all right.'

I say: 'Cricket takes all day. It's hard to stay angry for that long.'

I wonder about the tennis parents. Perhaps they're worse because tennis is an individual game. It's gladiatorial. One kid against another. None of the joy of a team: no collective delight, no shared despair. All that expectation on one pair of scrawny shoulders. No jokes. No joke.

Yet another friend, whose daughter goes to a ballet school, finds a girl, aged 10, crying in the toilets. The teacher has been very hard on the girl, which is why she is crying, so my friend comforts her. There's another mother in the toilet, who's been there the whole time. She says: 'You shouldn't do that. She needs to toughen up.'

More? Here's one. 'I took E to a swimming gala,' says a friend who lives in Manchester. 'There was a mother sat near me whose daughter must not have done as well in a race as she wanted. When the child – who had no towel – came up, dripping and shivering, she refused to give her the towel! Then she blamed her for all the money she'd spent on swimming, then told her she couldn't be bothered with her any more . . . The kid looked about 10.'

You tell your own kid she's worthless. You do the same, more aggressively, to someone else's. You actively wish harm on a small child.

A different sport, a different friend. She's watching her daughter – a small, skinny, 6-year-old – playing tag rugby for a local team. 'I can see it in my head,' she says. 'She's got the ball, she's making for the try line, when this father starts screaming, "Kill him, kill him!" at the top of his voice. It was so loud and so shocking that the other parents and I were stunned into silence. I didn't even tell him she's a girl.

'It was weird,' continues my friend, whose kids are of dual heritage, 'because rugby parents tend to be jolly good sorts and have a well-developed sense of fair play. Though I have heard some of them say, about my kids, "Oh, well. They're more naturally athletic than the rest of us."'

I've heard racist comments at P's football games, as have other parents I know. Not often, but we've heard them. Which means we've witnessed fully grown responsible adults getting so angry and frustrated about a children's play activity – a children's play activity in which they are not actually involved – that they feel justified in thinking racist comments about those children. In thinking those terrible things, and then saying them out loud.

Why does it matter to us how well our kids do in such competitions? These are out-of-school activities. They are meant to be a source of joy for the children, a time of relaxation and respite. Sport, music, art: if you can get into the flow of these pursuits, you can switch off from the rest of your life. If you're a child, you can forget your school and all its stresses, the strain of being shy, the pressure of being funny, the teachers you dislike, the constant academic assessment.

But that doesn't seem to be what the parents want. They don't want their child to relax into non-educational activities. They want them to succeed.

How have our achievements become so wrapped around those of our children? Is it because, in middle age, we sense our powers fading, even as we believe we can still reach the heights we desire? I wonder whether the feelings around midlife – the ebbing of potential, the still-present hope, the increasing frustration and discontentment – make watching children's sport more painful. The poignancy of witnessing your child, your mini-me, performing feats that you are no longer able even to attempt. Or the gut-stab of disappointment when they don't succeed. The regret, always present, flaring up once more.

*

'Football is the worst,' says my friend D, who runs a kids' team. 'I know there are other sports, but there's something about football.'

On the radio, I hear a professional sports commentator on the eve of his retirement. He says: 'I do believe that there's too much football now. And we cover it in too much depth. I love the game, and I love commentating on it, but there's too much of it and there's no room for other sports.'

A Football Association research project in 2010 revealed that 'children play football for intrinsic reasons', for 'self-worth and personal satisfaction'. When offered 16 statements around playing, the top 6 statements, across 40 groups of children under 12, were: 'Trying my hardest is more important than winning', 'I love playing football because it's fun', 'It's a really good game and I love it', 'It helps keep me fit and healthy', 'I like meeting new friends through football' and 'I like playing with my friends.'

D says: 'The parents can't believe that a game played by 7-year-olds isn't as competitive as the Premiership. They can't believe the kids just want to play a match, in a friendly way. The parents apply the same rules to a kids' match as they do when they're supporting a professional team. They shout abuse in the same way.'

Is there too much football? There are football matches every weekend, whether professional ones, trumpeted across the media, or amateur ones, ticking on from autumn to spring – rainy, muddy, miserable, relentless. Football is always in the papers, reported on as part of the news. It is a vital part of UK life. Part of the national conversation; part of the world's conversation. An international language. An Esperanto that people actually speak.

And so, if you're interested, you midlife footy fan, you can understand football. There's always something new to learn. It's not like other subjects, such as maths. At some point, you, a middle-aged person taught in a different era, will stop being able to help with your child's maths homework. This never happens with football. Or, at least, that's what you believe. With football, your knowledge is topped up every week, every day, by every newspaper and news bulletin and TV station in the land. You are certain you can help your child. With football, you and your opinions are always relevant. With football, you never get old.

At the end of each match, parents make little comments. 'Played a blinder, Donny!', 'Don't be scared of those big lads, don't pull out of tackles', 'Nice to see you looking for the clever pass.' Small-talk that reveals their hard-earned expertise. (Such expertise is less common when it comes to a gymnastics final, a chess tournament, an exercise in computer programming, a PowerPoint homework.)

Sometimes, parents make those comments during the match. Or worse. At one of P's matches, the referee had to speak to some parents. They were ranting about an off-side decision.

He said: 'That's the decision. It's been made. Get over it. If you don't like it, you can take it up with me at the end of the game. Until then, you have to be quiet. You don't say anything unless you're encouraging the kids. Or I'll stop the match.'

When we watch football club academy teams play, I notice that the mums and dads barely make a sound during matches. This is because parents of academy players sign contracts that specify acceptable behaviour from them, as well as their child. The contracts are specific. 'Encourage your child and others. Refrain from making any negative comments. Refrain from making any tactical or technical instructions. Praise is the only form of communication expected.' The parents watch with intensity, but they are the quietest football fans I know.

After one match, P says: 'I'm glad L's dad isn't here today. He's always shouting at us, telling us what to do.'

I hear of a mother who says, when her daughter is picked for a school team: 'She should know her own limitations.' When asked what this means, the mother explains that she doesn't see the point in her daughter competing in a sport when she isn't any good. The mother thinks there is no value in playing. Not unless you're going to win.

I speak to Dr Amanda Gummer, founder of the Fundamentally Children website. She's a psychologist who specializes in child development, play and parenting.

She says: 'There is a new breed of middle-aged parent out there. The trend is to have kids later, so people have had a career before they become parents. They're used to having appraisals within their career, so they approach parenting with appraisals in mind.'

Such parents regard their children as their new project. As their new career (especially if they've actually given up work).

'If they give up work, then the stakes are even higher,' says Gummer. 'Parenting becomes about how the rest of the world sees them, as the parent. The child is an extension of them.'

The problem with making your kids your project, with ferrying them to after-school clubs, getting them to scheduled activities, is that this adds to the burden of your life. You're busy anyway, because you're middle-aged, and in the middle of things, and then, says Gummer, 'you put all that effort into supporting your child. It takes a lot of effort and scheduling. It's yet more on your to-do list. You're more frazzled, more stressed and so you overreact to a situation that really doesn't matter. You get angry when you should be quiet. You ignore when you should respond.'

Parenting has become something else we must be good at. We must parent to the best of our abilities. This means that, due to the threat of traffic (real) and pervy strangers (not so much) and stupid drunks (random), and because we're of a generation which believes that to love your kid is to make sure they're safe, we are in a state of high tension at all times. On constant alert.

'Only a couple of generations ago, everyone lived close to their family,' says Gummer. 'So you had an aunty round the corner, Granny down the road and the kids were in and out of people's houses. There were no mobile phones, so you couldn't keep track of your kids. You had to assume they were OK, unless you heard otherwise.'

The real problem, says Gummer, is that there is a burgeoning mental-health crisis among teenagers. And, by taking their children's sports and music so seriously, parents can add to this. Over-involvement in your young kid's life leads to that child becoming an anxious teenager.

'Children are not allowed their autonomy,' she says. 'Children need the freedom to be themselves. They need the freedom to make mistakes, to have an off day and play badly, without being scrutinized. They know if they played badly anyway – they don't need a parent going nuts about it. Kids need the opportunity to fail and to pick themselves up again. They aren't given the credit they deserve.'

This despite the leagues, the trophies, the personal bests. We are awarding our kids medals, but not giving them credit.

We don't ignore our children in the way our parents did. We don't kick them outdoors at 9 a.m. on a Saturday and tell them not to come back until tea. We can't abandon them in the car outside the pub with a comic and a bottle of pop while we spend a couple of hours drinking with our mates. We have to take them places – play dates, sports training – and we have to stay and watch them do it, or make sure that other adults watch them for us. We are their carers, we are always vigilant. Is this a bad thing? Sometimes I think it is. Sometimes I don't.

I go to see my friend, whose kids are matey with mine. The children get giddy when they're together and it makes her nervous. 'Watch the road!' she says. 'Take my hand!' I ask her if her son walks to school. She says no. He doesn't walk anywhere on his own, not even to the local shop. He is 11.

Children are constantly monitored, by law. Teenagers are side-eyed, muttered about, CCTVed; too many of them in a shopping centre means that security is called. Babies are cooed over not just by family but by healthcare visitors and child-minders trained to spot abuse. Schools monitor their pupils' achievement, because pupil achievement is how schools themselves are monitored. There are constant checks: home-work, spelling tests, art competitions, team points. Teachers watch over children from the age of 3, checking to see if they can demonstrate an ability to share (PSED: personal, social and emotional development), or to colour in (EAD: expressive art and design). State schools get governmental directives that drill down into how they assess the children. These seem to change every couple of years. Private schools are obsessed with results. They bring parents in if their children aren't achieving.

The adults are watching, by law. The children are being assessed.

Part of being a child is the feeling of having your fun taken off you. I remember this feeling well. I would be absorbed in an activity – arguing with my brother, designing an imaginary house, playing with a tennis ball against a wall – and a grown-up would step in and change everything. An adult would watch us, decide that what we were doing wasn't right, and so stop it. Or, worse, take over. Grabbing the bat or the ball, muscling in on model-making, finishing off the Lego.

Some adults can't stop themselves. They believe they are helping. They believe they're making things better. You see their children, with their beautifully crafted models. Helped by their parents, monitored by their school, Insta-ed by their mates. Never alone.

'I don't want to know,' says S, about P. We're talking about a fall-out that has happened between P's friends. P is involved, on the periphery. We are talking it through, like good parents.

'I don't want to know,' says S. 'We know too much about what he's doing already. My mum and dad didn't have a clue what I got up to when I was his age.'

Later S says that he doesn't want to know what P's life is like, because if he does, he might want to sort it out himself, and that might get messy.

I think: But isn't it good to know what is going on in your children's lives? Isn't it good that he feels he can tell us? Friends of older children, of teenagers and university students, tell me that they can feel competition between other parents around how much their child confides in them. Their children say: 'Oh, G's mum is amazing. You can tell her anything.'

I think: How can I live my children's lives for them? I'm a 40-something woman from the chintzy suburbs of Manchester. I grew up with three channels on the TV, I walked to school on my own when I was 7. I used a phone that meant dialling a number (listening to the purr between each digit as the dial returned to its resting spot). I remember when cities had jagged holes in them left from Second World War bombs, when they were dirty, empty, litter-strewn, amateur.

What do I know of the life of a child or a teenager living in inner-city London in the twenty-first century? I recognize the emotions, but I don't understand the detail.

*

Monitoring children is all very well, but it leads to a desire for control. Why bother collecting the information if you can't change the result?

P sits innumerable exams, takes part in competitions – music, sport, English, maths – and I am constantly surprised at how stressed I feel about this. Even though I've told him that the results don't matter, as long as he does his best. And even though I genuinely believe this . . . I am stressed.

I am stressed because I worry that if P doesn't pass, if his team doesn't win, he will be upset. He doesn't always pass, he doesn't always win. He isn't upset. He says: 'I messed that up really badly. The alarm on my watch kept going off every five minutes and I couldn't work out how to switch it off. There's no way I passed.' Then we go for a pizza.

He plays in a football tournament where his team gets to the final. During the match, two of his team are badly injured: one is stretchered off and taken to hospital. His team loses. P is grumpy about it. But when we get home he says, 'Can I play FIFA?' and is fine within minutes.

I still have bad dreams about exams. In the dreams, I turn over a paper and realize that I have done no work at all on the subject. I panic. But why?

When P plays a match and it isn't going well, when his team is getting beaten, his coach says, at half-time: 'They won the first half. So we're going to win the second half.'

I think about this, sometimes. Here I am, halfway through my match. There's no coach telling me what to do. I'm sucking a piece of orange (they don't have oranges any more) on my own, wondering how I can make the game go better for me in the second half.

Another match. P's team are leading 6–0, with 10 minutes to go, when the opposing side's manager suddenly ushers his team off. Everyone is shocked. It takes a while to work out what is happening. The kids in the team were still playing hard, they still believed, their heads weren't down. But their manager walks on to the pitch, with his arms held wide, and shepherds them away. Later, he tells one of our parents he didn't like the way the match was going: he thought everyone was tackling too hard; he didn't want his team to be 'on the end of a big lose'.

Sometimes I look at the football coaches, the men – they are all men – who teach children how to play, and I wonder, Why are you doing this? Is it because it's the logical extension of talking about football? Is it because teaching gives you status in middle age, in a way that most jobs don't? Is it because it gives you a bit more control? Is it fun? Very few coaches make any money out of it. There is pleasure in building a team, but the children don't always listen; they are not always grateful. They don't do as they are told.

I know, from running a coding class for 9- and 10-year-olds, just how absorbed you can be when you are teaching a skill to children. It is utterly involving. You forget about everything else outside the task. Perhaps that's why the coaches do it. It takes you out of everything else that's going on. You are present in your life. You are useful.

But I also know how hard it is when a child doesn't choose to listen. Nothing happens. You are of no use at all. You are an old, mad person, repeating yourself over and over to a group of resentful brats who think you're too elderly to be relevant and can't wait to get away.

Some of P's friends are signed to professional clubs. A few have parents who have chosen to move house to facilitate this: away from where they thought they would settle, away from friends and family. One talented child switches school when his club suggests that he would be better off in a different

212 · **Out of Time**

secondary, one closer to the club's training ground. The club pays for a bus to collect him and a few other players, and take them to the new school every day.

But in his first year at his new school, this child gets a lot of injuries. His legs grow, his muscles struggle to stretch quickly enough to keep up with his bones. He doesn't play so much. His friends are all in other schools.

You mould your kid's life, but by how much? You mould your own, around your child's. How much, again?

P is playing a computer game. He wants me to play too. But I can't: I don't have the knack. I don't care enough to learn; the visuals make me travel sick. Computer games didn't thrill me when I was young – apart from the simple ones. I don't have the history, so I don't have the habit. I'm too stuck in my non-gaming ways. This makes P sad. His friends have parents who spend hours playing games with them on their Xbox or PlayStation.

I relent and play a fighting game with him. I used to play in arcades, a bit, so I can do that. (I have a sudden flash of memory, of playing Pacman and Space Invaders on those sit-down tables in pubs, too.) I choose to play as a two-dimensional dog. I button-mash throughout, and lose, but it's fun. I like my flat dog.

We play a few more bouts. P introduces other characters, which the computer plays. I get confused as to who's who, and lose every time. P is delighted.

'Let's do this a lot,' he says. 'Let's do it every day.'

For proper fans, for those who have followed their team since they were young, football is a thread that links their past with their present, their history with today. There's a connection, for S, with his young self, being forced to learn the names of every member of his team by his older brother.

'We had a picture of the team on the wall of our bedroom,' he says. 'And J would point at each player with a ruler and if I got the name wrong, he would whack me.'

S likes to say that he has loved his team longer than he has loved any girlfriend (or wife). This is true. The particular joy of supporting a football team is that you can love it for all of your life, and, though it will never love you back, it will always give you something new. It will give you friends, allies, something to talk about, a lived experience. It will give you something new each week, during the season (a result, a moving up or down the table, a potential missed, an opportunity seized); and, if you have satellite TV, or you read football gossip columns, it will give you even more. You can get a daily fix.

A football team is not like a musician, or a band. It doesn't go and die on you, from an unexpected overdose, from cancer. It doesn't reject its past or try to crack the States; it doesn't suddenly go and play a rubbish game, like American football, for a season or two. It might hark back to past glories, but it keeps on playing, every week, every week. Something new to obsess over, every week.

Even though every single member of his team has changed, over and over, even though some of his favourites are no longer alive, S still loves his team. It reminds him of his past (who he was, what he was doing when that goal went in, when they won the cup) and his future (the team is rebuilding, you can see what the manager's doing, we're going to win the cup) in a way that nothing else does. It is written through his life, it tells his story. He passes his story on to P.

The problem with being a football fan – of a professional team, of an amateur one, of your child's team, of one that's based in another country – is that you are not playing. You have no control over the game at all.

A memo is sent round with the school's weekly newsletter. A parent's friend has a child who has a rare cancer. The family needs £500,000 to get the child to the USA for treatment. I give money and I think: God, life is so unfair.

Part of coming to terms with middle age must be an acceptance of our lack of control. Because, really, we control so little in our lives, though we are taught otherwise. We are taught to believe that if we try hard, we will succeed; that if we are kind, karma will be kind back to us; that if we dream big, those dreams will come true. But we hit middle age and we look around and we realize that these beliefs are untrue. Look how hard I tried, how kind I was, how open and honest and yet . . . look where I am. Nowhere, really.

Now we know. We see clearly now. You can practise as hard as you can, but you don't automatically win the medal. Our ideas of balance, of proportionate recompense, are false. They may seem logical, but life is random and unfair.

Yet we are scared to teach the truth to our children. The truth is too big and scary. It may bite in the night. Instead, we repeat all the rules we were told when we were young. We keep the illusion alive.

Work hard, be kind, dream big. Practise and you will get better. I still believe those are useful tenets, but not because of the rewards. The joy is in the doing, not the results. The results are out of our control. Actually, they don't often matter.

You may have the football knowledge, but it makes no difference. You can shout, or not, up to you. No matter how hard you wish, you cannot affect the result.

The impossibility of living your child's life for him, or for her. Of making sure they don't get hurt, that they get it right. That they play it right.

I don't shout with the scary parents. I don't want to. Not

because I don't feel the same way – somewhere, deep down, I think I do – but because I don't dare to invest as much emotion as they do in the game. Because if I do, I can't cope with the disappointment.

16. Time

I have a coffee with a friend of mine, who is fifteen years younger than me. She says: 'I have all this time stretching out ahead, and I wonder how to fill it.' She is settled in her relationship; she enjoys her job; she has no children. She is happy, but also scared of becoming so content that she gets bored and does something drastic. Or that she gets bored and stays bored.

I go to a talk where an artist speaks, and he says: 'I think about all the books I haven't read, the art I haven't seen, all the knowledge that's out there. I want to absorb it, to know it all without having to take time to learn it. Because how am I going to fit it all in?'

F says: 'When is it my birthday?' and when I tell her – it's months away – she says: 'Is that tomorrow or the next day?'

The notion of time. Time passing, time past, time to come, time running out. I read a book called *Time Warped*, by Claudia Hammond, which attempts to get to grips with how we deal with time, how we approach it. I think about what reading does to time, and how much of my time is spent reading.

Luckily, *Time Warped* is a great read, and one of the chapters I enjoy most is about how we visualize time. Not everybody sees time – many people don't picture it at all – but those who do find it hard to change what they see. I see time, and I see it in a similar way to how I see numbers: in a very specific pattern, that twists around me. The number (and the age) 17 is in front of me, slightly to the right. Three is to my left. Fifty-five is over and behind my right shoulder; I'd have to turn to see it properly. 122 is behind my left ear. If you say a number to me, no matter how big, or small, even if it's a negative number, I know where it's located, where it is on my own personal number line.

The years are fixed, too. 1967 is to my left and down. 2016 is just slightly to the right. The months can squish, shuffle up together, stretch out according to which one I'm thinking of, but they, too, wrap around me and go from left to right.

In her book, Claudia says she has her own inner visualization of time, lived and historical, that doesn't change, that is located in space. Seeing time in space is a type of synaesthesia.

I contact Claudia and we meet for a quick chat. (She hasn't much time, ha.) She says that she sees time very clearly, and has ever since she was a child. But during the 90s, she had the disconcerting realization that, as the change of millennium approached, she had no picture of the future after 31 December 1999.

'It was strange,' she says. 'I could see the Middle Ages, the 1960s, the present day, but I couldn't picture the new millennium. I would check in my head and there was nothing. And then, gradually, there was something. And now I can see time again, stretching into the future.'

We talk about how, if you see time, your picture is partly cultural. The way we talk about time affects how we see it. So, from Claudia's research, the English and French say time is 'long' or 'short' (time as a distance), whereas Greek and Spanish people say 'much time' rather than 'long time' (time as an amount). It's the difference between seeing time as a long road and seeing it as a full jar.

Also, most English-speakers see the past as being to the left, the future to the right; but most Arabs and Israelis see time the other way around. This is because English is read from left to right, Arabic and Hebrew from right to left. What else? English-speakers tend to see time on a horizontal; Mandarin-speakers see the past as up, and the future as down, because their metaphors for time use the vertical plane. ('I know!' says Claudia. 'Completely the wrong way round.') They are eight times more likely than English-speakers to lay out time vertically.

When I was at school, I thought about numbers a lot more than I do now, and it seems to have affected my time vision. My numbers have a turning point at ten, and one at twenty, and those numbers, from one to twenty, are widely spaced (they take up more time/space, they take longer to pass through). Between twenty and thirty, they are nearer to each other, and get even closer after that.

I wonder if giving time a shape might be a problem. I talk to Claudia about it. If you can see all the years of your age laid out, like numbers, and you can see where you are within them, which number you're sitting on, then you're conscious of what has gone and what is left. My time surrounds me. It wraps around me: I can't duck and crawl out of its spiral.

Claudia says: 'I imagine if you really tried to train your mind, you could bring your present years round to the front, make them more spaced out.'

Perhaps I could but, to me, it sounds almost impossible. My visualization of time is fixed. It is part of me – and I see the years after 40 as short and very close together.

Time isn't how I see it, of course. It isn't fixed in space, it doesn't move around anywhere, particularly not around any-one in particular, that anyone being me. Time doesn't actually do anything at all: it just is.

The is-ness of time is hard to grasp. When people say, 'Time is the sixth dimension', that's hard to understand, even though we must live in that dimension. Mustn't we? Anyway. If you think of time, you probably understand it in terms of movement. Either you're moving through time, or time is passing by, and quite quickly at that.

(Claudia has a test for this. She gets people to think about this statement: 'Next Wednesday's meeting has had to be moved forward by two days.' When is the meeting? If you say Friday, then you have an ego-centred experience of time: you have a sense that you are moving along a timeline to the future. If you say Monday – which is obviously correct, by the way – then, for you (and me), time is moving towards you, as you stand still. Like me standing in a river, gathering water as it passes. Neither answer is correct, but they show our different approaches to time.)

One of the most universal perceptions among humans as we age is that time is speeding up, and it does so because we're getting older. The most common explanation of time's increasing speed is proportionality. A decade is the whole of a 10-year-old's life, but just 20 per cent of a 50-year-old's. So it's no wonder that a weekend seems so long to a 10-year-old, and so annoyingly brief to the middle-aged.

That feeling of time accelerating is why Claudia decided to write her book. And having done so, she is sure that proportionality is not a complete explanation. It's not even the only one. How we live affects how rapidly time seems to pass. Two habits, especially, have an effect: routine, and busy-ness. With a routine, you don't properly notice what you're doing, because you do something similar every day, so time passes quickly, as nothing is new. And when you're busy, you fill your hours with activity, leaving no space for tedium or slowness. Again, time goes quickly.

She says: 'But actually I'm happy for time to seem to go quickly now, because the opposite is so unpleasant. You really don't want your time to go slowly.'

We tend to moan about how quickly time goes. We can't get our heads round the years that have passed. We gasp at how swiftly children are growing ('I try not to do that,' says Claudia, 'because I remember how irritating I found it when I was young'). We think we're closer to our youth than we are. We don't believe it when someone says to us that the release of 'Love Me Do' is closer in time to the end of the Second World War (seventeen years) than it is to the release of 'This Charming Man' (twenty-one years).

But if you think about it, even for a short minute, you realize that time moving fast isn't all that bad a thing. Who wants to go back to those days of double RE, when you were so bored that every minute crawled by in slow motion? If you're enjoying yourself, if you're busy and useful, and you know what you're doing and when you're doing it, then – lucky you – time moves fast. If you're unhappy, it's impossibly slow.

Claudia says: 'Our minds construct how we experience time. Memory, attention and emotion are all important – if one of those is out of line to the way we usually experience them, then our sense of time is altered.' We are used to our own time experience.

We talk about the different compromises we make in our lives and how they might affect our notion of time. Claudia says: 'If you moved further out of the city where you work, in order to be able to afford a bigger house, then you might well find you get pleasure from your new larger home, with its extra rooms. But that pleasure is fleeting. You quickly absorb it into your everyday life. You stop noticing it. In contrast, the time you spend on a longer commute makes you unhappy every day. So you might want to consider that before making a major move.'

The enforced tedium of the long commute. When you watched the clock as the RE teacher droned on, the hands seemed to lock into position, to never move at all. Is the best way to freeze time, then, to be bored? This is hard to achieve, in these always-on, check-social-media, what's-the-wi-fi-code? days. Hard to achieve and, also, boring.

And, anyway, it isn't your boredom that slows time: it's your attention to time and the motivation behind your attention. Anyone who watches a sports game where the teams are evenly matched knows how slowly time can pass. When your team scrapes into the lead with ten minutes to spare, when it has to hold that lead until the final whistle, ten minutes can seem like an hour. And simultaneously, the opposing team's supporters are checking their watches and marvelling at how quickly the time is passing.

(My time is speeding up because I see – in a way I didn't before – that we're in the second half, and the match is going to end.)

Claudia, through her research, has pinpointed a few ways of making time go more slowly that don't involve being bored. She points out that boring experiences, such as being ill, drag on when they happen, but when you remember them, they seem to have taken no time at all. It's the opposite with exciting events: the time whizzes past but, in retrospect, all that activity seems to have taken ages. She calls this the Holiday Paradox.

She says: 'If you fill your days with as many new things as you can, you'll feel afterwards as though you have lengthened your time. If you did something different every weekend, you'd make so many new memories that the weeks would stop rushing past.'

Going on holiday is obviously one way to pack in new experiences, but also, says Claudia, if you vary your regular routine in just a few small ways, you will make time move less hurriedly. It's your attention, again. If you have to give something your attention, because it's unusual to you, then this will slow time. Routine and busyness both speed time as it happens, but afterwards, in your memory, only busyness – if it involves new experiences – will make your life seem longer.

'Walk a different way to work,' she says. 'Don't always have a cheese and coleslaw wrap for lunch. If you change your habits, the new experiences are a jolt, a surprise, and you remember them.' It's important to do new things, to learn something fresh, to put yourself out there, get scared or excited. New experiences create new memories and 'The more memories you can create for yourself in everyday life, the less the weeks will rush by,' says Claudia.

Sounds great. I'm up for excitement, for anticipation and recall. For experiences that make time flex. But . . . my life isn't all that flexible. The kids' school and their out-of-school interests lock us into a timetable. It's hard to have a varied, memory-making life, to pack it full of thrilling, time-stretching moments, when you're doing similar stuff every day, every week. And it usually involves packing and unpacking a rank sports bag.

'Yes,' says Claudia. 'You can do small things, though. Take them to a different park from the one you usually go to . . . Also, I sometimes deliberately don't pack my weekends with new things to do, because I'm tired and I want to relax.'

Maybe I could utilize the repetitiveness of our imposed routine and make it add up to something more. There must be a way of building your everyday, over-and-over memories around you, like stacking your bed with duvets and pillows and cosy coverlets, making your life warm and nest-y, so it is a haven. Making the same-old-same-old into something comfortable and nourishing, rather than tedious. A regulated life can be all of these things. Cosy, boring, sustaining, repetitive. Layer on layer on layer.

When I go to our local park, it's like I'm adding to my own history. There's no part of it that doesn't contain a memory. Over there is where the fair goes, but also the picnics and a few of the innumerable football parties that P has been to, many of which he's gate-crashed. This hill is where, at an ancient Pride, they laid out an AIDS blanket, an enormous, beautiful thing made of patchwork memorials to lives that were cut short, to people who never had the luxury of wondering about midlife and what it might mean.

The play park is where F disappeared for a terrifying, heart-stopping ten minutes; here is where I confronted a teenager who was about to hit a smaller kid; this building is where we hid when the wind and rain were so strong we couldn't actually get over the hill. This tree: I can draw this tree in my mind, where the branches broke off in high winds, how the remaining ones fit together so they can be climbed, but only so far. The lido alone is an ever-morphing memorial of my past and present.

If you are unhappy, you don't want to think about how long your unhappiness lasts. I listen to a podcast about a US soldier who was captured by the Taliban and imprisoned for seven years. He tried to escape, but was caught, and after that, his captors kept him in a cage, blindfolded, or with no light, or with the light switched on and off at random times. At one point, he was moved somewhere with a clock. He asked for it to be removed. He couldn't face how slowly the seconds were passing.

Time appearing to move quickly is a privilege, not a problem.

I go to a lunch and an editor tells me – almost bashfully – that his children are grown up now, they've left home and he and his wife are finding it hard. Not just with the physical space, the emptiness of rooms, the lack of noise, but with the amount of time they have. Their blank diaries. 'It's not too bad for me,' he says, 'because I work. But my wife is taking it hard.'

You might not want to dash through your life. You might not want it to be a race to the finish line. You might want to savour certain aspects, to make time stand still for a while.

The problem I have with time speeding up, with my busy-busy hustle towards my death, is the same problem I have with knowing that I have fewer years to live than I have lived. It makes me feel helpless and insignificant. And, of course, in the large scheme of things, this is true. I'm helpless to do anything about growing older, and I'm completely insignificant (except to a few people). It can make me wonder what the point is, really.

If your life whizzes past at a speed you can't control, if how you spend your days is how you spend your life, and how you spend your days is sorting out the kids and working and eating the same food as usual because you can't think of anything else, and going to the same places as you usually do because that's what the family likes, and nobody, not even you, notices or cares that your years are going past at warp speed . . . If this is what life is, then, yes, the speed of it can be a problem. The decades pass and then the kids leave and you have done . . . what? Anything? Nothing? What are you left with? Time? Space?

I remember something that Philippa told me. She said: 'Your brain is elastic. You can change the way you think. It's hard and it takes a long time, but you can change it.'

I interview Ruby Wax, and she says the same thing. Ruby has had depressive episodes and she has found that meditation – usually called mindfulness, these days – has helped her (though it doesn't cure depression). She took a post-graduate degree at Oxford to study mindfulness and what it does to the brain. She tells me that all the evidence shows it changes the way our brains work. It thickens our pre-frontal cortex (which is where we make our 'higher brain' decisions). It shrinks our amygdala (where our 'fight or flight' reactions are, those anger triggers). It helps us make better neural connections.

She is a huge meditation convert, Ruby Wax. Still, she's a realist. She says: 'Oh, you can't be mindful all the time. You'd never get anything done. It would be like if you were always in the gym. You know, you do your exercise and then you get back to real life.'

Stephen from MIND said something similar. He said: 'I'm not a hundred per cent sold on mindfulness, but I think there is something in being in the time that you find yourself. If you're washing dishes, wash dishes. If you're in that moment, live that experience, appreciate it for what it is.'

He said: 'You're at the life stage you're at. Accept it. If you have children, then all things have their season, and this is the season for staying in and looking after your children. Acknowledge where you are, accept where you are, move through it and enjoy it. Because the other option is to actively not enjoy your life.'

If you search for ways to change your relationship to time, then mindfulness comes up, over and over. If you focus on little details, train your attention to notice, then wonder at, what you're actually doing – sitting in a car, in traffic: how odd is that? – you'll find that the time you spend on that activity stretches and slows. The activity itself becomes more interesting, more memorable. If you can resist the temptation to check your texts, to call your mum, to daydream about the lottery, you can pull yourself out of the rushing moment, examine it properly, and see it for what it is.

A friend posts up some recently found pictures of her great-grandparents and their family. Formal Victorian line-ups, smudgy yet familiar faces.

People start to research their family tree when they hit middle age, and that can be to do with time passing. Somehow it becomes important to understand who you are and where you fit in in a wider sense, not just among random peers. You yearn to be part of a continuum. You wonder about the significance of your family's previous generations, of where you came from, of how your predecessors lived and what they did to get you to where you are now. But, unless you're upper class, your historical family knowledge will stop with your grandparents, or great-grandparents, if your family had their children young. So you start the research . . .

It's an attempt to make your life mean more. If you are part of a story that can be followed, traced back and placed within the past, your own short time is held within something more lasting and significant. Something longer. Your Museum of Me (the photographs, the baby clothes, the certificates for swimming twenty-five metres in your pyjamas) seems less like ridiculous hubris, more like a treasure trove for future generations.

I've never researched my own family tree, but we have our stories. My granny's dad was a gambler and a drunk, who ran away with a barmaid, taking whatever money there was with him. My mum's cousin was part of a family of music-hall performers, a troupe called the Elliot-Savonas that toured the north and went to America. There were around ten of them, and their act consisted of them all playing the saxophone and then – unbelievably – doing trick cycling. My dad's grandparents were missionaries. His mum, my other granny, was one of the first women to study maths at university. I haven't researched any of this. I have no idea how much of it is true (though there are pictures of the saxophone-playing/cycling troupe). But those are our family stories.

I'm not sure how I fit in. It's quite a lot to live up to, and perhaps the only way to respect our history and extend my time significance would be for me to become a cycling, saxophone-playing, gambling, mathematician preacher of the Lord. This would take . . . time.

I'm quite up for locating myself within a familial yarn, especially one that seems far more exciting than my own life. But, truthfully, what I'd really like to do is to take myself out of time. Remove myself from its relentless march. Is this possible? Can it be done? Can I freeze the moment, like a cartoon, hold everyone where they are, mid-chat, mid-snack, midlife and just duck under, sneak out for a bit?

It has taken me a long time to write this book. This is partly because I started it when F was very young, and there is nothing more time-hoovering and mind-shredding than a small child: they soak up your hours like a sponge, they fill your brain with mush. ('The longest, shortest time', as a podcast about families has it.) It's also because I fell into the middle of the middle-aged low. Time passed in between and around and via me, as I felt hopeless and panic-gripped or bored and unclever. The days, they seemed to fall through me and I just let them go. I unpicked, then re-stitched whatever crisis it was I felt I was in.

I kept on writing, even when I didn't want to, because I know writing is one of the few ways you can pull yourself out of whatever time you're in.

How do you want to think about time, about time everlasting, about your time, about what you can create during that time?

I want to stretch time, ping it, squish it. Make it pass *sloooooowly*, make it stop, make it speed up so fast it takes my breath away. I want to feel free of time's relentlessness. I can't control it, but I'd like to try.

A few things seem to help. Listening to new or old music or going to gigs. Reading. Having sex. Watching my children play an instrument or take part in a sport or perform in some way. Watching anyone who has practised for years play an instrument or take part in a sport or perform. Sport does something special to time, I find: watching it, having a go yourself. Sport's silly deadlines, the commitment, the belief, the intensity of a few vital minutes (seconds, sometimes), with all those years of dedication leading up to them.

Doing something – writing, drawing, building Lego – that requires you to be involved and committed and have an aim but not quite know what will come out. Not being distracted while you're doing it, that's important, too. My kids can bend time better than I can, so if I can bring myself to join in their games – properly join in, not just fiddle about with half an eye on my phone – then time slows and expands. We make cakes together. The timing matters.

Getting smashed used to help – it bent time so much that bits disappeared – but it doesn't help me any more. Out of time is good, out of everything not so much.

I am trying to change my vision of time. I can't, so far, alter how I see numbers or ages; I can't move forty-five back around the number line until it's in front of me, where fifteen is now. But I can use other visual metaphors, layer them on top. There are other ways to think about time, and it's not so hard to use all of them at once.

I can think of my life as a trajectory upwards, a straight, vertical line to outer space, like a rocket. Or downwards, towards my future, as if I were Chinese. I can think of it as a hill, which doesn't always help (in middle age, it can seem as though everything is downhill from now on). Still, it can feel good to think that, while you're on top of the hill, you can see everything laid out: future and past surrounding you, at your feet. You can feel grateful to be in the middle, with an almighty overview.

Or – and this is what seems to help most – I could remove my life from my fixed pattern and insert myself into a bigger picture, one that takes on the micro and macro. Some people do this through their religion. Most religions tell us that our lives are important, that we mean something and that death will not remove that meaning. Religion reassures us that we will live on in some way after our death.

I don't believe in an afterlife, though I've tried very hard to do so. But I like the idea that consciousness lives on in some way. Which it does, in the form of novels and films and photographs and our own memories of people who were and are loved.

And also, some scientists believe, in other ways. A friend sends me an article from outerplaces.com ('Where science meets science fiction'). It says: 'Prominent physics researchers from Cambridge University, Princeton University and the Max Planck Institute for Physics in Munich claim that quantum mechanics predicts some version of life after death. They assert that a person may possess a body-soul duality that is an extension of the wave-particle duality of sub-atomic particles.'

I read the article and get excited. Sub-atomic particles, meaning teeny-tiny, fundamental particles, such as photons and electrons, can be in one place, but also another at the same time. This is a function of them acting both like a wave and a particle.

The article says that some physicists think it's possible to extend this well-established theory to the idea of life after death. The argument goes like this. If there is a quantum code for all things, living and dead, then things will live on after death (in purely physical terms), because of the sub-atomic particles' wave-particle duality. If a particle writes all of its information on its wave function, as well as holding that information inside itself, then when the particle goes (dies) it doesn't matter because its information will live on in the wave.

Dr Hans-Peter Durr, former head of the Max Planck Institute, suggests that this might extend to us. We have all our information in our brain, the particle, and this is then written into the wave, which he calls the spiritual quantum field. This means that when the brain and body dies, the consciousness can live on. He says that beyond the material world 'is an infinite reality that is much bigger. Which this world is rooted in. In this way, our lives in this plane of existence are encompassed, surrounded by the afterworld already. The body dies but the spiritual quantum field continues. In this way, I am immortal.' I like this.

Another academic from the Max Planck Institute, Dr Christian Hellwig (from the Biophysical Chemistry Department; I am stealing his name for a cartoon baddie), found that information in our central nervous system is encoded in such a way that it allows lots of pieces of data to occupy the same moment in time. He points out that our thoughts and consciousness, our feelings all show properties that could be referred to as spiritual. And of those properties, not one directly interacts with the material world: they're not affected by forces like gravity or electromagnetism. 'However, these spiritual properties correspond exactly to the characteristics that distinguish the extremely puzzling and wondrous phenomena in the quantum world.'

Over at Princeton, Professor Robert Jahn, a physicist, also thinks that consciousness follows the tenets of quantum mechanics, but for different reasons. David Bohm, a quantum physicist who studied with Albert Einstein and was his friend, thought something similar.

He said: 'The results of modern natural sciences only make sense if we assume an inner, uniform, transcendent reality that is based on all external data and facts. The very depths of human consciousness is one of them.'

These ideas may be baloney. They may well appeal to me because they chime with the ideas of rave culture, or because I was brought up going to church so, as a child, I was indoctrinated with an idea of a bigger consciousness. I'm OK with that. If you've ever felt united with strangers at a festival, or looked at the sky at night, then you know how amazing it is to feel small and yet – at the same time – part of a bigger thing. To be insignificant and monumental in the same instant. Musicians understand that. And so do certain quantum physicists.

What are the other ways of pulling time about? How can we make time stretchier? Fill it when we need to? Empty it, sometimes? Move quickly and then more slowly?

Repetitive action, the same movement over and over, can change how we feel in time. Running, yoga, singing, chanting. Sit-ups. Only ten more to go, only five . . . And the act of creating is a real time-twister. You can fill your days, right up to the brim, through creativity – gardening, writing, making music – and there is something about that headspace, when you are truly immersed, that makes time bend. The flow, some people call it. Hours pass, days sometimes. Time changes. Routines disappear. You forget to eat. And when you come out, and someone asks you what you've been doing, you're in a daze. What have you been doing? You're not sure.

That's why it's best to keep what you've created. Even if you don't show anyone except yourself. It's evidence. It's the small prize after the hours of puzzle. If your creation doesn't end up as anything, then it's easy to believe that your time has been wasted. When it hasn't. It's been stretched and tested, not wasted.

Learning something you find difficult, that will do it too. A man tells me about flying a microlight, a tiny, insubstantial aircraft, with wings and a cockpit – it seems like a chair in the air. When he's flying his microlight, he thinks only of what he has to do with the controls, what he must do, so that he doesn't die. Other than that, he looks around, at the earth spread out beneath him, at the beautiful, glorious world below, natural and people-made, with none of the tedious detail, the imperfect close-up human failures. He has escaped. And time means nothing, and his heart is full.

I talk to a woman who has terminal cancer. She is young, in her forties. She has two children and a husband and an interesting career. But she is dying. I talk to her about death and tell her that I'm going to call my book *Out of Time*. She gets excited about this. I'm surprised, because she's running out of time herself (more rapidly than she lets on when I talk to her).

She says: 'Out of time is great. Out of time is what you want, really. You want to extricate yourself from how long you've lived, and how long you have, or haven't, got left to live. Pull yourself out of that idea of a fixed time. You have to do it, really, or everything seems cruelly absurd and meaningless.'

17. Long-term

When we first met, we would get up around midday, have breakfast together. A fry-up, or coffee and the remains of a takeaway, depending on how hungover we were and what there was in the fridge and whether we had enough cash to go to the shop. We would leave the flat – to do what? Trawl round second-hand shops, limp off our hangovers, see a film, walk across a park, play pool in a bar. At about 4.30, 5, we would be ravenous. We would try to find somewhere to eat, always difficult. It would be a weekday, because he worked at the weekends, so most places weren't open. Those that were open didn't want us to eat at that time. It was before London became bewitched by eating out, before burgers were re-invented as the fodder of young gods, before 'slow' or 'dirty' were compliments, food-wise. We sat in the pub with packets of crisps ripped open on the table.

Was that what we did? Sometimes. We went away whenever we could afford it. Ryanair, easyJet, to places we'd never been before. Or we drove long days to stay with friends: Cornwall, Leeds, Glasgow. Work was about earning chunks of money and fitted around everything else we found important: everything else meaning, going out. We would go to clubs, gigs, anywhere off-peak, sharing cheap flights with jokey elderly people who zoomed between European cities to sit on coaches that trundled them around the sights.

I would write all day and all night and all day and all night, sleeping for a few hours in my clothes, swallowing handfuls of diet pills bought in US pharmacies. Then I would stop working and sleep, or take more pills and socialize. We had too much living to do to fit in too much work. Time shifted, stretched and shrank, according to our deadlines and desires.

For a couple of years, when P was little, S opted out of the routine. This is easy to do when you have one child, who doesn't have to be anywhere in particular. We both opted out then because the routine was portable. Though P needed a certain regularity, a rhythm, we could continue some of our pre-child lives: going clubbing, up-and-leaving on off-peak holidays. But when circumstances really changed, when P had to go to school, S continued to live by his own timetable. He got up late, he went out late, he managed his days according to what he wanted to do. And, gradually, his life shifted away from me, and first one, then two kids, from our small, detailed world of places to be, at particular times, with bags packed correctly and in the appropriate uniform.

For a while, it was like he was a lodger, or a ghost. We lived in parallel universes. He wasn't aware of what any of us were doing, even though we did the same thing, at the same time, every week. I would go to bed not knowing when he'd be back, but knowing that it wouldn't make much difference to our daily life anyway. I would go to bed knowing that everything was up to me: that if I stopped, it all stopped.

This seems like a lifetime ago. Now, when he's at home, the routine is his too; we have different roles and specialities within them. He cooks, he supervises homework, he goes to football matches, he picks the kids up from school, takes them swimming or cycling or wherever they need to be. In many ways, he's better than I am at the routine; he doesn't sweat the small stuff.

*

In cafés and sports halls, I listen to younger mums, and they discuss their partners. They make jokes about how their husband sent their daughter to school without a skirt on, how he gets cross in the morning when the children are noisy ('I think I'm just used to the chaos!'). They list the little things he forgets (the name of the head teacher, that the middle child won't eat cheese, the nappies, for God's sake). And it's all easy and cheerful, and what strikes me is that these women don't sound indignant, they sound happy.

They are indulgent of their husband's ways, because those ways don't really matter. If you are in control of the minutiae of a family – which injections the kids have had, the password to the bank account, who needs to be where and when – then you are the boss. You might not be doing paid work, but you are the maypole around which the whole family dances. It's a role that suits some people more than others.

I think it can be easier if one person is in charge of a family's routine and details, because otherwise all the strands get tangled. It can be easier, but that doesn't make it right for everyone. Most job shares are tricky to coordinate, but they work. Also, gender has nothing to do with who should be in charge. I'd like it noted that I didn't apply for the job.

Still. Sometimes I text S just before he has to pick up the kids, because I can't quite believe he's going to turn up as he said he would. He turns up, as he said he would.

There is a way that older couples can be with each other. When the woman – it is usually the woman – talks about her husband as though he isn't present, when she diminishes him in company by describing what he does wrong all the time, or just what he does all the time. My mum does this, sometimes. 'Listen to him! He doesn't even know which button to press on the washing-machine!'; 'He drove all the way to the hospital. But he'd left the letter on the bed.' She addresses her remarks to me, or to the other women around us, because all men are the same, aren't they? Men are like children, to be jollied along and checked up on and protected from the real world and its consequences.

The indulgence of the young mums has gone, replaced by low-level exasperation. Perhaps it's because the power has gone, too. Once children don't need your organizational whizz, once the routine has been demystified, handed over, once you are not the CEO of the household, then you are in control of a situation so familiar that it seems as though you have no power at all. So you look for other things to organize. You bicker over details.

My mum and dad love each other. They have a partnership. He sorts the bins, gets the car MOT'd, he's in charge of the garden. She cooks, does the laundry, books the holiday, sends birthday cards. This works well, usually. But she would like to drive, occasionally; he fancies a different meal, every so often.

The same thing, over and over, with the same person, can make that person boring. Even though it's not the person who is dull. It's the routine, and the routine is needed and the routine is resented and the routine is what keeps the family ticking over.

In our bedroom, there is a photo of us standing on a bridge. Behind us is a swollen, rushing river; we're somewhere in America. The photo was taken around the time we first met. He is wearing a hat and pulling a silly face. I am grinning; I look elated, overjoyed.

For ages the photo reminded me of something I couldn't quite recall. I know it now. It's a picture in my parents' bedroom of my dad, where he has the same expression as I do. The photo was taken on their wedding day. He is wearing a hat, but his hair flops over his eye; I have the same hairstyle now as he did then. He is young, and he looks like me and his dad and my brother and my son, and the past and the future and all of us are mixed up in there. And he is wildly, wonderfully happy.

When you meet someone and fall in love, everything is uncertain. You don't know how your affair will work out. You don't know who your new love is, or who you will be together. Time flickers, stands still, races ahead. No history yet; no habits.

Gradually, as you spend more time together, jokes arrive, phrases you use as shorthand, as a way of smoothing over an awkward moment, of avoiding a row. You have favourite songs and places, you know an opinion from the set of a head. You think: I'll get him that, he'll love it. Or: There's no point in even asking, there's no way she'll want to go. The surprise of your most loved person fades away and you move around each other with knowledge, flowing together and apart, holding hands when you fall asleep, manoeuvring from worktop to fridge, like no-contact dancers, without a bump. What keeps us close after all these years? Are we held together by irritation, by familiarity? Are we just bound by habit? Is routine keeping us safe, or should we shatter it, carve a hole in our heads, let some blood drip, expose our regimented brains to the air?

Recently, we went to see a play – a modern farce – that was a massive smash hit. Everyone we knew who had seen it had absolutely loved it. They'd quote lines at us, start laughing when describing certain scenes. The play was a critical success, too: five-star reviews, awards for the main actors, people helpless with laughter.

We sat at the end of the back row in the stalls. The play began. There was a lot of falling over, some talking to the audience that seemed impromptu but wasn't, acting so big that initially I thought it must be part of a joke, a play within a play. About twenty minutes in, as everyone around us clasped each other's forearms, wiped tears from their eyes, doubled over from laughing so hard, I asked S if he was enjoying himself.

He said: 'No. I fucking hate it. It's shite.'

So did I. I thought exactly the same. We were the only two people in the whole of the theatre that weren't in fits of hilarity. United, as one: together in our rotten hatefulness.

We left and went for a sandwich. We bitched about the play to obscene, appalling, murderous levels. We had a lovely time. Oh, it was great.

18. Death

'I knew a woman who had cancer,' says a woman I know, who has cancer. 'She wore a wig, had her eyebrows tattooed on and wore false eyelashes. And she said that, during the day, she just passed as normal and tried not to think about it. But at night, when she was peeling off her eyelashes and taking off her wig, and lying down . . . in that sort of coffin posture . . . that made her anxious. She decided to stop lying down and sit up all night instead.

'The problem was that her doctor had said to her, "Don't worry too much. You'll probably pass away in your sleep." So she simply refused to go to sleep.'

If you start to count how many years you have left, then what you're counting to is death. This is true even if you've sold your soul to the devil so you can live to 100, and he's given you a signed centenarian guarantee, like a birthday card from the Queen. It's the final countdown. Feel free to add the music in your head.

'Why are you writing about death?' says my friend. 'I thought your book was about the middle of life, not the end of it.'

'You don't want to dwell on it, do you, really?' says another. 'We all know it's coming, and there's too much of it about these days.'

I have a very dear friend who stopped visiting his mum when she was terminally ill because she lived a long way away and he couldn't bear to see her in such a reduced state. We disagreed about this – I thought he should visit her more – but she died anyway. He didn't regret his decision. 'I want to remember her when she was herself, not when she wasn't really there,' he says. 'When she was alive, not dying.'

Alive, not dying.

Even if you're not counting, others are. (Though they can be doing it in the opposite direction: 'I can remember when you were born. You were a funny little scrap,' says my mum. 'I can't believe I have a daughter as old as you.') I go to see a financial consultant. Financial consultants are people who love counting. This financial consultant tells me that, once you hit 55, the banks see your mortgageable worth not as how much you earn per year but as how much your pension will bring in. At the moment, S and I do not have much to count.

There are plenty of artists – plenty of people – who have got to midlife and found themselves wrestling with the idea of death. The death maths hits them, as it does us all, and they consider what they have and haven't done, and what they can't do any more.

Leo Tolstoy struggled badly when he hit 50, losing confidence in his own ability and sinking into depression. He could find no purpose, no meaning to his life. He wrote about it in *The Confession*. It's a hard read. Easier is 'The Death of Ivan Ilyich', one of his short stories. Ilyich is a rich, well-regarded, self-satisfied 45-year-old. He works in the law. He is married, with a child. He has a lovely house. Ilyich is, if we're honest, the kind of smug middle-aged man you don't want to be sitting next to during a long meal. Anyway, when he's 45, he bangs his side and ends up with an intestinal illness. He ignores it, but after a while he goes to the doctor, who tells him he may have a 'loose kidney'. Gradually, the illness reveals itself to be terminal.

At a certain point, death seems close, but Ilyich cannot believe it: 'At the bottom of his heart, Ivan Ilyich knew that he was dying; but so far from growing used to this idea, he simply did not grasp it – he was utterly unable to grasp it. The example of the syllogism that he learnt in Kiseveter's logic – Caius is a man, men are mortal, therefore Caius is mortal – had seemed to him all his life correct only as regards Caius, but not at all as regards himself.'

Those who work with the terminally ill have said that Tolstoy's depiction of Ilyich's process of dying is astonishingly accurate. The various states Ilyich goes through before death might, these days, be described as the stages of grief – denial, anger, bargaining, depression, acceptance – except that such a description isn't nearly enough. Ilyich is more than those stages, he is himself: silly and petty and self-centred. And human. As he ails, we begin to understand him.

Ilyich lies on his deathbed, eking out the hours to his end. One by one, his influential friends stop coming round to visit him; his wife doesn't understand the desperation of his illness; his riches cannot cure him; his good works will not be remembered after his death, and neither will he. He is tormented, in physical and personal agony.

A poor servant boy, Gerasim, cares for Ilyich as he suffers. Gerasim, in Ilyich's eyes, becomes an exemplary character, almost a living angel. Here, thinks Ilyich, is a person who has lived life as he should, modestly, providing care for others, unlike Ilyich, whose selfish materialism has brought him untold riches but no spiritual wealth. Ilyich has spent his life not doing the right things. If only he had understood this earlier!

This moral epiphany doesn't stop Ilyich dying, but that's how death rolls.

Instead, there is an awful crescendo to his agonies until, in his final hours, he understands that there is something he can do, a 'right thing'. Ilyich's final, redeeming act is to feel kindness towards his wife and child, to feel sorry for them and not himself, and to set them free by dying.

'The Death of Ivan Ilyich' is full of insight and intimacy. It offers no answers but it lays out the questions. Still, I think there is something unseemly about a rich man judging a poorer man's life as better than his own. Gerasim serves Ilyich because Ilyich is his employer; if Gerasim had more money, he wouldn't be tending him. Ilyich reminds me of those City types who hit 43, throw up their hands and say, 'Oh, no, I've made a fortune, and now I've realized that money doesn't bring happiness!' Then they quit and use their spare change to live in an eco-mansion and to set up a mountaineering charity for underprivileged children. That always seems less like middle-aged revelation to me, and more like a carefully managed early retirement. I am aware of how bitter this sounds.

Reading 'The Death of Ivan Ilyich' makes me feel better, because it is a great piece of writing; and worse, because it reveals how bleak death is, even a fictional one that is monitored and alleviated by a caring friend.

Irvin D. Yalom is an existential psychotherapist and writer, and I am advised to read some of his work. Yalom believes that the 'primal stuff of psychotherapy is always existence pain' (as opposed to repressed emotions, or the need to unpick a traumatic past). He thinks we should stop worrying about whether we fancy our mother and start thinking about how much we're messed up by the very fact of being here. Hence, 'existential psychotherapy'.

In *Love's Executioner and Other Tales of Psychotherapy*, Yalom writes: 'I have found that four givens are particularly relevant to psychotherapy: the inevitability of death for each of us and for those we love; the freedom to make our lives as we will; our ultimate aloneness; and, finally, the absence of any obvious meaning or sense to life.'

Yes. Yes, I know.

I get an email from a friend, telling me she has cancer. Telling me not to worry, they've caught it early, they're operating and then there will be chemo and maybe radiotherapy, and it's a bit of a shocker, but the kids seem to be coping, and honestly, not to worry.

I worry. I'm old enough now to understand that doctors do not always know about cancer, meaning they don't know if they've caught it all, or what that means. Doctors talk in percentages, when it comes to cancer, and what are you meant to make of that death maths?

Part of what Yalom believes is that we need to confront the reality of our deaths. If we don't, then, like Ivan Ilyich, we will spend much of our lives aiming at goals that don't matter. If we're lucky, we might even achieve them (look at us, having sex with scores of different, younger partners! Brandishing our genuine Burberry handbag! Buying a house that is bigger than our parents'! Buying a house at all!). But, even if we do, our achievements will not make us fundamentally happy. They will mean little, and will crumble when the sharp glare of imminent death reveals them for the chimera they are.

This does not make me feel good about life, or death.

However, Yalom's book makes me feel better because the stories of his clients are interesting, and because he names the dread that lives in the pit of your stomach and bubbles into your mind.

And he talks about meaning. The meaning that death gives to your life. Death can take away meaning, but it can give meaning too.

I listen to a podcast where the presenter talks to Jeb Corliss, a professional BASE jumper, which means he is paid money to jump off tall buildings. He has jumped off the Eiffel Tower. In the podcast, Corliss remembers when he had a bad accident.

He says: 'I was laying in bed in the hospital, totally shattered and broken, but alive. And I was thinking, "Wow, that didn't kill me, maybe I just won't die? What happens if I live to 50?" And that was actually a scary thought. My out's always been death.'

A couple of years ago, on holiday in France, I was driving along a fast, winding road. There were two lanes on our side, for overtaking; only one on the other. I had P and F in the car, and an older friend of theirs. It was raining – just spitting, really – and as I steered the car around a long bend, the wheels hit some oil and we spun. We spun, it seemed, very slowly, once around, across the overtaking lane, over the central line and into the approaching traffic, with me braking and trying to steer and nothing seeming to make any difference at all. We decelerated from 60 m.p.h. to a standstill.

We stopped, with the nose of the car against the passenger wheel of an enormous MPV. The MPV had stopped too, a long line of traffic behind it. There was a child in the passenger seat. I can see his face now, all eyes and open mouth.

And then, we carried on.

F said, from her child seat: 'Again, again! Around again!'

I try to think like Yalom, to let death help me make my remaining life more meaningful, but it is hard. I sense the countdown, but life keeps getting in the way. Packed lunches, overdue tax bills, a new song that seems to speak of everything, sports socks that are impossible to put on anyone's foot, especially if its owner won't stay still . . . All that. I wonder if those who are facing imminent death can understand better.

I interview Wilko Johnson, the guitarist and singer who played with Dr Feelgood. In January 2013, Wilko was diagnosed with terminal pancreatic cancer, and given ten months to live. Refusing any form of chemotherapy, he embarked on a farewell tour, and made an album with Roger Daltry. And then, eleven months after his diagnosis ('In extra time,' he says to me), a fan, who happened to be a doctor, put him in touch with an oncologist. The oncologist successfully operated on Wilko's cancer.

So now Wilko is back where he was before. He's back to being like the rest of us. He's going to die, but he doesn't know when. His life is like a thriller movie, where the countdown to the exploding bomb is stopped with two seconds to go.

I interview him on stage, in front of fans. I wondered if this might make him less open, but that's not Wilko's style. He is very honest; also clever and tough and brimming with emotion.

He says: 'Everyone's imagined it: what would I feel if the doctor told me I had months to live? And I tell you what, it was nothing like I imagined. I'm sitting in this room, and the doctor says to me, "You've got cancer." It takes probably less than a second to say those words. And suddenly the whole universe has changed, irrevocably. And yet I felt absolutely calm.' He puts out his hand, flat, in front of him. 'Not a tremor. It was as if he was talking about someone else. The doctor said a little bit to me – there was a short conversation. And then we left, to walk home. It was a beautiful winter's day and I looked up at the trees against the sky. I suddenly felt this rush of emotion. I thought, I'm ALIVE! I was just looking round everything, going, I'M ALIVE! By the time we got home, I was almost ecstatic.

'Then I felt that this was maybe a shock reaction, and any moment I was going to come plunging down . . . but, no, I didn't. It was the beginning of a most extraordinary year and a bit for me. Just crazy. It's crazy, sometimes you get the high and – I've actually done this – you stand on Canvey sea wall, shouting, 'I'm alive, I'm alive!' You wouldn't put it in a film, it's too crummy.'

Oddly, this is exactly what was put in a film (a non-crummy one) about Wilko, by Julien Temple. The film is a documentary called *The Ecstasy of Wilko Johnson*, and the opening scenes show Wilko on a sea wall at Canvey Island, explaining much of what he said to me: his elation at being alive, and at seeing life around him. That bliss is what people remember about Wilko's short death sentence. Perhaps we remember it because it's a comforting notion: to think that, when you're told you have a short time to live, you can live that time filled with joy.

Wilko says to me: 'I've never been a person that's learnt to meditate, but that's what you have to do: live in the moment. There is no future. Anything you do, don't do it in reference to the future. And as far as the past goes, you haven't got time to make amends for all the things you wished you'd done . . . all your sins. You've got to forget about the past, you haven't got a future, you've got to live in that moment.

'But,' he says, 'you get the other side, too. When it's three o'clock in the morning . . . That's the thing with cancer, it does make you feel alone. It's very lonely, in the early hours. All I can say is, if you know anybody who's got cancer, always be there for them. Be there for them, because they are feeling lonely.'

*

I send texts to my friends, the ones whose brothers die suddenly, who are diagnosed with a big bad illness, whose parents are wasting away in an institution. They don't always reply.

Yalom has written about this day-night contrast; about how, now he is in his seventies, he is upbeat during his days, and makes sure he doesn't waste his time. He doesn't go for lunch with anyone he doesn't really want to see; he spends his days writing, which he enjoys; he is kind to his wife, recognizing that she, like him, is just an ageing animal, trying to live.

But at night, things are harder. At night, when he tries to face up to the reality of his death, it is too much for him, too terrifying and sad.

Yalom has treated people who are facing imminent death. He says that they tend to allay their fears in one or both of two ways. They have 'two beliefs, or delusions, that afford a sense of safety. One is the belief in personal specialness; the other, the belief in an ultimate rescuer.'

The impressive thing about Wilko is that he had neither. He didn't think he was special; he didn't think he would be rescued. And then he was.

Wilko was 65 when he was diagnosed. His wife died of cancer in 2004. He has two sons, and they are grown up. These are important factors in your approaching death, because they are important factors in your life.

Wilko has said that, after he was cured, he found it hard to readjust to the idea of not dying. He misses his wife terribly.

I go to see Gillian Howie, an academic who works in Liverpool. She has studied how people react to being told that they have a terminal illness. She found that, instead of instantly realizing that they should appreciate the beauty around them, or rushing around trying to tick off a bucket list of fabulous experiences, the terminally ill mostly react in another way.

'The most common reaction is denial,' says Gillian. 'Complete denial.'

They go early Ilyich. Even when they're given the results of the test, and the results say, 'Six weeks to go'?

'Yes,' she says. 'Denial, denial, denial. People get the test results, then busy themselves with appearing as though everything is normal, getting on and doing the everyday . . . But they take tranquillizers and sleeping pills at night, because that's when it's quiet and they can think about what's really happening. That's my sense of it.'

The night terror. As I'm writing this chapter about death, and what it does to your head when you try to think about it, David Bowie dies. I surprise myself with how upset I am. I burst into tears over my Weetabix and remain slightly weepy for days.

As is well known now, Bowie released his last album, *Black Star*, on his birthday, 8 January. He died of cancer three days later. He knew he was dying. He was diagnosed as terminal and lived for eighteen months after his diagnosis. But instead of visiting Machu Picchu or organizing a party for all his old friends, he kept his cancer very quiet and took his daughter and wife on a trip around his childhood haunts. Then they all went back to New York, to their home, and he concentrated on his art. He scored a Broadway musical based on *The Man Who Fell to Earth*, and he made *Black Star*.

Two of the tracks from his album were accompanied by a video: 'Black Star' and 'Lazarus'. In the 'Lazarus' video, Bowie comes out of a wardrobe dressed in the striped suit he wore on the back of his 1976 *Station to Station* album. He sits at a table having ideas and writing them down excitedly. There is a skull on the table, but he ignores that. He also ignores another, older, frailer Bowie, who lies behind him, with bandages around his eyes and buttons where his eyes should be.

This Bowie writhes on a metal bed, seems to rise towards the ceiling, falls back. He looks frightened, tortured. Underneath his bed lies a pale woman. She taps on his bedstead. She is calling him, she wants his attention. The night terror. At the end of the song, the vital, creative, stripe-suited Bowie walks backwards into the wardrobe and shuts the door.

Life and death exist alongside each other. They laugh, flail, fight, create alongside each other, though they don't often acknowledge that they're in the same room. Then life returns to where it came from.

The darkness of the wardrobe. Some people believe that there's another door, in the back, out to Narnia.

People talk about a good death, or a bad one. My granny lived to 101 ('a good innings') but her death was not good. She went into hospital for a minor illness and caught *Clostridium difficile* while in there, though this was not mentioned on her death certificate. In the few weeks she was in hospital, she lost so much weight we couldn't recognize her when we visited. No one seemed to be feeding her. We found the ward set-up confusing; we never met a consultant; most of the nurses were casual and cold-hearted. Within minutes of my granny dying, someone stole her gold necklace from around her neck.

We complained. We were sent up through the system to meet the people who run the hospital. They assured us that improvements would be made, that explanatory leaflets would be left at each bedside. Nothing like that would happen again. We believed them.

I don't believe them now. I don't care about that now. I don't think about it.

Now, this is what I think. I think we should have kicked in the doors, lifted my granny from her hospital bed, eased the tubes from her limbs, removed the catheters and the drip-drip killer morphine. We should have wrapped her in a soft blanket and carried her poor, tiny, broken body home to let her die in her own bed. And we should have punched those fucking nurses to the floor on our way out.

Irvin D. Yalom says this, about a loved one's death: 'If one is guilty about not having done something that one should have done, then it follows that there is something that could have been done. A comforting thought that decoys us from our pathetic hopelessness in the face of death.'

My brother-in-law's brother, A, died a couple of years ago. He was young, just 53. Before we knew he was ill, we saw A on a visit. He seemed happy and seemed slim. 'You've lost weight!' we said, congratulating him. (Now, when I see someone my age who has lost a lot of weight, I'm worried. I think: Cancer. And if they have put on a lot of weight, especially around the face, I think: Treatment.)

After several tests, A was diagnosed as terminal and given six months to live. He and my brother-in-law went on a trip across America, while he was still relatively well. They did a lot of fantastic, memorable things: they saw the Grand Canyon, went to Las Vegas, took in a Broadway show. But A got tired a lot, and there were days when he slept for fourteen hours straight. This was harder for my brother-in-law to cope with than it was for A. He wanted to make everything good for A, whether that was sorting out an amazing holiday or making sure he was on the right medication or pushing for him to be moved from hospital to his own home for his final weeks . . .

I talk to Gillian Howie about this transference, the desire for control in a situation where you have no control at all, where you are powerless to change what is happening, and what is happening is the worst thing you can imagine. She tells me that in New Zealand, a type of care planning has been introduced – 'assisted dying', she calls it – so that while patients are well enough, they can set down principles around what they want to happen as they become more ill. This means that how they are cared for as they approach their death has something of them in it, that they are present as they disappear.

'One of the shocking things about all this,' says Gillian, 'is that your body is doing something that you are not in control of. You realize that you, yourself, who you are really are, are somehow different from the organism that's killing itself, and you.'

We can influence what's happening around death, we can make it more comfortable, more appropriate to the person who is dying. We can ensure that they spend their days near a window, that they can see a tree, or a plant. Gillian says: 'When you're growing things and touching non-human nature, there is a sense of cultivation, a tending and a growing, and that attention is very healing. If you could tend yourself in the same way as you would tend your geranium . . .'

We can play the music they love; we can make sure that people are with them who care about their welfare. People who love them. People who love you.

But we can't control much more than that. We can't control the happening of our death and we can't control the happening of other people's. We believe we can, that something can be done, but it can't, not really.

P likes comparison questions, and he says: 'Which would you rather? A good death when you're young, or a bad death when you're old?' I would have found this a hard question when I was younger. Not now. I don't want to die before I get old.

Afterwards, I wonder what he means by a good death. I think he might mean one with a fancy funeral. Or an unexpected one, maybe? The careless step out from the kerb, the unseen lorry? The heart attack? Good for the dead person.

Not so much for those left. But a death that drags on, the agony of Alzheimer's, the gradual withdrawal from all that is familiar, the loss of self, the slow fade to black . . . Is that any better?

Is a good death one that doesn't hurt? Years ago, a friend drowned when he was 31, and I was 30. Someone said to me, trying to comfort, that drowning was one of the best ways to die, that before you drown, you go into a bliss state and become ecstatic as you lose your life. 'He wouldn't have suffered,' they said.

I remember thinking: So *what*? So what, really? He's still dead.

Bowie's talent and persona seemed to tell many people – individually – that they could be special, that they didn't have to blend into the normal, that they could be wonderful. But when he died, that special person, we realized that, actually, he *was* normal. He was extraordinary, but ordinary, too. He was mortal. So, what of us, who are mortal, but – as it turns out – not really so special?

I listen to an old interview of Bowie's, about his song 'Heathen'.

He says: 'The words started coming and I just couldn't control them, and I was in tears at the end of the thing . . . I think it was a traumatic epiphany. A man confronting the realization that life is a finite thing, and he can already feel it: life itself going from him, ebbing out of him, the weakening of age. And I didn't want to write that. I didn't want to know that I do feel that. Who does?

'It's not the age itself. Age doesn't bother me – so many of my heroes are older guys. It's the lack of years left that weighs far heavier on me . . . It's having to let go of it all . . . There's such a cloud of melancholia from knowing that I'm going to have to leave my daughter on her own. I don't know what age that's going to be, thank God, but it just doubles me up in grief.

'I embrace ageing. It doesn't faze me at all, ageing. It's the death part that's a drag.'

Bowie said this when he was 55.

Kyoki Mori wrote an essay about death: 'I used to claim that I was afraid of dying and not of death. It was the process I dreaded, not the result. I didn't want to suffer pain, look ugly or feel panicked and helpless . . . I wouldn't mind being dead, I insisted, if I could die suddenly, unexpectedly, painlessly, and (perhaps most important) unknowingly from a heart attack, or a tree falling on my car. Or in my sleep at a very old age . . . Sometime in my forties, I came to admit the truth: the main problem with death isn't dying but being dead. Much as I'm afraid of the process, the result is unimaginably worse.'

I have read books about how authors feel when their most beloved person dies. *Levels of Life*, by Julian Barnes. *The Year of Magical Thinking*, by Joan Didion. An essay by Joyce Carol Oates in a book called *The Inevitable*.

Didion's book is about the sudden death of her husband, the writer John Gregory Dunne, and the year after it. It is also about the illness of their only daughter, Quintana. Quintana doesn't die in the book, but she does after it's published. In the book, Didion writes that her husband's death 'cut loose any fixed idea I had ever had about death, about illness, about probability and luck, about good fortune and bad, about marriage and children and memory, about grief, about the ways in which people do and do not deal with the fact that life ends, about the shallowness of sanity, about life itself'.

Joyce Carol Oates was also married to a writer, Ray Smith, who dies. 'Interminable days have passed, and interminable nights, and I am still here. This is amazing to me.' She stops living in the whole of their house. She does not eat at the table. She retreats into her bed, 'the nest', which is a swirl of pillows and bedclothes and work and Ray's books. When she is in the nest, she does not undress properly because she is cold, but also because she thinks, somewhere inside her, that if she keeps her socks on, she will not have to waste precious seconds pulling them on when she gets the phone call from the hospital about Ray. Who is not in a hospital. Who is dead.

Julian Barnes writes: 'Perhaps grief, which destroys all patterns, destroys even more: the belief that any pattern exists.'

These are dignified, intelligent people, able to articulate what is going on. They are smashed to the floor by their grief. Their lives are ripped into tiny pieces and they find it very hard to pick up even a few pieces.

There are many ways to think about death in philosophy and psychology. Here are two I find interesting. One is familiar: that mortality gives meaning to your life. Because we know that our lives are finite, our everyday events and rituals are given meaning and purpose. If you reflect on the fact that you're mortal, you become more engaged with life now. This is the Irvin Yalom and Wilko approach. It says that death – especially imminent death – chooses how you live your life.

The second way of thinking about death turns this idea around. It says that how you live your life chooses your death. If you live as a Buddhist, you approach death in a certain way (you believe you will be reincarnated). If you live as a hedonist, you give death a different meaning (a risk you're willing to take). So, if you change the way you live your life, it will change the way you see your dying.

By the way, I know several Buddhist hedonists. They're confused, as we all are.

Many Buddhist monks believe it is good to study death more intimately, and perform the Nine Cemetery Contemplations, where they consider the various stages of decomposition of a dead body. Their deep understanding of the process of death means, they believe, that they can understand their life more completely. Their knowledge of death and life is circular, one informing the other.

I'm not sure that I care so much about what happens to my body after it has killed me. I have an organ donor's card. I'd like to return to the amazing earth that bore me, but I don't mind in what form.

I wonder about the Buddhist hedonists. I wonder about all of us who have no strong beliefs, one way or another. Surely the problem is, if you really know that you are really going to die, then that knowledge, instead of giving meaning to the here and now, can take the meaning away.

It's all pointless, if we're going to die. If we're all footprints in the shifting sand of time, then nothing we do matters at all.

I speak to Claire and Rupert Callender, who run the Green Funeral Company. They've been involved in death professionally since 2000, but Rupert's life was dogged by it for many years. His dad died unexpectedly when he was 7, and within six months his two remaining grandparents died, then a slew of family friends; when he was 25, and only just coming to terms with his dad's death, his mum died. He hadn't gone to his father's or grandparents' funerals.

He says: 'I'm terrified of death. That what's brought me to the job. I never went through that immortal teenage stage. I knew you could walk out of the door, like my dad did, and not come back.'

Claire says: 'Not like me, drunkenly walking halfway across Archway Bridge in my teens.'

I'd hoped, I suppose, that being involved with death would make Claire and Rupert immune to its bleak truth, but they tell me that they think about it all the time, and it makes them very frightened.

Rupert says: 'I still consider death an outrage and a terrible thing, and I would stop it if I could . . . if the alternative wasn't living for ever. It doesn't get any easier. I'm running towards the fire. I think about it all the time. It's always there.'

Claire says: 'This job has massively increased my fear of people I love dying. Seeing the impact of a child dying on a mother, seeing her ten years on, it never goes away. And I really hoped that being an undertaker would make me come back home every day and be in a state of bliss as a parent, but that hasn't happened. I'm still shouting about wet towels left on the floor.'

They are both inspired by music, a little: Claire was involved in punk (she used to work at an independent record label) and Rupert's life was changed by rave. Rave opened him up. 'Rave saved me from a prolonged frozen grief,' he says. 'It allowed me to access emotions. I knew that it was based around the drugs and the music, but that didn't matter. It was still valid. You just need the intention.'

The funerals they provide are inspired by the people who are left. If the person who died was a violent alcoholic, or if they committed suicide, or if they were young and should have lived longer, and their parents are still alive, Claire and Rupert help the people left behind to work out what they want to do. They say that the emotion that is most often not dealt with is anger, that by the time someone dies, there's usually a massive fissure in the family, a searchlight on the difficult times that have been papered over.

Claire says: 'The thing I take away from working with death is that every single one of us, every normal person has this incredible core of strength and light. We all have it and, come that terrible moment, then people are amazing. We live in amazing communities and they rise up and they bring round casseroles and they walk the dog and they wash the kitchen floor. Your community is there to hold you. This incredible love-filled thing happens around total tragedy.'

I ask them what they think happens after we die. Where do we go? Claire is more materialist, Rupert spiritual. He wonders if time is looping on itself, that we will eventually become our ancestors. He has a hope that we're always alive and always dead at the same time. When they have arguments, the difference in their beliefs sometimes comes up. Rupert says, 'Well, I might be on a spiritual plane looking for you, and, because you don't believe you'll carry on, you'll just be using your time to have a rest. I'll be bashing on a Perspex door and you won't be listening.'

I tell Rupert and Claire about the quantum physics theory of life after death, because I think Rupert will like it. And he does. Claire says, 'I don't think it matters what you believe, really, just pick a belief.' She also says: 'No one will know who you are in seventy-five years. Three generations on, you will be forgotten, so there's no point in paying for a lease on a grave for longer than that.'

I like to think of myself as part of a bigger life – the continuing existence of humans, for instance, or the ongoing journey of Earth, or of the planets – because if I do, that helps me change the meaning of my life. I don't expect anyone to read my work after I'm dead. I haven't contributed enough in any other walk of life to make any long-term difference. I have children, but so do many people. Still, I will go into the earth, and I will become part of the natural cycle of things, the seasons, the death and rebirth of the plants and flowers, the wild grasses. And the pollen will lift on the wind, some part of what I once was.

It is hard, if you're not religious, to make sense of your living contribution. What we do, what we're capable of achieving, is so small and irrelevant. We are not David Bowie. Our children won't be David Bowie either. We make tiny contributions, in our short lives, and don't we make a fuss about it?

But we could make a few people's lives happier. We could contribute to the enormous total of people's kindness; we could add a little more to the vast, everlasting human empathy. That is one of the ways we can overcome death. Or, at least, it can make us stop thinking about it so much. Another way is to discover what we like doing, and – as long as it isn't harming others, so put down that hamster – to do it quite a lot. I try to think as hard as I can, and by doing so, I can contribute to the total of human consciousness, according to those cheerful quantum physicists. We are free to make our life as we want, and that is a frightening but amazing prospect.

Irvin Yalom again: 'The fear of death is always greatest in those who feel that they have not lived their life fully. A good working formula is: the more unlived life, or unrealized potential, the greater one's death anxiety.'

19. Generations

All life is a time of turmoil, of gathering and shedding, of shifting. Your movement through it, and life's movement through you, means that you change all the time. We are as malleable as Play Doh. We'd have to be, or we wouldn't get through.

But in middle age, somehow, your flexibility is not recognized. Because your circumstances are more settled, you seem set (in stone, in your ways). Like the grown-ups we knew as children, the ones who appeared to be without doubt or problem, unchanging, if we were lucky, and staying, not leaving. In middle age, we can choose to be as those adults seemed to be. We tell ourselves, 'That's the way I am', as though our character was there from birth, or stayed frozen after childhood and adolescence, a rigid, identifiable entity, named and labelled. No alarms and no surprises. No further developments, thank you for asking.

I read a book called *The Inevitable*, a collection of essays about death. In it, Sallie Tisdale writes: 'It is our peculiar punishment that we know things change and we want this to be otherwise. We want to hang on to what is going away, keep our conditions as they are, people as they are, ourselves as we are.'

We have reached a state of being: we are who we are. We are certain of what we like and don't like, how we will react when put into certain situations. We avoid people and places that don't suit us, as much as we can. We are rigid in our fear of variation. We refine and refine, and restrict and restrict, until we're left alone every Saturday night, watching *Match of the Day* in an armchair that nobody else in the family is allowed to sit on. It's safer that way.

The idea of an unchanging person also applies to the people we are closest to. Transformation is frightening. How can a carefree happy child grow into a sullen teenage fuck-up? What happened to the long-haired lover who overwhelmed you with their beauty, their wit, their untrammelled sexiness? Who is that elderly person walking effortfully up the road? They are your child; your partner; your parent. In the end, they are you.

My dad, so swift and sporty in middle age, is slow now; his hair is white, his eyes rheumy. He can still throw and catch a ball with surprising agility, but he is past the age where he can speak the language of young children for very long. He can't deal with ours too well, unless P talks to him about football, or F sings a song he knows. They, of course, don't notice whether he can cope. They are kids: they talk and sing regardless; they broadcast. But their noise agitates him; their sudden boisterousness makes him anxious. He withdraws into his crossword, goes to the corner shop for a pint of milk and another newspaper.

Sometimes, I have caught him looking at P and F with such love and wonder, it's as though they were angels sent to keep his heart beating. Sometimes he is so vague in their company that I wonder if he actually knows their names.

Staying at our house the other day, he announced he was going for a quick drive. To a town that is 50 miles away, near where my brother lives. We pointed this out. I said, 'You know we're in London? This is London.' He said, 'Oh, really? I'll just pop to the shop and get a paper then.'

When we have a meal together, my dad will break into the daily rattle of conversation to talk about subjects completely unrelated to anything that anyone has mentioned so far. The noise of the doodlebug bombs that came over his house in the war. The political situation in India. The difference in sensibilities between a middle-class man from Surrey and a working-class one from Salford. He talks of ideas, of experiences in the past. And football, too, of course. The family Esperanto.

My mum seems young for her age. She looks young, and she is becoming younger in the way she accedes to others; she is less sure of herself and what she knows. She can be as easily cast down as a teenager.

Our kids are her only grandchildren and she loves to spend time with them: she takes them to the park, to soft play, to the zoo, to museums; a retired teacher marshalling an educational day out. She engages P in marathon games of Monopoly and Scrabble. Her love has wonder, too: it can seem as if she admires the kids as much as she loves them, as though she's their low-status friend, deferential. 'Shall I sit here?' she asks F. 'Is the pasta all right?' Once, I caught her sitting on my bed, looking at F in her cot as F rolled around, yelling. Just looking. Just watching.

When I get in, she tells me everything that has happened throughout the day. All the detail, like a toddler. 'We met L at the park and she was with her little girl, who had a very unusual name. And she and F played in the sandpit. And tell Mummy what we did on the way home, F! What did we do? We had an ice-cream! And what flavour was it? It was chocolate, wasn't it?'

As they age, my parents seem to move away from me and at the same time get closer. We have less in common, but they need me more. They are bewildered by the way we use phones and iPads. They are uncertain around the internet; they phone me or my brother and ask us to book tickets, or print off travel documents. When they come to stay, they are very present because they need looking after, despite their active natures. They like to be reassured. Plans have to be explained in full detail. I have to talk my mum through every tube stop, each road junction. She makes lists. She puts on her glasses to peer at her small *A–Z*.

She wants to be close to me, as I do to my children, to my family. She wants to be relevant and important, vital to what is going on. 'I just like to feel useful,' she says, as I make a packed lunch while she noisily unloads the dishwasher and puts everything away. But there are implements and crockery with homes she doesn't know, so she leaves them piled high on the counter, right next to my elbow.

Before my granny died, we would go up to see her, in Cumbria, alone in her house. We would check her cupboards for food, throw away the out-of-date containers in the fridge, make fresh food and freeze it, replace old with new. We would clean the house, everywhere, including her. My brother didn't clean her, but I did. I would help her with dressing and undressing, untucking her vest, using baby wipes where she wasn't properly clean, carefully creaming her crevices with Sudocrem. Her skin was soft and dry, her hair a-fluff, the style mussed by her cardie, hoicked over her head to save undoing the buttons. All her colours were pale and faded, as though she was wrapped in muslin.

But elderly people are not babies. They are bigger, they are harder to manoeuvre, they are angrier. Their smells are not so sweet. Their nails are sharp, and their tongues. They reproach you when they talk – 'What do you think you're doing with that? What *are* you on about?' – and also by being the age they are, weakening before your eyes as you stride around your life, as you make plans and follow them through, as you rule your small domain.

I think of my granny, and I think of my parents. My parents are not old. They are active. They are together. But they are not, not by any stretch, young.

Once, my mum was the centre of our family, the maypole around which we all danced. Once, her schedule was impossible, too; she was pulled in all directions by her kids, her husband, her mother, her work. Her middle age was busy busy busy. Now she calls me and leaves long answerphone messages, telling me that nothing much has been happening, really, it's been raining again and your dad hasn't cleared out the shed, even though he promised he would.

20. Now

It is tempting to force a narrative sense on to our lives, to tell our story according to established form. To make it fit into the rhythms and patterns we love. I read F stories every night and, though the characters change – a wayward child, a silly cat, a charismatic, possibly bulimic, tiger – the stories all have a shape, a purpose. But lives, our lives as they are lived, aren't like that. Even if you manage to tell the tale you wish during your lifetime, death will not arrive when you desire. It will arrive, don't doubt that – there's always a page with 'The End' on it – but it doesn't arrive on cue. It won't gather and tie all your loose ends, the straggle, the knots, into a beautiful bow.

I can give you the bad stats, we can work out the death maths together, we can have a laugh about it. And then we can walk out of the door, like we always do, and one of us might not come back. The truth is, I don't know how long I have left, and neither do you. Even if you tell me you're going to live to 100. Even if you usually get your own way.

So, we might not be in the middle of our lives. But we are in the accepted centre. The dip of the U, the top of the mountain, halfway up the stairs. Stuck in the middle. Of everything: of our lives, our families, our own time. Is that so bad?

I think it is not. We can remember what has been, we can relate to what might be. We are not so young, but not so old. We can write a letter and we can send an email. We know about the Second World War and we know about social media; we understand why our parents find mobile phones tricky, but get why kids like gaming. We can see young people's future and old people's past. Because they are our future, our past.

We can see it all, spread out around us, if we just bother to look for a moment. That is a proper privilege. We are lucky to be in the thick of things. The middle of life is busy and full, and though that can stop us appreciating it, perhaps we should relish that silly hectic-ness. Or commit to it, anyway.

This is not a book that claims to be a self-help book. This is because I'm not qualified for such things, and because I believe that any book you enjoy, from *The Gruffalo* to *Ulysses*, is a self-help book.

However, I would say that the process of writing this non-self-help book, this book of uncertain questions and un-qualified almost-answers, has helped me negotiate my midlife stage. It hasn't been easy. Midlife crisis is only easy and wink-wink-hilarious to those who are not in middle age. Tell the jokes, if you want, but they don't sound so funny when the punchline is you.

But I am here to tell you that the crisis ends, mostly because nobody can live in a state of crisis for too long. Wilko's bliss, an upbeat form of crisis, disappeared once there was no agreed end point. When that was taken away, he had to revert to normal, to a non-bliss state. When Homer Simpson thinks he's going to die from eating fugu sushi, he resolves to live his life to the full. But when he doesn't, he's back on the sofa, eating pork rinds. Claire Callender said she thought that creating and helping with so many funerals for young people would make her a constantly beatific mother. That didn't happen. We can only live with the knowledge that time is running out if we don't consider it too often. It's too panicky to exist any other way.

Still. If you consider it, as I have done, as I still do, twisting around myself to try to catch a glimpse, like a puppy chasing its tail, then after you stop spinning there are areas you might start to think about.

You might think about freedom. About how we are free, all of us, to make our lives as we want. The immensity of that, and the vast responsibility . . .

And the downright lie of it, too. We are not free, not practically, not in our everyday existence. We are tied to timetables, and to work, and to each other, to the people we love and who love us. I am as likely to up and leave my children so that I can better express my true purpose in life as I am to learn how to skydive.

It can be good to consider those restrictions. Perhaps even write them down. Here is the heading: 'What I cannot change'. And what you find, once you move away from the love responsibilities of friends and family, the necessity of money, is that, if you're honest with yourself, you can change some things about your middling life. But, if you're being even more honest with yourself, you don't want to. For instance, you might want to run a marathon. Except that, for some reason, you don't appear to be getting up an hour earlier every day to do the training. That's OK. It just means you don't really want to run a marathon. You want to *have run* a marathon, and that's different.

Once you realize that, you can fast forward a bit. And on, a bit further. You can pull yourself forward through time right to your deathbed and you can consider what, when you're there, you might want to have done. Maybe a marathon isn't on that list. But perhaps a book is. Perhaps you can get up an hour early every day to write a book. Or to read a book. Or you could hear the alarm, think, Sod it, and you could have a bonus lie-in.

Bear in mind that if you want to have a legacy project, to create something that will outlast you, it is going to take up a lot of your time. You will have to give up on sleep, on seeing your friends, on hanging out with your children during the few short years that they're young. None of that is a problem, if it's what you want to do. You might find that it isn't. You might find that swimming in the cold, cold sea on a hot day is what you want to do instead.

You might think about time. If you want to have a lot of memories on your deathbed, then you're going to have to get disruptive. Change your regular sandwich, book a theatre visit, take the kids to a different park. Make time for an art gallery, try a band you don't know much about. Drink a martini or two. Go out dancing.

All that. That is what I'm good at. I'm not so good at working around the other, more practical stuff I Cannot Change. But as soon as I finish this book, properly put it away instead of hanging on to it, in an effort to keep young and not to fail and never to put myself anywhere other than in the shadows, with the cynical people, assessing instead of doing, then, *then*, I am going to look at the adult stuff. I've booked a meeting with a financial adviser, and I'm going to insure myself, S and the kids against whatever random acts life can throw at us. I am going to consider what will happen to my work once newspapers go completely online, when I'm deemed too old to know what I'm meant to know, even though I only know anything through research and asking other people.

I will spend days on the phone talking to builders. I will get a better fuel deal. I will weigh up the price of a garden against the price of living somewhere further away, away from all the people we love, and all the things we like to do.

If I look at S, as I do most days, I can picture him when I met him. He was skinny and he had stupid hair and messed-up teeth and piercings in inopportune places. He looks different now. He's a man who likes to play with his appearance and he's changed his hair and beard and clothing style many, many times since I've known him. And he has got older. His hair has changed colour – I think it's changed colour – and he wears glasses sometimes. If I turn my eyes away from him, I can't remember if he has his glasses on or not. I see him and I don't see him. I know when he's in the room, and I can tell his mood without lifting my head.

I look at P, and he flashes between babyish and full-grown, strobes between life stages. He slumps like a teenager, laughs like a little kid, drops a comment that makes me think he might be an old man.

And F, wild, hilarious, violently loving little F, who has been here only a few short years, she, too, is changing.

We change but we still know each other. We'd recognize each other anywhere.

I read this, by Sallie Tisdale, who is a Buddhist: 'The Buddha taught us that nothing is permanent. He taught us this in a great many ways, but most of what he said came down to this: things change; change hurts; change cannot be avoided.'

We cannot avoid the changing time we are in. We cannot avoid the transformation of our future. We cannot undo our fixed past, our heedlessness, our deliberate cruelty and our ludicrous beliefs, all the stupidity and brilliance that led us here.

When P and F were small, when they were at that bustling, hazardous, incessant age that starts the moment children begin moving around by themselves and doesn't stop until they have been accepted into Reception at school – then I used to think of myself as being in a small rowing boat. The weather was not good, the waves were choppy, it was dark and raining. I couldn't see the shore I'd left, and I couldn't see the shore I was going to. In that situation, there is only one thing to do. You have to keep rowing. So I did. And after a while, the weather got better and I could see the place I was aiming for.

This feeling happens over and over in midlife. It happens in most personal crises. There is a horrible time when you don't know why you're bothering to continue, when you can't see where you're going. And you have the aw-fuck-this moment, the chuck-it-in episode when all you want is to stop rowing the boat (stop making meals, stop answering emails, stop picking up and comforting and finding lost things) and somehow be spirited away to a different, sunnier shore that you've reached without all that back-breaking, over-and-over effort.

Or maybe you fancy a different picture. Here's one. You're on a tightrope and you've managed to point your toes, keep your balance and your nerve, and continue moving forward. And now you're all the way out in the middle. You've done amazingly, but now you're out here, you can feel the wind all around, and you sense the space beneath and above you, and you worry that you might wobble. Oh, God, you do wobble. No wonder, given that you're negotiating the tight-rope while carrying several large suitcases from the past, plus a few significant others, who are clinging to you and growing to enormous sizes. So you freeze.

What can you do? You can fall off. You can turn back. Or you can carry on, step by step by step, to the other side. This is not a self-help book. But here are a few things that helped me continue to push the oars through the water, stop wobbling on the wire, keep on keeping on.

Running, slowly

I'm not going to repeat why I like running, the endorphins it releases, the suspension of age and time it offers. The joy of the pad-pad-pad of feet and heart. Instead, I'll tell you about my first ever Park Run.

P joins a running club at school and discovers that he really enjoys it. So he and I decide to try out our nearest five-kilometre Park Run. P is extremely excited, and does well. Out of a field of 418, he comes 209th and is first in his age category. I run at my usual snail pace. I am lapped by the fastest runners. They thunder past me, young men with long, strong strides. I don't care. I never ran at school. I'm happy just to be there.

When I finish, I'm given a piece of paper that says 365. I think: Not bad! I'm as elated as usual, my rush feels great. But then, when the website publishes the results, I discover that I have not come 365th. I have come 414th. Out of 418 runners. I realize that I know who came after me, as well. Two were a mother and her young daughter, who kept stopping to walk. One was a lady who had never run before. Very possibly the final person was a dog-walker who'd wandered into the race by mistake.

I send an email to ask about my placing, and the organizers explain there were so many participants (it was the first Saturday after New Year) that they'd had to hand out some numbers twice, reuse the pieces of paper. But my time didn't lie. I was very slow. I was 414th.

Running, slightly faster

For around a day, I am secretly gutted about my 414th place, and irritated with myself for feeling gutted. What's my problem? I could see everyone pulling away when we set off so, really, what did I expect? I know I'm slow and I actively try to switch off my competitiveness when I run, and I still got my high afterwards, so everything should be fine. Am I still so driven by comparison with others? Am I still trying to com-

pete? Is there some small part of me that relates to the tri-
athlon madmen? How sad.

But something else is bothering me, a feeling that's not
quite as egotistical as competitiveness with other people. It's
the realization that telling everyone I'm a really slow runner
is an excuse. It gets me off the hook. I've been coasting, not
trying, giving up when I've only just started. The girl who was
running with her mother was running as fast as she could.
I wasn't.

P is very sweet, and slightly patronizing about my result. I
say, 'I always run at the same speed.'

He says, 'Just try going a little bit quicker, see what happens.'

So I do. I go running by myself a week later and I try to
speed up a little. It works. I run the fastest I ever have. I'm still
very, very slow, but I'm a bit faster. I don't run any more Park
Runs. I don't want to compete with younger, swifter people,
who may well force me into a sad attempt at showing off and
ultimately into having a heart attack. I run against myself, to
see if I can get a little bit better.

Get out of your head

Once getting out of your head through drink and drugs
becomes unthinkable, due to hangovers fast-forwarding into
the shattering disintegration of your soul, plus the days and
days it takes to reassemble your soul afterwards, how do you
stop getting bored with yourself and your thoughts? How can
you lose your mind, or at least leave it behind for a short time?

Having sex is an obvious one. But what if there's no one
nearby who you fancy, or you've had a row with your partner,
or you're out and about in a south London supermarket, and
they're in Stoke, for some godforsaken reason, and you're not
feeling that turned on anyway? What's the quickest shortcut
to an out-of-mind experience?

One of the easiest is to watch a live performance. What an amazing thing, to be able to immerse yourself in a communal, transcendent activity that requires nothing more of you than to turn up and watch. You join in by being present. You become part of a bigger thing, even if you don't enjoy that bigger thing so much. Comedy and theatre and sport do this, but live music is the best way.

And so are nightclubs. If you find one you like, and you're allowed to get there early enough, a two-hour burst on the dance floor will always sort you out. Plus: remembering how mangled the other punters were, and what mad outfits they had on, will keep you stimulated for days afterwards.

Reading, going to art galleries

I am always astonished by how much enjoyment and revelation I can get out of going to a public art gallery for fifteen minutes. You can just walk in and stand in front of a painting, a sculpture, an offering that someone made for others – for you and me – to consider. You can look at it and it can revolutionize your day. And books. I forget the detail of almost every book I read, but when I'm inside one, I'm absorbed, living a different life, in tears on the tube. Public transport is the best place to read. You are moving forward, to a new place, without doing any work of your own. And you are in another place as you do so. You are entirely on the move.

Listening to musicians

Although my job might be becoming increasingly irrelevant, talking to older musicians has helped me a lot. These interesting, fantastic people, who created songs and sounds that changed other people's lives, who would be fascinating however old they are, they've all said things that I've remembered.

Viv Albertine, who was the in The Slits when she was young, suggested that I should think about what I liked to do when I was in my teens and early twenties. That time when you're all over the shop, but you're brave and you're instinctively pushing for what you want. Many middle-aged people – especially women, who find themselves taking time out to care for others – forget what they used to do, what they liked to do. And the more I thought about this, the more sense it made. So I suggest it to you.

Take some time to think about what you really, honestly, enjoy. And if you can't think of anything, then do what Viv says. Think about what you liked to do in your late teens and early twenties. Then discard the deviant sexual practices and the over-reliance on alcohol and drugs (or don't – it's up to you) and consider the other stuff. Did you like playing the guitar? Did you like dancing, or going camping in the wild? Maybe you were happiest when you were wandering around second-hand shops, or sitting in olde-worlde pubs, or cycling along back roads, wiggling through a city.

Other people who have helped are Wilko, John Lydon, Paul Weller.

Paul Weller said, 'Obviously I'm conscious of how old I am, but if I don't think about it, then I don't feel any sort of age, really. I don't feel like an old person, and I don't feel like a young person. I just feel . . . I'm just me.'

John Lydon said, 'What would I be if punk never happened? I would be a punk.'

Listening to music

Always, always, always, ALWAYS. Music tells your hidden stories, it beats alongside your heart. It speaks for you when you have no words. There is room for you in music, in a way that there isn't in novels and films, in stories. Music knows you and what you're going through.

Committing to something you would once have found laughable

As I've said, I help run a computer coding club for 9- and 10-year-olds. I have never played a computer game. I don't enjoy them at all; I think they're pointless. But I enjoy learning how to use simple programming languages and then helping children learn them. They pick them up so much more quickly than I do, it makes me laugh. The hour I spend with them at Code Club is engaged and absorbing and full-on and takes me out of myself more quickly than anything else I do.

Teaching

Teaching is consistently undermined. But people in middle age, those of us who lived through the 90s, with their open-mindedness about outsiders and what they can bring to the mainstream, we could be good at teaching people. You don't have to become a qualified teacher. You just need to speak publicly when you're asked, to mentor, to try to help people who haven't worked as long as you – who haven't had all those experiences, special to you – to find their way through what they're up to. Plus, people younger than you are interesting. Listen to them, they know a lot.

Though there is a warning around teaching, especially for men. The middle-aged man who teaches from the standpoint of letting everyone else know how great he is, who is wired for broadcast but not for reception: that man is not the teacher anyone wants.

Shedding, forgetting

The only way to feel lighter and better about going into the second half of your life – the second half, if you're lucky – is to forget most of what you've done before. It's in the past. It's gone now. And if other people bring it up, that's fine, and we can talk about it if you want, but it is no more. The feelings remain: the long friendships, the understandings built up over years, our shared history and what it did to us all. But the facts: they're not so important. They really aren't.

So shed the clothes you never wear, forget them. Call the people you've always liked, meet up with them and deliberately don't talk about the past. Let go of the ones who have moved on. It's OK. Give away your possessions (well, your clothes and all those old books you never read any more; maybe even your vinyl): give them to other people, to young people with no money – you were once one of them.

Have a think about your resources. What were you good at when you were 18, 19, 20? Are you still interested in that now? What's stopping you?

We all have dreams and fantasies. They are part of what makes us who we are. But we are not very good at achieving them. We get diverted, we lose confidence. They were the wrong dreams in the first place. The truth is, in middle age, we can't do everything we once thought we could. We don't have the time, and we don't have the capabilities. At some point, you have to say, 'This is as good as I can be, as good as I can be right now.' You don't have to be happy about it, but I would recommend that you are.

If you can understand your restrictions, recognize them, hold them up to the light and accept them, you're every age and no age at all.

We live, as everyone always does, in particular times. We are confined by outside factors. Politics, economics, jobs. You can't move house if every house out there is too expensive. You can't change your spouse unless they want to change themselves. You can't stop work if you need the money. You can't get work if there isn't any. You can't prevent your kids from growing up and away from you, and you can't stop them making all the mistakes you hoped they wouldn't. You can't make them grateful, either. And none of this is your fault (unless you voted Tory). It just is.

You want change? Great. You've got it wrong? Make it right. But remember that the old way of middle-aged revolution – the classic midlife crisis – requires a lot of strength and certainty in your choice, and those may fade. Chucking in your whole life for a new one that appears different, but will end up as the same life in new clothes? That isn't always such a good idea. Breaking up a marriage is a violent thing to do, and sometimes it's very necessary. But nobody truly gets away with it, the negation of the love that was, that lasted such a long time. Nobody truly gets away with hurting someone else, especially if that someone is a child, and especially if that someone is your child. So take on the hurt, if you have to. Love and hurt are ours to take and to receive.

In so many ways, we are not free to make our life as we want. But in so many other ways, we are.

We can decide to be happy. We can make tiny changes. We can take on the kinds of responsibilities that we shirked when we were young. We can be patient with people who have no power and angry with those who have power. We can use our patience and our anger to fuel us.

We can decide to reclaim our body from outsiders: to ignore what we're meant to look like, how we're supposed to treat that body and adorn it and cover it with unguents, and instead concentrate on how it feels. How does your body feel, to you? Accept its limitations and strengths, work with them. Dress it however you bloody well like. At the moment, we're lucky: our body and our self are intertwined. When we become ill, the body will take over. So it's best to fuel its energy for that time. Keep it moving, fast and flexible.

We can change our brain, through learning or through

being present in the moment. We can throw out our old ways of thinking.

We can pull ourselves out of time by enjoying our time. We can work really hard and we can meditate, if we can be bothered, and we can shriek into the howling abyss, and we can read and make our kids laugh, and we can dance and we can make time stand still by staring out at the sea or into someone else's eyes. We can make time stretch.

We are our past, our present and our future all at once; we are always all of these things. It's only that, as we age, the proportions change. My past is more of me than my future, but it's my present that I'm involved in.

All around, friends, heroes, parents, children are being picked out at random, and they die. They fall over and bang their head, they get knocked down by a car, they become terminally ill, and we say, 'Why them? Why us? Why me?'

But why not?

Why not? Midlife is different from youth and it's different from elderly. But all of life is living with death flickering and glittering somewhere to the side, around our blind spot, where we can't quite see. Life is like that, no matter how old we are.

So, I think again about that chess game. I look at the chessboard in my mind, I see the pieces that remain, I mourn the ones I squandered. I feel the atmosphere change when I ask if I can start the game again . . .

Still. All those pieces! On the board! Waiting for me to move them.

I think about that, and I feel . . . better.

Because, yes, this is the game. This is our life. This is it. Let's play, with whatever we've got left.

Acknowledgements

Writing a book is an isolating, maddening, ridiculous, pointless, appalling, arse-thickening process. But of those, it's mostly isolating. So thank you to everyone who talked to me about middle age, whether formally or anonymously or when I brought it up, desperately, during conversation.

Thank you to my all-the-aces agent Kirsty McLachlan and everyone at David Godwin Associates.

Thank you to Ruaridh Nicoll, who commissioned the piece that set this book in motion, and to Jane Ferguson and Sarah Donaldson, who gave me time off to write it.

Thank you to Jenny Berglund for fabulous, on-the-money research and Allie Dickinson for transcription and insightful opinion.

To Louise Haines, Sarah Thickett, Julian Humphries and Patrick Hargadon at HarperCollins, especially Louise, who waited and never shouted.

To Matt Writtle for the impromptu photos, sorry for delaying your Brighton trip.

Massive, bottom-of-my-heart thanks to everyone who has looked after my children or ferried them around so I could work, especially Dee Ceesay, Julie Foy and Steph Williams, who have stepped in to help more times than I can count. The afterschool-club crew: Mrs Antonio, Miss Humpage, Big Miss Murnin, Little Miss Murnin. Also: Jim T-W, Hannah T-W, Sarah Galliford, Anne Rodgers, Clara Veneri, Monika and Michael Nollet, Emily and Matt Waller, Larissa and Richard Avery, Shananne Lane, Michael Palmer, Marco and Steph Cesai, Tim Weeks, Jennifer Sawyer, Dick Sawyer, Toby Sawyer, Jonathon Holmes, Amanda Freeman, Patricio Sanchez, Lizzie Wilson, Shirley Fosu, Terri Sinclair, Leona Fitzgerald, Jack and Liz Murphy, Thom Chesser, Merrilees Smiley . . . so many, many people.

To Chris Lock and everyone at Carpe Diem FC, the best football club in the land.

To the people who kept me going: Louise de Lemos, Amanda Freeman, Lulu Le Vay, Louise McKinney, Richard Benson, Ekow Eshun, Saskia Reeves, Clint Dyer, Chloe Fox.

To Facebook and Twitter friends who helped me with titles and made me laugh when I was in book despair.

To everyone who would rather go out than stay in. Me too. It's a big world out there.

To Brockwell Park Lido Café and the British Library, the best places to work.

To my mum and dad, who know all about this but choose not to dwell.

To P and F, midget gems, shooting stars, reasons to live, all the everythings.

And Smiley, who is sailing through middle age with aplomb and a fancy wardrobe. How irritating.